FOUNDATIONS *for* MINISTRY SERIES

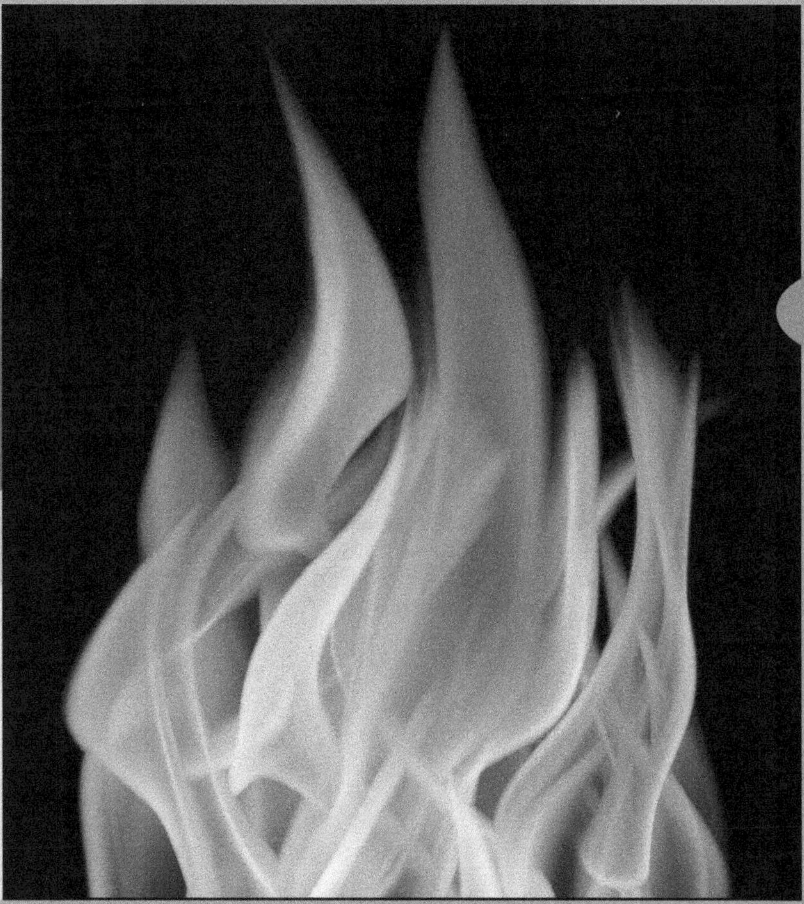

Biblical Studies

THE BIBLE AND THE FUTURE

Dr. Don L. Davis

T2-140

TUMI WORLD IMPACT

The Urban Ministry Institute, a ministry of World Impact, Inc.

© 2019. The Urban Ministry Institute. All Rights Reserved. Copying, redistribution and/or sale of these materials, or any unauthorized transmission, except as may be expressly permitted by the 1976 Copyright Act or in writing from the publisher is prohibited. Requests for permission should be addressed in writing to:

The Urban Ministry Institute
3701 E. 13th Street
Wichita, KS 67208

ISBN: 978-1-62932-415-9

The Urban Ministry Institute is a ministry of World Impact, Inc.

All Scripture quotations, unless otherwise noted, are from The Holy Bible, English Standard Version, copyright © 2001 by Crossward Bible, a division of Good News Publishers. Used by permission. All Rights Reserved.

Contents

- 5 — About the Author
- 7 — Preface
- 11 — *Session 1*
  The Importance of the Doctrine of Last Things:
  The Second Coming of the Lord Jesus Christ
- 21 — *Session 2*
  The Kingdom of God and the Historic Hope of the Church
- 59 — *Session 3*
  Physical Death, Immortality, and the Intermediate State
- 87 — *Session 4*
  The Signs of the Time, the Rapture, and the Tribulation
- 123 — *Session 5*
  The Second Coming and the Need to Watch
- 155 — *Session 6*
  The Wrath of God during the Tribulation and Millennial Views of Revelation 20
- 183 — *Session 7*
  The Resurrection, Final Judgment, and Eternal Punishment
- 229 — *Session 8*
  The Blessed Hope: The New Heavens and Earth and the Consummated Kingdom of God
- 265 — Appendix
- 306 — About Us

About the Author

Rev. Dr. Don L. Davis is the Executive Director of The Urban Ministry Institute and a Senior Vice President of World Impact. He attended Wheaton College and Wheaton Graduate School, and graduated summa cum laude in both his B.A. (1988) and M.A. (1989) degrees, in Biblical Studies and Systematic Theology, respectively. He earned his Ph.D. in Religion (Theology and Ethics) from the University of Iowa School of Religion.

As the Institute's Executive Director and World Impact's Senior Vice President, he oversees the training of urban missionaries, church planters, and city pastors, and facilitates training opportunities for urban Christian workers in evangelism, church growth, and pioneer missions. He also leads the Institute's extensive distance learning programs and facilitates leadership development efforts for organizations and denominations like Prison Fellowship, the Evangelical Free Church of America, and the Church of God in Christ.

A recipient of numerous teaching and academic awards, Dr. Davis has served as professor and faculty at a number of fine academic institutions, having lectured and taught courses in religion, theology, philosophy, and biblical studies at schools such as Wheaton College, St. Ambrose University, the Houston Graduate School of Theology, the University of Iowa School of Religion, the Robert E. Webber Institute of Worship Studies. He has authored a number of books, curricula, and study materials to equip urban leaders, including *The Capstone Curriculum*, TUMI's premiere sixteen-module distance education seminary instruction, *Sacred Roots: A Primer on Retrieving the Great Tradition*, which focuses on how urban churches can be renewed through a rediscovery of the historic orthodox faith, and *Black and Human: Rediscovering King as a Resource for Black Theology and Ethics*. Dr. Davis has participated in academic lectureships such as the Staley Lecture series, renewal conferences like the Promise Keepers rallies, and theological consortiums like the University of Virginia Lived Theology Project Series. He received the Distinguished Alumni Fellow Award from the University of Iowa College of Liberal Arts and Sciences in 2009. Dr. Davis is also a member of the Society of Biblical Literature, and the American Academy of Religion.

Preface

The Urban Ministry Institute is a research and leadership development center for World Impact, an interdenominational Christian missions organization dedicated to evangelism and church planting in the inner cities of America. Founded in Wichita, Kansas in 1995, the Institute (TUMI) has sponsored courses, workshops, and leadership training events locally for urban leaders since 1996. We have recorded and reformatted many of these resources over the years, and are now making them available to others who are equipping leaders for the urban church.

Our *Foundations for Ministry Series* represents a significant portion of our on-site training offered to students locally here in Wichita. We are thankful and excited that these materials can now be made available to you. We are confident that you can grow tremendously as you study God's Word and relate its message of justice and grace to your life and ministry.

For your personal benefit, we have included our traditional classroom materials with their corresponding audio recordings of each class session, placing them into a self-study format. We have included extra space in the actual printed materials in order that you may add notes and comments as you listen to the recordings. This will prove helpful as you explore these ideas and topics further.

Remember, the teaching in these sessions was actually given in class and workshop settings at our Hope School of Ministry. This means that, although the workbooks were created for students to follow along and interact with the recordings, some differences may be present. As you engage the material, therefore, please keep in mind that the page numbers on the recordings do not correspond to those in the workbook.

Our earnest prayer is that this *Foundations for Ministry Series* course will prove to be both a blessing and an encouragement to you in your walk with and ministry for Christ. May the Lord so use this course to deepen your knowledge of his Word, in order that you may be outfitted and equipped to complete the task he has for you in kingdom ministry!

Course Description and Objectives
The purpose of this course is to explore the biblical teaching and current theories surrounding the theme of the Second Coming of Christ, and all of the rich textured topics which revolve around it. The theme of the future is arguably one of the most significant, rich, and profitable subjects for preaching and teaching, although it fails to receive the kind of attention it deserves in many pulpits today. Although the theme of biblical prophecy suffers from much abuse in many sectarian arenas, the informed and enlightened preacher, evangelist, or Christian worker must strive to master the material, and consistently reference this glorious teaching in every phase of their discipling and ministry. Special emphasis in this course will be placed on the practical meaning of this teaching for discipleship, especially in urban communities which so desperately need the ministry of hope in its congregations and neighborhoods. We will critically assess the biblical evidence for the various dimensions of the future, the intermediate state, and the final judgments, and close with a close look at the eternal state of believers, and the hope of eternal life to come at the *parousia*, or Second Coming of our Lord Jesus.

As a result of taking this course, each student should be able to:
- Recognize the significance and prominence of the Second Coming and its related themes in the biblical materials of both Old and New Testaments
- Articulate for others the importance of the Second Coming of Christ as the great hope of the Church and the desire of the saints of all the ages
- Give a brief overview of some of the recent trends in biblical and theological studies in Eschatology, or the doctrine of Last Things, and relate them to each other in terms of credibility and clarity
- Distinguish between the different theories of the Kingdom of God as present, as future, and as both present and future, and implications of each theory for ministry and justice in the world today
- Identify the main principles and dimensions underlying the theories of Tribulationism, the Rapture, and the millennial theories associated with the coming of Christ
- Memorize selected texts on the Second Coming of Christ and its relevance for our lives today
- Discover ways to preach and teach biblical prophecy of the future without resorting to making guesstimates about current events as present-day fulfilment of biblical truth

- Outline some of the critical truths associated with the major topics connected to the Second Coming of Christ, i.e., physical death and immortality, the intermediate State, the Millennium, the Resurrection of the Body, the Final Judgment, Eternal Punishment, and the Paradise to come

Assignments and Grading

For our TUMI satellites, all course-relevant materials are located at *www.tumi.org/foundations*.

Each course or workshop has assigned textbooks which are read and discussed throughout the class. We maintain our official *Foundations for Ministry Series* required textbook list at *www.tumi.org/foundationsbooks*.

For more information, please contact us at *foundations@tumi.org*.

Lesson One
The Importance of the Doctrine of Last Things: The Second Coming of the Lord Jesus Christ

The Final Purposes of the Lord God: The Destiny to Come

The final goal of God's purposes for the world includes, negatively, the destruction of all God's enemies. Satan, sin and death, and the elimination of all forms of suffering (Rev. 20.10, 14–15; 7.16f.; 21.4; Isa. 25.8; 27.1; Rom. 16.20; 1 Cor. 15.26, 54). Positively, God's rule will finally prevail entirely (Zech. 14.9; 1 Cor. 15.24–28; Rev. 11.15), so that in Christ all things will be united (Eph. 1.10) and God will be all in all (1 Cor. 15.28, av). With the final achievement of human salvation there will come also the liberation of the whole material creation from its share in the curse of sin (Rom. 8.19–23). The Christian hope is not for redemption from the world, but for the redemption of the world. Out of judgment (Heb. 12.26; 2 Pet. 3.10) will emerge a recreated universe (Rev. 21.1; cf. Isa. 65.17; 66.22; Matt. 19.28), 'a new heavens and a new earth in which righteousness dwells' (2 Pet. 3.13).

The destiny of the redeemed is to be like Christ (Rom. 8.29; 1 Cor. 15.49; Phil. 3.21; 1 John 3.2), to be with Christ (John 14.3; 2 Cor. 5.8; Phil. 1.23; Col. 3.4; 1 Thess. 4.17), to share his glory (Rom. 8.18, 30; 2 Cor. 3.18; 4.17; Col. 3.4; Heb. 2.10; 1 Pet. 5.1) and his kingdom (1 Tim. 2.12; Rev. 2.26f.; 3.21; 4.10; 20.4, 6); to be sons of God in perfect fellowship with God (Rev. 21.3, 7), to worship God (Rev. 7.15; 22.3), to see God (Matt. 5.8; Rev. 22.4), to know him face to face (1 Cor. 13.12). Faith, hope, and especially love are the permanent characteristics of Christian existence which abide even in the perfection of the age to come (1 Cor. 13.13), while 'righteousness and peace and joy in the Holy Spirit' are similarly abiding qualities of man's enjoyment of God (Rom. 14.17). The corporate life of the redeemed with God is described in a number of pictures. the eschatological banquet (Matt. 8.11; Mark 14.25; Luke 14.15–24; 22.30) or wedding feast (Matt. 25.10; Rev. 19.9), paradise restored (Luke 23.43; Rev. 2.7; 22.1f.), the new Jerusalem (Heb. 12.22; Rev. 21). All these are only pictures, since 'no eye has seen, nor ear heard, nor the heart of man conceived, what God has prepared for those who love him' (1 Cor. 2.9).

R. J. Bauckham, "Eschatology" in The New Bible Dictionary. (3rd ed.).
D. R. W. Wood and I. Howard Marshall, eds.
Downers Grove, Il.: InterVarsity Press, 1996.

I. **The Prominence of the Second Coming in the Scriptures**

Eschatology = from the Greek word **eschatos** *meaning 'last', the term refers to the 'doctrine of the last things.' The Bible teaches that the God of the Scriptures is moving all things, all history toward the fulfillment of his purposes for his creation. The God and Father of our Lord Jesus Christ has not abandoned creation, but has determined to consummate the entirety of all things in the coming of his Son. Nothing can stop this–it is moving towards us with speed and certainty.*

> Titus 2:11-13 – For the grace of God has appeared, bringing salvation for all people, [12] training us to renounce ungodliness and worldly passions, and to live self-controlled, upright, and godly lives in the present age, [13] waiting for our blessed hope, the appearing of the glory of our great God and Savior Jesus Christ

Martin Luther said he only had *two days* on his calendar: *today* and *"that day."*

A. General facts about doctrine of last things, those themes associated with the Second Coming of Christ:

1. It is posited that one out of every 30 verses in the Bible mention this doctrine.

2. For every single mention of the first advent of Messiah into the world there are eight mentions of the Second Coming of Christ.

3. Texts related to the Second Coming are mentioned in 318 references in Scripture, made in 216 chapters of the Bible.

4. Entire books of the New Testament (NT) are devoted to dealing with its content (e.g., 1 and 2 Thessalonians), along with entire chapters focused on the particulars surrounding the coming of our Lord (e.g., Matthew 24; Mark 13; Luke 21, etc.).

5. The Old Testament (OT) prophets, although they tended to merge the two comings in their prophetic utterances, devote entire sections of their writings to the theme of the Second Coming of Messiah, and its meaning for the people of God and the created order.

B. Jesus of Nazareth taught consistently and witnessed boldly about the certainty and quality of his second advent.

1. Matthew 24:29-31 – Immediately after the tribulation of those days the sun will be darkened, and the moon will not give its light, and the stars will fall from heaven, and the powers of the heavens will be shaken. [30] Then will appear in heaven the sign of the Son of Man, and then all the tribes of the earth will mourn, and they will see the Son of Man coming on the clouds of heaven with power and great glory. [31] And he will send out his angels with a loud trumpet call, and they will gather his elect from the four winds, from one end of heaven to the other.

2. Luke 21:34-36 – "But watch yourselves lest your hearts be weighed down with dissipation and drunkenness and cares of this life, and that day come upon you suddenly like a trap. [35] For it will come upon all who dwell on the face of the whole earth. [36] But stay awake at all times, praying that you may have strength to escape all these things that are going to take place, and to stand before the Son of Man."

3. John 14:3 – And if I go and prepare a place for you, I will come again and will take you to myself, that where I am you may be also.

C. The angels of the Ascension bore testimony that Jesus would in fact appear again a second time. (cf. Heb.2.2)

Acts 1.11 -- "Men of Galilee, why do you stand looking into heaven? This Jesus, who was taken up from you into heaven, will come in the same way as you saw him go into heaven."

D. The apostles, who were eyewitnesses of the glory and majesty of the Risen Lord, testified constantly of the truth of Christ's second appearing.

1. The coming of Jesus of Nazareth, the risen Lord, will be personal.
   1 Thess. 4:16-17 – For the Lord himself will descend from heaven with a cry of command, with the voice of an archangel, and with the sound of the trumpet of God. And the dead in Christ will rise first. [17] Then we who are alive, who are left, will be caught up together with them in the clouds to meet the Lord in the air, and so we will always be with the Lord.

2. His coming is associated with deliverance and salvation of his own.
   Hebrews 9:28 – so Christ, having been offered once to bear the sins of many, will appear a second time, not to deal with sin but to save those who are eagerly waiting for him.

3. We are exhorted to live in such a manner as not to be ashamed of him when he appears.
   1 John 2:28 – And now, little children, abide in him, so that when he appears we may have confidence and not shrink from him in shame at his coming.

4. The apostolic witness of the Second Coming emphasizes his coming to judge the ungodly.
   Jude 1:14-15 – It was also about these that Enoch, the seventh from Adam, prophesied, saying, "Behold, the Lord came with ten thousands of his holy ones, [15] to execute judgment on all and to convict all the ungodly of all their deeds of ungodliness that they have committed in such an ungodly way, and of all the harsh things that ungodly sinners have spoken against him."

> **"When Christ returns, how awful to know that all of it was true, and that it is too late to do anything about it."**
> – C. S. Lewis

II. The Second Coming of Jesus is the Blessed Hope of the Church

The Second Coming of our Lord Jesus must be at the center of our worship, celebration, preaching, and discipleship, for it is the doctrine which provides us with the greatest incentive to sacrifice all we have and are in this world for the coming glory ahead.

A. The status of the Blessed Hope of the Coming of Christ:

1. It is the hope of *eternal life* promised to those who believe in Jesus before the ages began, Titus 1:2 in hope of eternal life, which God, who never lies, promised before the ages began.

2. The hope relates to the theme of sharing eternal glory with God in the presence of Christ forever.

   a. Titus 3:7 – so that being justified by his grace we might become heirs according to the hope of eternal life.

   b. Col. 1:27 – To them God chose to make known how great among the Gentiles are the riches of the glory of this mystery, which is Christ in you, the hope of glory.

   c. 2 Tim. 2:10 – Therefore I endure everything for the sake of the elect, that they also may obtain the salvation that is in Christ Jesus with eternal glory.

3. This hope produces a sure and steadfast anchor of the soul, one which provides stability, clarity, and endurance in the midst of persecution and tribulation.
   Hebrews 6:18-19 – so that by two unchangeable things, in which it is impossible for God to lie, we who have fled for refuge might have strong encouragement to hold

fast to the hope set before us. [19] We have this as a sure and steadfast anchor of the soul, a hope that enters into the inner place behind the curtain

4. The hope is rooted on the historical fact of Jesus' resurrection from the dead.
1 Peter 1:3 – Blessed be the God and Father of our Lord Jesus Christ! According to his great mercy, he has caused us to be born again to a living hope through the resurrection of Jesus Christ from the dead

5. This hope produces energy for holiness and separation unto the Lord's purposes and will.
1 John 3:3 – And everyone who thus hopes in him purifies himself as he is pure.

B. Implications of the Blessed Hope for our lives:

1. We are eagerly awaiting his coming.
Titus 2.11-14 -- For the grace of God has appeared, bringing salvation for all people, [12] training us to renounce ungodliness and worldly passions, and to live self-controlled, upright, and godly lives in the present age, [13] waiting for our blessed hope, the appearing of the glory of our great God and Savior Jesus Christ, [14] who gave himself for us to redeem us from all lawlessness and to purify for himself a people for his own possession who are zealous for good works.

2. We are to turn our backs on the darkness of the present age.
1 Thess. 5:2-10 – For you yourselves are fully aware that the day of the Lord will come like a thief in the night. [3] While people are saying, "There is peace and security," then sudden destruction will come upon them as labor pains come upon a pregnant woman, and they will not escape. [4] But you are not in darkness, brothers, for that day to surprise you like a thief. [5] For you are all children of light, children of the day. We are

not of the night or of the darkness. [6] So then let us not sleep, as others do, but let us keep awake and be sober. [7] For those who sleep, sleep at night, and those who get drunk, are drunk at night. [8] But since we belong to the day, let us be sober, having put on the breastplate of faith and love, and for a helmet the hope of salvation. [9] For God has not destined us for wrath, but to obtain salvation through our Lord Jesus Christ, [10] who died for us so that whether we are awake or asleep we might live with him.

3. We are to love neither the world nor the things within it.
1 John 2:15-17 – Do not love the world or the things in the world. If anyone loves the world, the love of the Father is not in him. [16] For all that is in the world—the desires of the flesh and the desires of the eyes and pride in possessions—is not from the Father but is from the world. [17] And the world is passing away along with its desires, but whoever does the will of God abides forever.

4. We are to watch and pray always that we may be counted worthy to escape the things which are destined to come upon the world, and to stand before the Son of man, our Lord Jesus Christ.
Luke 21:34-36 – But watch yourselves lest your hearts be weighed down with dissipation and drunkenness and cares of this life, and that day come upon you suddenly like a trap. [35] For it will come upon all who dwell on the face of the whole earth. [36] But stay awake at all times, praying that you may have strength to escape all these things that are going to take place, and to stand before the Son of Man.

5. We are to derive comfort to our hearts in the midst of loss and difficulty in the world.
1 Thess. 4:13-18 – But we do not want you to be uninformed, brothers, about those who are asleep, that you may not grieve as others do who have no hope. [14] For since we believe that Jesus died and rose again, even so, through Jesus, God will bring with him those

who have fallen asleep. [15] For this we declare to you by a word from the Lord, that we who are alive, who are left until the coming of the Lord, will not precede those who have fallen asleep. [16] For the Lord himself will descend from heaven with a cry of command, with the voice of an archangel, and with the sound of the trumpet of God. And the dead in Christ will rise first. [17] Then we who are alive, who are left, will be caught up together with them in the clouds to meet the Lord in the air, and so we will always be with the Lord. [18] Therefore encourage one another with these words.

C. Why, in light of the above teaching, is the doctrine of "last things" so disparaged, ignored, and/or neglected in the church today?

1. Extravagant, bizarre correlations are made regarding the *specific and particular fulfillment of prophetic scripture in light of current events.*

2. Doubt and the culture of skepticism and unbelief is rampant in many sectors of believers today.
2 Peter 3:3-4 – knowing this first of all, that scoffers will come in the last days with scoffing, following their own sinful desires. [4] They will say, "Where is the promise of his coming? For ever since the fathers fell asleep, all things are continuing as they were from the beginning of creation.

3. Ignorance of the biblical testimony of the Second Coming is due to the systematic neglect of many pulpits to tell the entire story of salvation – beginning, middle, and end.

4. There is worldliness and lack of awareness of the time of his coming. Drained passion for Christ has resulted in a love of this world while pretending to cling to the hope of the next one

a. John 12:24-25 – Truly, truly, I say to you, unless a grain of wheat falls into the earth and dies, it remains alone; but if it dies, it bears much fruit. [25] Whoever loves his life loses it, and whoever hates his life in this world will keep it for eternal life.

b. Matthew 24:42-44 – Therefore, stay awake, for you do not know on what day your Lord is coming. [43] But know this, that if the master of the house had known in what part of the night the thief was coming, he would have stayed awake and would not have let his house be broken into. [44] Therefore you also must be ready, for the Son of Man is coming at an hour you do not expect.

5. Today we are experiencing numbness and drowsiness regarding the signs of the times.
Mark 13:33-37 – Be on guard, keep awake. For you do not know when the time will come. [34] It is like a man going on a journey, when he leaves home and puts his servants in charge, each with his work, and commands the doorkeeper to stay awake. [35] Therefore stay awake—for you do not know when the master of the house will come, in the evening, or at midnight, or when the cock crows, or in the morning— [36] lest he come suddenly and find you asleep. [37] And what I say to you I say to all: Stay awake."

III. Conclusion: "Even so, come, Lord Jesus!" Rev. 22.20

The distinctive feature of Christian eschatology is its *Christ-centeredness.* Christ's second coming marks the completion of his work begun in Bethlehem and at Calvary. The resurrection of believers depends on the resurrection of Jesus (1 Cor. 15.20–22). Christian hope is not mere wish-fulfilment, because it looks for fulfilment of a plan already in operation. The kingdom of God is not mere compensation for present miseries, but rather the full experience of blessings already experienced in part through the Spirit, "who is a deposit guaranteeing our inheritance" (Eph. 1.14). Eschatology concerns the vindication of God's purposes for all creation. It calls people not so much to contemplate their individual destinies, as to allow the perspective of hope to influence the whole of life.

S. H. Travis. "Eschatology," *The New Dictionary of Theology.*
S. B. Ferguson and J. I. Packer, eds. (electronic ed.).
Downers Grove, Il.: InterVarsity Press, 2000.

2 Tim. 4:8 – Henceforth there is laid up for me the crown of righteousness, which the Lord, the righteous judge, will award to me on that Day, and not only to me but also to all who have loved his appearing.

A. *Heed the call* to watch, to be ready, to stay awake.

B. "You'd better get ready; you'd better get right . . . "

In the NT the sudden and unexpected nature of Jesus' return is captured in the image of the thief who comes in the night (Matt. 24.43; Luke 12.39; 1 Thess. 5.2, 4; Rev. 3.3; 16.15), the master who returns after a long journey (Mark 13.34–36; Luke 12.35–38, 42–48) and the bridegroom who arrives in the middle of the night (Matt. 25.1–13). Jesus and his first followers thus employ scenes from everyday life to depict his return. In these examples, darkness plays an obvious role. No doubt this is due both to the tendency to relate light and dark by analogy to God and Satan, respectively (e.g., Acts 26.18; Col.1.13), and to the normal rhythm of life that has us active during the day and sleeping during the night (cf. Mark 4.27). While highlighting the abruptness of the second coming, then, these images also underscore the necessity of constant readiness, symbolized in the call to stay awake.

Leland Ryken, J. Wilhoit, et al. "Second Coming."
Dictionary of Biblical Imagery. (electronic ed.).
Downers Grove, Il.: InterVarsity Press, 2000.

Lesson Two
The Kingdom of God and the Historic Hope of the Church

The Kingdom of God as Present and Future

Summing up, then, we may say that the kingdom of God both in the teaching of Jesus and in that of the Apostle Paul is a present as well as a future reality. Our understanding of the kingdom must therefore do full justice to both of these aspects. George Eldon Ladd stresses the importance of seeing these two aspects: "The central thesis of this book [The Presence of the Future] is that the Kingdom of God is the redemptive reign of God dynamically active to establish his rule among men, and that this Kingdom, which will appear as an apocalyptic act at the end of the age, has already come into human history in the person and mission of Jesus to overcome evil, to deliver men from its power, and to bring them into the blessings of God's reign. The Kingdom of God involves two great moments: fulfillment within history, and consummation at the end of history." Herman Ridderbos makes a similar point. He suggests that at the beginning of his ministry Jesus placed more emphasis on the presence of the kingdom in fulfillment of Old Testament prophecy, whereas toward the end of his ministry he laid more stress on the future coming of the kingdom." Ridderbos insists, however, that the future and present aspects of the kingdom must never be separated: " . . . In this preaching [that of Jesus the element of fulfillment is no less striking and essential than that of expectation. . . . For the future and the present are indissolubly connected in Jesus' preaching. The one is the necessary complement of the other. The prophecy about the future can only be rightly viewed from the standpoint of the Christological present, just as the character of the present implies the necessity and certainty of the future." One who is a believer in Jesus Christ, therefore, is in the kingdom of God at the present time, enjoying its blessings and sharing its responsibilities. At the same time, he realizes that the kingdom is present now only in a provisional and incomplete state, and therefore he looks forward to its final consummation at the end of the age. Because the kingdom is both present and future, we may say that the kingdom is now hidden to all except those who have faith in Christ, but that someday it shall be totally revealed, so that even its enemies will finally have to recognize its presence and bow before its rule.

Anthony A. Hoekema, *The Bible and the Future.*
Grand Rapids: William B. Eerdmans Publishing Company, 1979, pp. 51-52.

I. Eschatology and the Old Testament

Eschatology did not arise when people began to doubt the actuality of God's kingship in the cult, but when they had to learn in the greatest distress to rely, in faith alone, on God as the only firm basis of life and when this realism of faith was directed critically against the life of the people so that the coming catastrophe was looked upon as a divine intervention full of justice and also so that it was confessed that the Holy God remained unshakeable in His fidelity and love to Israel. . . . Eschatology is a religious certainty which springs directly from the Israelite faith in God as rooted in the history of its salvation.

Hoekema, The Bible and the Future, p. 4.

A. The Coming Redeemer is expected.

1. The promise of a future redeemer begins the cosmic drama and narrative of the sacred scripture.
   Gen. 3:15 – I will put enmity between you and the woman, and between your offspring and her offspring; he shall bruise your head, and you shall bruise his heel."

2. The serpent is here associated with the person and workings of Satan, the archenemy of God and humankind.

   a. Rev. 12:9 – And the great dragon was thrown down, that ancient serpent, who is called the devil and Satan, the deceiver of the whole world — he was thrown down to the earth, and his angels were thrown down with him.

   b. Rev. 20:2 – And he seized the dragon, that ancient serpent, who is the devil and Satan, and bound him for a thousand years

3. This is the *proto-evangelium* (the first telling of the Gospel in Scripture), and, God's revelation *in a nutshell* "of his saving purpose with his people," (Hoekema, p. 5)

4. Note the coming one is the "seed of the woman" who is further seen as the seed of Abraham.
(Gen. 22.18; 26.4; 28.14)

5. The coming one would be of the tribe of Judah.
(Gen. 49.10)

6. Of the families of Judah, the coming redeemer would be of the household and lineage of David.
2 Samuel 7:12-13 – When your days are fulfilled and you lie down with your fathers, I will raise up your offspring after you, who shall come from your body, and I will establish his kingdom. [13] He shall build a house for my name, and I will establish the throne of his kingdom forever.

B. The Coming One would be the *archetype* of the roles of prophet, priest, and king.

1. The coming prophet:
Deut. 18:15 – The Lord your God will raise up for you a prophet like me from among you, from your brothers—it is to him you shall listen

2. The priest after the order of Melchizedek:
Psalm 110:4 – The Lord has sworn and will not change his mind, "You are a priest forever after the order of Melchizedek."

3. The King will come to his temple:
Zech. 9:9 – Rejoice greatly, O daughter of Zion! Shout aloud, O daughter of Jerusalem! behold, your king is coming to you; righteous and having salvation is he, humble and mounted on a donkey, on a colt, the foal of a donkey.

4. This figure will constitute the *coming of God in the midst of his people*. Isaiah 9:6-7 – For to us a child is born, to us a son is given; and the government shall be upon his shoulder, and his name shall be called Wonderful Counselor, Mighty God, Everlasting Father, Prince of Peace. [7] Of the increase of his government and of peace there will be no end, on the throne of David and over his kingdom, to establish it and to uphold it with justice and with righteousness from this time forth and forevermore. The zeal of the Lord of hosts will do this.

C. The coming redeemer is embodied as the Suffering Servant of Yahweh.

1. The Isaiah texts dealing with the servant motif include Isa. 42.1-4; 49.5-7; 52.13-15; chapter 53.

2. He will be anointed and sanctified by the Spirit of the Lord. Isa. 42.1-4; cf. 61.1ff.

3. He will be chosen as a light to the nations, a beacon to the Gentiles. Isa. 49.5-7

4. He will deeply humble, a stumbling block to the proud nations which do not know him. Isa. 52.13-15

5. He will be bruised for our iniquities, wounded for our transgressions, and his sacrifice will be Yahweh's sacrifice for the guilt of his redeemed. Isa. 53

D. The Coming Redeemer will be the divine Son of Man who will establish God's rule forever.

Daniel 7:13-14 – I saw in the night visions, and behold, with the clouds of heaven there came one like a son of man, and he came to the Ancient of Days and was presented before him. [14] And to him was given dominion and glory and a kingdom, that all peoples, nations, and languages should serve him; his dominion is an everlasting dominion, which shall not pass away, and his kingdom one that shall not be destroyed.

1. This person comes with the clouds of heaven, and appears before the Ancient of Days. (v. 13)

2. To this one who is like a "son of man" is given dominion, glory, and a kingdom. (v. 14a)

3. All peoples, nations, and languages should serve *him*. (v. 14b)

4. The duration of his dominion is eternal; it shall never pass away, and his kingdom shall never be destroyed. (v. 14c)

5. Jesus of Nazareth used the term "Son of Man" as his favorite term regarding himself, and associated it directly with his role as Messiah and Lord.

    a. Matthew 12:8 – For the Son of Man is lord of the Sabbath.

    b. Matthew 12:40 – For just as Jonah was three days and three nights in the belly of the great fish, so will the Son of Man be three days and three nights in the heart of the earth.

    c. Mark 8:38 – For whoever is ashamed of me and of my words in this adulterous and sinful generation, of him will the Son of Man also be ashamed when he comes in the glory of his Father with the holy angels.

    d. Mark 9:31 – for he was teaching his disciples, saying to them, "The Son of Man is going to be delivered into the hands of men, and they will kill him. And when he is killed, after three days he will rise."

  e. Luke 12:8 – And I tell you, everyone who acknowledges me before men, the Son of Man also will acknowledge before the angels of God.

  f. John 8:28 – So Jesus said to them, "When you have lifted up the Son of Man, then you will know that I am he, and that I do nothing on my own authority, but speak just as the Father taught me.

E. The OT speaks of the Coming Kingdom of God.

1. "Though the term 'kingdom of God' is not found in the OT, the thought that God is king is found, particularly in the Psalms and in the prophets." Hoekema, p 7

2. God is referred to as the King in the OT.

  a. As King of his people Israel. (e.g., Deut. 33.5; Ps. 84.3; 145.1; Isa. 43.15)

  b. As King of the whole earth. (e.g., Ps. 29.10; 47.2; 96.10; 97.1; 103.19; 145.11-13; Isa. 6.5; Jer. 46.18)

3. Kingdom = *malkuth*, refers to the *authority and right to rule* of a sovereign, and only secondarily to the *realm* over which the sovereign presides.

4. Daniel 2 provides one of the clearest articulations of the nature and scope of the kingdom of the coming redeemer:

  Daniel 2:44-45 – And in the days of those kings the God of heaven will set up a kingdom that shall never be destroyed, nor shall the kingdom be left to another people. It shall break in pieces all these kingdoms and bring them to an end, and it shall stand forever, [45] just as you saw that a stone was cut from a mountain by no human hand, and that it broke in pieces the iron, the bronze, the clay, the silver, and the gold. A great God has made known to the king what shall be after this. The dream is certain, and its interpretation sure."

    a. God will set up *a kingdom that shall never be destroyed*, nor shall the *kingdom be left to another people*. (v. 44)

    b. It shall destroy all other earthly kingdoms, bringing them to an end. (v. 44b)

    c. This kingdom established by God will *stand forever* – i.e., it is an eternal rule of Yahweh God. (v. 44c)

F. The eschatological vision of the OT is also embodied in the language of the *New Covenant*.

  1. The notion of covenant is critical to understanding the spirit and power of the OT:

    a. The Noahic covenant.
Gen. 9:9-10 – Behold, I establish my covenant with you and your offspring after you, [10] and with every living creature that is with you, the birds, the livestock, and every beast of the earth with you, as many as came out of the ark; it is for every beast of the earth.

    b. The Abrahamic covenant.
Gen. 12:1-3 – Now the Lord said to Abram, "Go from your country and your kindred and your father's house to the land that I will show you. [2] And I will make of you a great nation, and I will bless you and make your name great, so that you will be a blessing. [3] I will bless those who bless you, and him who dishonors you I will curse, and in you all the families of the earth shall be blessed."

    c. The covenant at Sinai.
Exod. 20:1-3 – And God spoke all these words, saying, [2] "I am the Lord your God, who brought

you out of the land of Egypt, out of the house of slavery. [3] "You shall have no other gods before me.

2. The people of Judah and Israel disobeyed the covenant of God at Sinai, where God gave the law, due to their sin and idolatry.
Jeremiah 31:31-32 – "Behold, the days are coming, declares the Lord, when I will make a new covenant with the house of Israel and the house of Judah, [32] not like the covenant that I made with their fathers on the day when I took them by the hand to bring them out of the land of Egypt, my covenant that they broke, though I was their husband, declares the Lord.

3. God promises in the eschatological vision of the OT to establish a new covenant where his spirit would be placed within them, and the law would be written on their hearts.
Jeremiah 31:33-34 – But this is the covenant that I will make with the house of Israel after those days, declares the Lord: I will put my law within them, and I will write it on their hearts. And I will be their God, and they shall be my people. [34] And no longer shall each one teach his neighbor and each his brother, saying, 'Know the Lord,' for they shall all know me, from the least of them to the greatest, declares the Lord. For I will forgive their iniquity, and I will remember their sin no more."

4. In the person of Jesus of Nazareth, the new covenant promised in the OT has come to its completion and fulfillment, ushered in through his death and resurrection. (cf. Heb. 8.8-13; 1 Cor. 11.25.)

G. Israel will be restored in the eschatological vision of the OT.

1. The scattered, judged, and broken people of Israel would be regathered to their land by the Lord's own hand.
Jeremiah 23:2-3 – Therefore thus says the Lord, the God of Israel, concerning the shepherds who care for my people: "You have scattered my flock and have driven

them away, and you have not attended to them. Behold, I will attend to you for your evil deeds, declares the Lord. [3] Then I will gather the remnant of my flock out of all the countries where I have driven them, and I will bring them back to their fold, and they shall be fruitful and multiply.

2. The Lord himself will bring back his people to the land "a second time."
Isaiah 11:10-11 – In that day the root of Jesse, who shall stand as a signal for the peoples—of him shall the nations inquire, and his resting place shall be glorious. [11] In that day the Lord will extend his hand yet a second time to recover the remnant that remains of his people, from Assyria, from Egypt, from Pathros, from Cush, from Elam, from Shinar, from Hamath, and from the coastlands of the sea.

3. Israel will be dramatically transformed and restored spiritually by the Spirit of God.
Ezekiel 36:23-28 – And I will vindicate the holiness of my great name, which has been profaned among the nations, and which you have profaned among them. And the nations will know that I am the Lord, declares the Lord God, when through you I vindicate my holiness before their eyes. [24] I will take you from the nations and gather you from all the countries and bring you into your own land. [25] I will sprinkle clean water on you, and you shall be clean from all your uncleannesses, and from all your idols I will cleanse you. [26] And I will give you a new heart, and a new spirit I will put within you. And I will remove the heart of stone from your flesh and give you a heart of flesh. [27] And I will put my Spirit within you, and cause you to walk in my statutes and be careful to obey my rules. [28] You shall dwell in the land that I gave to your fathers, and you shall be my people, and I will be your God.

H. The OT vision of The End reveals the outpouring of the Spirit on the world.

1. The prediction of the manifestation of God's Spirit is the dynamic and central sign of the end's manifestation. Joel 2:28-32 – "And it shall come to pass afterward, that I will pour out my Spirit on all flesh; your sons and your daughters shall prophesy, your old men shall dream dreams, and your young men shall see visions. [29] Even on the male and female servants in those days I will pour out my Spirit. [30] "And I will show wonders in the heavens and on the earth, blood and fire and columns of smoke. [31] The sun shall be turned to darkness, and the moon to blood, before the great and awesome day of the Lord comes. [32] And it shall come to pass that everyone who calls on the name of the Lord shall be saved. For in Mount Zion and in Jerusalem there shall be those who escape, as the Lord has said, and among the survivors shall be those whom the Lord calls."

2. The gift of the Holy Spirit upon the believers on the day of Pentecost is the fulfillment of this prophecy, and represents *this present age* as the literal *eschaton,* the final age of God's salvific work in the world.

    a. Peter identified the outpouring of the Spirit at Pentecost as the fulfillment of the Joel text.
    Acts 2:14-18 (ESV) – But Peter, standing with the eleven, lifted up his voice and addressed them, "Men of Judea and all who dwell in Jerusalem, let this be known to you, and give ear to my words. [15] For these men are not drunk, as you suppose, since it is only the third hour of the day. [16] But this is what was uttered through the prophet Joel: [17] " 'And in the last days it shall be, God declares, that I will pour out my Spirit on all flesh, and your sons and your daughters shall prophesy, and your young men shall see visions, and your old men shall dream dreams; [18] even on my male servants and female servants in those days I will pour out my Spirit, and they shall prophesy.

    b. We therefore are presently in the *eschaton,* the last time.

1 John 2:18 – Children, it is the last hour, and as you have heard that antichrist is coming, so now many antichrists have come. Therefore, we know that it is the last hour.

3. The presence of the Spirit in the church is the pledge and assurance of the future possession of eternal life promised to those who believe in the person of Jesus Christ.

   a. 2 Cor. 1:21-22 – And it is God who establishes us with you in Christ, and has anointed us, [22] and who has also put his seal on us and given us his Spirit in our hearts as a guarantee.

   b. Eph. 1:13-14 – In him you also, when you heard the word of truth, the gospel of your salvation, and believed in him, were sealed with the promised Holy Spirit, [14] who is the guarantee of our inheritance until we acquire possession of it, to the praise of his glory.

   c. Eph. 4:30 – And do not grieve the Holy Spirit of God, by whom you were sealed for the day of redemption.

I. The Day of the Lord, as described in the OT:

1. It will involve swift destruction upon the enemies of God and Israel.
   Joel 2:1-2 – Blow a trumpet in Zion; sound an alarm on my holy mountain! Let all the inhabitants of the land tremble, for the day of the Lord is coming; it is near, [2] a day of darkness and gloom, a day of clouds and thick darkness! Like blackness there is spread upon the mountains a great and powerful people; their like has never been before, nor will be again after them through the years of all generations.

2. The Lord comes on that Day with fierce wrath and anger.
   Isaiah 13:9-11 – Behold, the day of the Lord comes, cruel, with wrath and fierce anger, to make the land a desolation and to destroy its sinners from it. [10] For the stars of the heavens and their constellations will not give their light; the sun will be dark at its rising, and the moon will not shed its light. [11] I will punish the world for its evil, and the wicked for their iniquity; I will put an end to the pomp of the arrogant, and lay low the pompous pride of the ruthless.

3. It is a day of divine visitation and judgment.
   Amos 5:18-20 – Woe to you who desire the day of the Lord! Why would you have the day of the Lord? It is darkness, and not light, [19] as if a man fled from a lion, and a bear met him, or went into the house and leaned his hand against the wall, and a serpent bit him. [20] Is not the day of the Lord darkness, and not light, and gloom with no brightness in it? (cf. Isa. 2.12, 17; Zeph. 1.14-15; Mal. 4.5)

4. The Day of the Lord will bring transformation, blessing, and deliverance to those who fear the Lord.

   a. Malachi 4:1-2 – "For behold, the day is coming, burning like an oven, when all the arrogant and all evildoers will be stubble. The day that is coming shall set them ablaze, says the Lord of hosts, so that it will leave them neither root nor branch. [2] But for you who fear my name, the sun of righteousness shall rise with healing in its wings. You shall go out leaping like calves from the stall.

   b. Psalm 92:12 – The righteous flourish like the palm tree and grow like a cedar in Lebanon.

   c. Isaiah 55:12-13 – "For you shall go out in joy and be led forth in peace; the mountains and the hills before you shall break forth into singing, and all the trees of the field shall clap their hands. [13] Instead of the thorn shall come up the cypress; instead of the brier shall come up the myrtle; and it shall make a name for the Lord, an everlasting sign that shall not be cut off."

    d. Jeremiah 31:9-14 – With weeping they shall come, and with pleas for mercy I will lead them back, I will make them walk by brooks of water, in a straight path in which they shall not stumble, for I am a father to Israel, and Ephraim is my firstborn. [10] "Hear the word of the Lord, O nations, and declare it in the coastlands far away; say, 'He who scattered Israel will gather him, and will keep him as a shepherd keeps his flock.' [11] For the Lord has ransomed Jacob and has redeemed him from hands too strong for him. [12] They shall come and sing aloud on the height of Zion, and they shall be radiant over the goodness of the Lord, over the grain, the wine, and the oil, and over the young of the flock and the herd; their life shall be like a watered garden, and they shall languish no more. [13] Then shall the young women rejoice in the dance, and the young men and the old shall be merry. I will turn their mourning into joy; I will comfort them, and give them gladness for sorrow. [14] I will feast the soul of the priests with abundance, and my people shall be satisfied with my goodness, declares the Lord."

    e. Hosea 14:5-7 – I will be like the dew to Israel; he shall blossom like the lily; he shall take root like the trees of Lebanon; [6] his shoots shall spread out; his beauty shall be like the olive, and his fragrance like Lebanon. [7] They shall return and dwell beneath my shadow; they shall flourish like the grain; they shall blossom like the vine; their fame shall be like the wine of Lebanon.

J. The eschatological vision of the OT envisions new heavens and a new earth.

  1. God himself will create new heavens and a new earth, and the former world will no longer come to mind. Isaiah 65:17-18 – "For behold, I create new heavens

and a new earth, and the former things shall not be remembered or come into mind. [18] But be glad and rejoice forever in that which I create; for behold, I create Jerusalem to be a joy, and her people to be a gladness.

2. God has sworn that this universe will be remade, remolded, and refashioned, even as his people shall be. Isaiah 66:22 – "For as the new heavens and the new earth that I make shall remain before me, says the Lord, so shall your offspring and your name remain.

3. This promise of the new heavens and earth is incorporated into the NT vision of Christ's finishing saving work.
2 Peter 3:13 – But according to his promise we are waiting for new heavens and a new earth in which righteousness dwells.

4. According to the *progressive revelation of the apostles,* this new heaven and new earth will be accompanied with the very dwelling of God where the redeemed shall live forever.
Rev. 21:1-3 – Then I saw a new heaven and a new earth, for the first heaven and the first earth had passed away, and the sea was no more. [2] And I saw the holy city, new Jerusalem, coming down out of heaven from God, prepared as a bride adorned for her husband. [3] And I heard a loud voice from the throne saying, "Behold, the dwelling place of God is with man. He will dwell with them, and they will be his people, and God himself will be with them as their God.

K. Summary

Let us now sum up what we have learned about the eschatological outlook of the Old Testament. At the very beginning, there was an expectation of a coming redeemer who would bruise or crush the head of the serpent. As time went on, there was a growing enrichment of eschatological expectation. The various items of this expectation were certainly not all held at once, and they assumed various forms at various times. But

> if we may think of these concepts in a cumulative way, we may certainly say that at various times the Old Testament believer looked for the following eschatological realities in the future: (1) the coming redeemer, (2) the kingdom of God, (3) the new covenant, (4) the restoration of Israel, (5) the outpouring of the Spirit, (6) the day of the Lord, (7) the new heavens and the new earth. All these things loomed on the horizon of expectation."
>
> Hoekema, pp. 11-12.

Everyone's driving habits change when they catch sight of the police squad car, so surely the idea of the Lord's sure return, and his fear, is the *beginning* of wisdom. – Anonymous

II. **The Kingdom Story as Cosmic Drama**

The Second Coming of our Lord Jesus must be at the center of our worship, celebration, preaching, and discipleship, for it is the doctrine which provides us with the greatest incentive to sacrifice all we have and are in this world for the coming glory ahead.

> Num. 24:17-19 – I see him, but not now; I behold him, but not near: a star shall come out of Jacob, and a scepter shall rise out of Israel; it shall crush the forehead of Moab and break down all the sons of Sheth. [18] Edom shall be dispossessed; Seir also, his enemies, shall be dispossessed. Israel is doing valiantly. [19] And one from Jacob shall exercise dominion and destroy the survivors of cities!"

A. Components of a guiding worldview (from Arthur Holmes):

1. It has a *holistic* goal. (Where did we come from and where are we going?)

2. It is a *perspectival* approach. (From what vantage point do we see things?)

3. It is an *exploratory* process. (How do we continue to understand our lives?)

4. It is *pluralistic*. (What other views are suggested by our collective vision?)

5. It has *action outcomes*. (What ought we to do in light of our mythic vision?)

B. How the world works: the power of a mythology.

1. Where did we all come from? *Cosmology and origins*

2. What is the purpose of life? *Teleology*

3. How ought we then to live? *Morality*

4. Where do we go when we die? *Metaphysics and transcendence*

C. The wonder of story: when philosophy and narrative marry one another.

1. The centrality of human experience

2. The richness of human affections

3. The use of sanctified imagination

4. The power of concrete image, action, and symbol

5. The immediacy of heightened reality

6. The enjoyment of artistic craftsmanship

D. Key Propositions of Story Theology

William J. Bausch lists ten propositions related to story theology that help us understand the significance and importance of the study of stories and the understanding of Bible and theology: (William J. Bausch, *Storytelling and Faith*. Mystic, Connecticut: Twenty-Third Publications, 1984.)

1. Stories introduce us to *sacramental presences.*

2. Stories are always more important than *facts.*

3. Stories remain *normative (authoritative)* for the Christian community of faith.

4. *Christian traditions* evolve and define themselves through and around stories.

5. The stories of God precede, produce, and empower *the community of God's people.*

6. Community story implies *censure, rebuke, and accountability.*

7. Stories produce *theology.*

8. Stories produce *many theologies.*

9. Stories produce *ritual and sacrament.*

10. Stories are *history.*

III. The Story of "Thy Kingdom Come:" Living Under God's Reign

A. The distinctiveness of Jesus' gospel: "The Kingdom is at hand." Mark 1.14-15

B. Jesus and the inauguration of the Age to Come into this present age:

1. The coming of John the Baptist. Matthew 11.2-6

2. The inauguration of Jesus's ministry. Luke 4.16-21

3. The confrontation of Jesus with demonic forces. Luke 10.18ff.; 11.20

4. The teaching of Jesus and His claim of absolute authority on earth. Mark 2.1-12; Matt. 21.27; 28.18

Christ's death for our sins — His payment of the penalty declared against us — was His legal victory whereby He erased Satan's legal claim to the human race. But Christ also won dynamic victory. That is, when He was justified and made alive, adjudged and declared righteous in the Supreme Court of the universe, Satan, the arch foe of God and man, was completely disarmed and dethroned. Christ burst forth triumphantly from that age-old prison of the dead. Paul says that He "spoiled principalities and powers" and "made a show of them openly, triumphing over them in it." (Colossians 2.15)."

Paul Billheimer, *Destined for the Throne*, p. 87.

---

5. "The Kingdom has come, and the strong man is bound." Matt. 12.28,29

6. The kingdom of God "has come." – *pleroo*

7. The meaning of the Greek verb: "To fulfill, to complete, to be fulfilled, as in prophecy."

8. The invasion, entrance, manifestation of God's kingly power.

9. Jesus as the binder of the strong man:
Matt. 12:25-30 – Knowing their thoughts, he said to them, "Every kingdom divided against itself is laid waste, and no city or house divided against itself will stand. [26] And if Satan casts out Satan, he is divided against himself. How then will his kingdom stand? [27] And if I cast out demons by Beelzebul, by whom do your sons cast them out? Therefore they will be your judges. [28] But if it is by the Spirit of God that I cast out demons, then the kingdom of God has come upon you. [29] Or how can someone enter a strong man's house and plunder his goods, unless he first binds the strong man? Then indeed he may plunder his house. [30] Whoever is not with me is against me, and whoever does not gather with me scatters.

C. Two manifestations of the Kingdom of God: The "Already/Not Yet" Kingdom (Oscar Cullman, *Christ and Time*; George Ladd, *The Gospel of the Kingdom*)

1. The *first advent*: The rebellious prince is bound and his house looted, and God's reign has come.

2. The *second advent*: The rebellious prince is destroyed, and his rule confounded with the full manifestation of God's kingly power in a recreated heaven and earth.

IV. **The Christocentric Order: Messiah Yeshua of Nazareth as Centerpiece in Both God's Revelation and Rule**

> Jesus' message was the Kingdom of God. It was the center and circumference of all He taught and did. . . . The Kingdom of God is the master-conception, the master-plan, the master-purpose, the master-will that gathers everything up into itself and gives it redemption, coherence, purpose, goal.
>
> E. Stanley Jones, *Is the Kingdom of God Realism?*

A. Messiah's *mission*: to destroy the works of the devil. 1 John 3.8

B. Messiah's *birth*: the invasion of God into Satan's dominion. Luke 1.31-33

C. Messiah's *message*: the Kingdom's proclamation and inauguration. Mark 1.14-15

D. Messiah's *teaching*: Kingdom ethics. Matt. 5-7

E. Messiah's *miracles*: His kingly authority and power. Mark 2.8-12

F. Messiah's *exorcisms*: His defeat of the devil and his angels. Luke 11.14-20

G. Messiah's *life and deeds*: The majesty of the Kingdom. John 1.14-18

H. Messiah's *resurrection*: The victory and vindication of the King. Rom. 1.1-4

I. Messiah's *commission*: The call to proclaim His Kingdom worldwide. Matt.28.18-20

J. Messiah's *ascension*: His coronation. Heb.1.2-4

K. Messiah's *Spirit*: The "arrabon" (surety, pledge) of the Kingdom. 2 Cor.1.20

L. Messiah's *Church*: The foretaste and agent of the Kingdom. 2 Cor.5.18-21

M. Messiah's *session in heaven*: The generalship of God's forces. 1 Cor. 15.24-28

N. Messiah's *Parousia (coming)*: The final consummation of the Kingdom. Rev. 19

....

God's Kingdom means the divine conquest over His enemies, a conquest which is to be accomplished in *three stages;* and *the first victory has already occurred.* The power of the Kingdom of God has invaded the realm of Satan–the present evil Age. The activity of this power to deliver men from satanic rule was evidenced in the exorcism of demons. Thereby, Satan was bound; he was cast down from his position of power; his power was "destroyed." The blessings of the Messianic Age are now available to those who embrace the Kingdom of God. We may already enjoy the blessings resulting from this initial defeat of Satan This does not mean that we enjoy the fullness of God's blessings, or that all that is meant by the Kingdom of God has come to us. . . . the Second Coming of Christ is absolutely essential for the fulfillment and consummation of God's redemptive work. Yet God has already accomplished the first great stage in His work of redemption. Satan is the god of This Age, yet the power of Satan has been broken that men may know the rule of God in their lives.

George Ladd, *The Gospel of the Kingdom*, p. 50.

V. The Kingdom of God Is Present and Offered in the Midst of the Church

A. The *Shekinah* has reappeared in our midst as His temple. Eph. 2.19-22

B. The people (*ekklesia*) of the living God congregate here: Christ's own from every kindred, people, nation, tribe, status, and culture. 1 Pet. 2.8-9

C. God's *Sabbath* is enjoyed and celebrated here: freedom, wholeness, and the justice of God. Heb. 4.3-10

D. The *Year of Jubilee* has come: forgiveness, renewal, and restitution. Col. 1.13; Matt. 6.33; Eph. 1.3; 2 Pet. 1.3-4

E. The Spirit (*arrabon*) indwells us: God lives here and walks among us here. 2 Cor. 1.20

F. We taste the powers of the Age to Come: Satan is bound in our midst; the *Curse* has been broken here; deliverance is experienced in Jesus' name. Gal. 3.10-14

G. We experience the *shalom* of God's eternal kingdom: the freedom, wholeness, and justice of the new order are present here. Rom. 5.1; Eph. 2.13-22

H. We herald the Good News of God's reign (*evanggelion*). We invite all to join us as we journey to the full manifestation of the Age to Come. Mark 1.14-15

I. Here we cry *Maranatha!* Our lives are structured by the living hope of God's future and the consummation. Rev. 22.17-21

> When Christ took his seat in the heavens, He proved conclusively that Satan's devastation was complete, that he was utterly undone. Hell was thrown into total bankruptcy. Satan was not only stripped of his legal authority and dominion, but by an infinitely superior force he was stripped of his weapons also. But this is not all. When Jesus burst forth from that dark prison and "ascended up on high," all believers were raised and seated together with Him "But God . . . brought us to life with Christ. . . . And in union with Christ Jesus he raised us up and enthroned us with him in the heavenly realms." (Ephesians 2.4-6 NEB)
>
> Paul Billheimer, *Destined for the Throne*, p. 87.

VI. The Already/Not Yet Kingdom

    A. Through the Incarnation and the Passion of Christ, *Satan was bound*.

        1. Jesus has triumphed over the devil. 1 John 3.8

        2. Jesus is crowned as Lord of all. Heb. 1.4; Phil. 2.5-11

        3. Satan is now judged. Luke 10.17-21

        4. Satan's power has been severely curtailed. James 4.8

        5. His authority has been broken. 1 Pet. 5.8

        6. His minions are being routed. Col. 2.15

        7. His system is fading away. 1 John 2.15-17

8. Those he enslaved are being set free. Col. 13-14

9. His eventual doom has been secured. Rom. 16.20

B. Although Satan has been defeated, he is *still lethal and awaits his own utter destruction.*

1. "Bound, but with a long rope." 2 Cor. 10.3-5; Eph. 2.2

2. "A roaring lion, but sick, hungry, and mad." 1 Pet. 5.8

3. Satan continues to be God's active enemy of the Kingdom:

    a. Blinds the minds of those who do not believe. 2 Cor. 4.4

    b. Functions through deception, lying, and accusation. John 8.44

    c. Animates the affairs of nations. 1 John 5.19

    d. Distracts human beings from their proper ends. cf. Gen. 3.1.ff.

    e. Oppresses human beings through harassment, slander, fear, accusation, and death. Heb. 2.14-15

    f. Resists and persecutes God's people. Eph. 6.10-18

C. Satan's final doom is *certain and future.*

1. He has been both spoiled and utterly humiliated in the Cross. Col. 2.15

2. His final demise will come by Christ at the end of the age. Rev. 20

3. Missions is the announcement and demonstration of the defeat of Satan through Christ:

   a. The ministry of reconciliation. 2 Cor. 5.18-21

   b. The ministry of disciple-making. Matt. 28.18-20

II. **Special Characteristics of the NT Kingdom Framework: The Story of God** (Hoekema, pp 14-54)

   A. The NT declares and testifies that the predicted OT eschatological event has been fulfilled in the person of Jesus of Nazareth.

   1. The virgin has given birth to Immanuel.
      Matt. 1.20-23 with Isa. 7.14

   2. The Messiah was born in Bethlehem.
      Matt. 2.5-6 with Micah 5.2

   3. The Redeemer fled to Egypt for safety.
      Matt. 2.14-15 with Hos. 11.1

   4. The King enters into Jerusalem.
      Matt. 21.4-5 with Zech. 9.9, etc.

B. The events recognized as singular in the OT prophetic vision are represented in <u>two stages</u> in the NT:

- The present *Messianic Age* (fulfilled in Jesus of Nazareth).

- The *Age of the Future* (where Jesus will consummate his work already begun).

1. The powers of the Age to Come have been and are being tasted in the Church of God. Heb. 6.5

2. The Holy Spirit is the very pledge (down payment) and seal of the future inheritance, the hope of eternal glory. (cf. Eph. 1.13; Eph. 4.30; 2 Cor. 1.22)

3. Christ has appeared to humankind at the end of the ages to put away sin, and will appear the second time for full deliverance of his people. Heb. 9.26-28

C. The blessings of the Age to Come (which are being experienced right now in the church) are the pledge, guarantee, and seal of the "greater blessings to come."

1. The First Coming is the pledge and brings certainty of the Second.
   Acts 1:11 – "Men of Galilee, why do you stand looking into heaven? This Jesus, who was taken up from you into heaven, will come in the same way as you saw him go into heaven."

2. The Holy Spirit in the Church and in the Christian is the seal of the inheritance to come.
   Eph. 1:13-14 – In him you also, when you heard the word of truth, the gospel of your salvation, and believed in him, were sealed with the promised Holy Spirit, [14] who is the guarantee of our inheritance until we acquire possession of it, to the praise of his glory.

3. Believers "occupy till he comes," living between the two comings of Christ, bearing witness to his name in the world.
Titus 2:11-14 – For the grace of God has appeared, bringing salvation for all people, [12] training us to renounce ungodliness and worldly passions, and to live self-controlled, upright, and godly lives in the present age, [13] waiting for our blessed hope, the appearing of the glory of our great God and Savior Jesus Christ, [14] who gave himself for us to redeem us from all lawlessness and to purify for himself a people for his own possession who are zealous for good works.

4. Kingdom teaching is the ultimate point of reference. "Oscar Cullman uses a well-known figure: the Christian believer lives between D-day and V-day. D-day was the first coming of Christ, when the enemy was decisively defeated; V-day is the Second Coming of Christ, when the enemy shall totally and finally surrender." — Hoekema, p. 21

....

The hope of the final victory is so much the more vivid because of the unshakably firm conviction that the battle that decides the victory has already taken place.

George Ladd, *The Presence of the Future*, p. 337.

....

D. The meaning of history: (Hoekema, p. 23f)

1. History is the outworking of God's purposes. (*Heilsgeschichte* versus *Historie*)

2. The triune God is the Lord of history, ruling over all. Ps. 103.19; 2 Chron. 20.6; Eph. 1.11

3. Jesus of Nazareth is the center of history itself. (The coming of Christ into the world is the "central fact of history.")

   a. History is dominated by Christ: God was in Christ reconciling the world to himself. 2 Cor. 5.18-21

   b. In Jesus, the final victory over the curse, death, evil, and the devil are won decisively and finally. Col. 2.15

   c. The Lamb alone is worthy to take the scroll from the hand of him on the throne and set God's salvific purpose into motion. Rev. 5

4. The new age has been ushered in with the presence of Jesus of Nazareth. Luke 7.28

5. Augmented Hoekema:
   All of history is moving toward a goal: *the totalizing summary of God as all-in-all in the new heavens and new earth after every enemy of Christ has been placed under his feet.*
   1 Cor. 15:23-28 – But each in his own order: Christ the firstfruits, then at his coming those who belong to Christ. [24] Then comes the end, when he delivers the kingdom to God the Father after destroying every rule and every authority and power. [25] For he must reign until he has put all his enemies under his feet. [26] The last enemy to be destroyed is death. [27] For " God has put all things in subjection under his feet." But when it says, "all things are put in subjection," it is plain that he is excepted who put all things in subjection under him. [28] When all things are subjected to him, then the Son himself will also be subjected to him who put all things in subjection under him, that God may be all in all.

III. **Tua Da Gloriam: "The Historic Hope of the Church"**

Ps. 115.1-3 – Not unto us, O Lord, not unto us, But to Your name give glory, Because of Your mercy, And because of Your truth. Why should the Gentiles say, "Where now is their God?" But our God is in heaven; He does whatever He pleases."

....

From Before to Beyond Time
Adapted from Suzanne de Dietrich, *God's Unfolding Purpose*.
Philadelphia: Westminster Press, 1976.

A. *Before Time* (Eternity Past)
   Ps. 90:1-3

   1. The Eternal Triune God
      Ps. 102:24-27

   2. God's Eternal Purpose
      2 Tim. 1:9; Isa. 14:26-27

      a. To glorify His name in creation.
         Prov. 16:4; Ps. 135:6; Isa. 48:11

      b. To display His perfections in the universe.
         Ps. 19:1

      c. To draw out a people for Himself.
         Isa. 43:7, 21

   3. The Mystery of Iniquity: The Rebellion of the Dawn of the Morning (*Lucifer*)
      Isa. 14:12-20; Ezek. 28:13-17

4. The Principalities and Powers
   Col. 2:15

B. *The Beginning of Time* (The Creation)
   Gen. 1-2

   1. The Creative Word of the Triune God.
      Gen. 1:3; Ps. 33:6,9; Ps. 148:1-5

   2. The Creation of Humanity: The Imago Dei.
      Gen. 1:26-27

C. *The Tragedy of Time* (The Fall and the Curse)
   Gen. 3

   1. The Fall and the Curse.
      Gen. 3:1-9

   2. The *Protoevangelium*: the Promised Seed
      Gen. 3:15

   3. The End of Eden and the Reign of Death.
      Gen. 3:22-24

   4. First Signs of Grace.
      Gen. 3:15, 21

D. *The Unfolding of Time* (God's Plan Revealed Through the People Israel)

   1. The Abrahamic Promise and the Covenant of Yahweh (Patriarchs).
      Gen. 12:1-3; 15; 17; 18:18; 28:4

2. The Exodus and the Covenant at Sinai:
   Exodus

3. The Conquest of the Inhabitants and the Promised Land:
   Joshua to 2 Chronicles

4. The City, the Temple, and the Throne:
   Ps. 48:1-3; 2 Chron. 7:14; 2 Sam. 7:8ff.

   a. The role of the prophet: *to declare the word of the Lord.*
      Deut. 18:15 -- The Lord your God will raise up for you a prophet like me from among you, from your brothers—it is to him you shall listen

   b. The role of the priest: *to represent God and the people.*
      Heb. 5:1 -- For every high priest chosen from among men is appointed to act on behalf of men in relation to God, to offer gifts and sacrifices for sins.

   c. The role of the king: *to rule with righteousness and justice in God's stead.*
      Ps. 72.1-2 -- Give the king your justice, O God, and your righteousness to the royal son! [2] May he judge your people with righteousness, and your poor with justice!

5. The Captivity and the Exile:
   Daniel, Ezekiel, Lamentations

6. The Return of the Remnant:
   Ezra, Nehemiah

E. ***The Fullness of Time*** (**Incarnation of the Messiah Yeshua [Christ Jesus]**)
   Gal. 4:4-6

1. The Word Becomes Flesh.
   John 1:14-18; 1 John 1:1-4

2. The Testimony of John the Baptist:
   Matt. 3:1-3

3. The Kingdom Has Come in the Person of Jesus of Nazareth.
   Mark 1:14-15; Luke 10:9-11; 10:11; 17:20-21

   a. Revealed in His person.
      John 1:18 -- No one has ever seen God; the only God, who is at the Father's side, he has made him known.

   b. Exhibited in His works.
      John 5:36 -- But the testimony that I have is greater than that of John. For the works that the Father has given me to accomplish, the very works that I am doing, bear witness about me that the Father has sent me.
      (cf. John 3:2; 9:30-33; 10:37-38; Acts 2:22; 10:38-39)

   c. Interpreted in His testimony. (Matt. 5-7)

4. The Secret of the Kingdom Has Been Revealed.
   Mark 1:14-15 -- Now after John was arrested, Jesus came into Galilee, proclaiming the gospel of God, [15] and saying, "The time is fulfilled, and the kingdom of God is at hand; repent and believe in the gospel."

   a. The Kingdom is already present.
      Matt. 12:25-28 -- Knowing their thoughts, he said to them, "Every kingdom divided against itself is laid waste, and no city or house divided against itself will stand. [26] And if Satan casts out Satan, he is

divided against himself. How then will his kingdom stand? [27] And if I cast out demons by Beelzebul, by whom do your sons cast them out? Therefore they will be your judges. [28] But if it is by the Spirit of God that I cast out demons, then the kingdom of God has come upon you.

b. The Kingdom is not yet consummated.
Matt. 25:31-34 -- When the Son of Man comes in his glory, and all the angels with him, then he will sit on his glorious throne. [32] Before him will be gathered all the nations, and he will separate people one from another as a shepherd separates the sheep from the goats. [33] And he will place the sheep on his right, but the goats on the left. [34] Then the King will say to those on his right, 'Come, you who are blessed by my Father, inherit the kingdom prepared for you from the foundation of the world.

5. The Passion and Death of the Crucified King:
Matt. 26:36-46; Mark 14:32-42; Luke 22:39-46; John 18:1ff.

   a. To destroy the devil's work: *Christus Victor.*
   1 John 3:8; Gen. 3:15; Col. 2:15; Rom. 16:20; Heb. 2:14-15

   b. To make atonement for sin: *Christus Victim.*
   1 John 2:1-2; Rom. 5:8-9; 1 John 4:9-10; 1 John 3:16

   c. To reveal the Father's heart.
   John 3:16; Titus 2:11-15

6. *Christus Victor:* The Resurrection of the Glorious Lord of life.
Matt. 28:1-15; Mark 16:1-11; Luke 24:1-12

F. *The Last Times* (The Descent and Age of the Holy Spirit)

1. The *arrabon* of God: The Spirit as Pledge and Sign of the Kingdom's presence
   Eph. 1:13-14; 4:30; Acts 2:1-47

2. Peter, at Pentecost, and the Presence of the Future: "This is that."

   a. The Church as foretaste and agent of the Kingdom.
      Phil. 2:14-16; 2 Cor. 5:20

   b. The present reign of Messiah Jesus.
      1 Cor 15:24-28; Acts 2:34; Eph. 1:20-23; Heb. 1:13

   c. The ushering in of God's kingdom community "in-between the times".
      Rom. 14:7

3. The Church of Messiah Jesus: Sojourners in the Already and the Not Yet

   a. The Great Confession: Jesus is Lord.
      Phil. 2:9-11

   b. The Great Commission: Go and make disciples among all nations.
      Matt. 28:18-20; Acts 1:8

   c. The Great Commandment: Love God and people.
      Matt. 22:37-39

4. The Announcement of the Mystery: Gentiles as Fellow-Heirs of Promise. Rom. 16:25-27; Col. 1:26-28; Eph. 3:3-11

   a. Jesus as the *Last Adam,* the Head of a New Human Race.
      1 Cor. 15:45-49

   b. God drawing out of the world a New Humanity.
      Eph. 2:12-22

5. In-Between the Times: Tokens of *Age of Sabbath and of Jubilee.*
   Acts 2:17 ff.; cf. Joel 2; Amos 9; Ezek. 36:25-27

G. *The Fulfillment of Time* (**The *Parousia* of Christ**), 1 Thess. 4:13-17

   1. Completion of World Mission: the evangelization of the world's *ethnoi.* Matt. 24:14; Mark 16:15-16; Rom. 10:18

   2. The apostasy of the Church.
      1 Tim. 4:1-3; 2 Tim. 4:3; 2 Thess. 2:3-12

   3. The Great Tribulation.
      Matt. 24:21ff; Luke 21:24

   4. The Parousia: the Second Coming of Jesus
      1 Thess. 4:13-17; 1 Cor. 15:50-58; Luke 21:25-27; Dan. 7:13

   5. The Reign of Jesus Christ on earth
      Rev. 20:1-4

6. The Great White Throne and Lake of Fire.
   Rev. 20:11-15

7. "For He Must Reign:" The final placement of all enemies under Christ's feet.
   1 Cor. 15:24-28

H. *Beyond Time* (Eternity Future)

1. The Creation of the New Heaven and Earth.
   Rev. 21:1; Isa. 65:17-19; 66:22; 2 Pet. 3:13

2. The Descent of the New Jerusalem: The Abode of God Comes to Earth.
   Rev. 21:2-4

3. The Times of Refreshing: the Glorious Freedom of the Children of God.
   Rom. 8:18-23

4. The Lord Christ Gives Over the Kingdom to God the Father.
   1 Cor. 15:24-28

5. The Age to Come: The Triune God as All-in-All.
   Zech. 14:9 & 2:10; Jer. 23:6; Matt. 1:23; Ps. 72:8-11; Mic. 4:1-3

I. Implications of the *Already/Not Yet Kingdom Drama of All Time*

1. God's Sovereign Purpose Underwrites All Human History.

a. Whatever he pleases, he does.
Ps. 135:6

b. God's counsels and plans stand forever, to all generations.
Ps. 33:11; Ps. 115:3

c. God declares the end of all things from the beginning.
Isa. 46:10

d. Nothing and no one can withstand God's plan for salvation and redemption.
Dan. 4:35

2. God is the Central Character in the Unfolding of the Divine Drama. Eph. 1:9-11

3. Missions is the *Recovery of that Which Was Lost* at the Beginning of Time.

   a. God's sovereign rule.
   Mark 1:14-15

   b. Satan's infernal rebellion.
   Gen. 3:15 with Col. 2:15; 1 John 3:8

   c. Humankind's tragic fall.
   Gen. 3:1-8 cf. Rom. 5:5-8

   d. Making disciples among all nations is *fulfilling our role in the script of Almighty God!*

IV. Conclusion: "There's Plenty Good Room in My Father's Kingdom!"

Though Christ has ushered in the new age, the final consummation of the new age is still future. The Bible therefore sees history as directed toward a divinely ordained goal. The Bible therefore sees history as directed as directed toward a divinely ordained goal. . . . The New Testament believer, therefore, is aware that history is moving toward the goal of this final consummation. This consummation of history, as he [sic] sees it, includes such events as the Second Coming of Christ, the general resurrection, the Day of Judgment, and the new heavens and new earth. Since the new heavens and new earth will be the culmination of history, we may say that all history is moving toward this goal.

Hoekema, *The Bible and the Future*, pp. 31-32.

Isaiah 65:17 – For behold, I create new heavens and a new earth, and the former things shall not be remembered or come into mind.

- The ancient Kingdom promise of a coming redeemer has been fulfilled in the person of Jesus of Nazareth.

- All that we are and all that we do must be done in light of the "already but not yet" Kingdom.

The Bottom Line: _____

Lesson Three
Physical Death, Immortality, and the Intermediate State

Archie Bunker and A Unique Idea of Death

"When you gotta go, you gotta go. You because he wants you. And when he wants you. And he don't want no quack doctors putting new hearts into you and keeping you here against his will, 'cause it throws him off schedule. It throws him all off. Now you do that to him . . . throw his schedule off like that, and when you get up there, you'll have to answer to him won't you? Because he'll want to know why you didn't come up when you were called. Why you were late. Why you ignored him."

Spencer Marsh, God, Man and Archie Bunker
(New York: Harper and Row Publishers, 1975).

I. Physical Death

Death is now viewed in the light of the resurrection of Jesus. In 75 places nekros is the object of egeiro, "to awaken," or anastasis, "to raise" (NIDNT 1: 445), and Christ is called the first (in importance, not time) from the dead (Col 1.18; Rev 1.5). Death does not "separate us" from Christ (Rom 8.38–39); so death is spoken of as being "at home with the Lord" (2 Cor 5.8), as "gain" (Phil 1.21), and "to depart and to be with Christ" (Phil 1.23), and as to have "fallen asleep" (John 11.11). In the NT death is more than a terminus to life. It can affect life as it moves to that end. One can experience a living death, or a "body of death," Rom 7.24. Existentially, one who has encountered Christ is said to have eternal life even during this present life (John 3.36); whereas, one who has not yet encountered Christ is said to be "dead" in sin (Eph 2.1; cf. Col 2.13; Rev 3.1). Passing from death to life, experientially, is spoken of as the new birth (John 3.3–8). To a degree, then, eternal life (the opposite of death) is given now, but not in fullness. "For as in Adam all die, so in Christ all will be made alive" (1 Cor 15.22). The tension between the "already" and the "not yet" maintains an "eschatological reserve," for "the last enemy to be destroyed is death" (1 Cor 15.26). The final generation, living at the Parousia, will be translated without experiencing death (Matt 16.28). Evidently the translated, and those resurrected, begin the fullness of eternal life at the Parousia (1 Thess 4.16–18). They will be beyond death (Rev 20.6).

Norman R. Gulley. "Death," The Anchor Bible Dictionary.
New York: Doubleday Publishers, 1996.

Psalm 39:4 – O Lord, make me know my end and what is the measure of my days; let me know how fleeting I am!

A. Definition: Physical Death is the termination of physical life in various aspects.

1. The dust returning to the earth.
   Eccles. 12:7 – and the dust returns to the earth as it was, and the spirit returns to God who gave it.

2. Our breath taken away.
   Psalm 104:29 – When you hide your face, they are dismayed; when you take away their breath, they die and return to their dust.

3. Our earthly house being put off.

   a. 2 Cor. 5:1 – For we know that if the tent, which is our earthly home, is destroyed, we have a building from God, a house not made with hands, eternal in the heavens.

   b. 2 Peter 1:13-14 – I think it right, as long as I am in this body, to stir you up by way of reminder, [14] since I know that the putting off of my body will be soon, as our Lord Jesus Christ made clear to me.

4. Being unclothed.
   2 Cor. 5:3-4 – if indeed by putting it on we may not be found naked. [4] For while we are still in this tent, we groan, being burdened– not that we would be unclothed, but that we would be further clothed, so that what is mortal may be swallowed up by life.

5. Falling asleep.
   Psalm 76:5 – The stouthearted were stripped of their

spoil; they sank into sleep; all the men of war were unable to use their hands.

6. Going and not returning from the land of darkness. Job 10:21 – Before I go—and I shall not return—to the land of darkness and deep shadow

B. An unusual viewpoint from Karl Barth: *Death is a part of God's good creation.*

1. Barth, summarized:

    a. The death of humankind was not the result of fall into sin, but an aspect of God's good creation.

    b. God planned from the beginning that the life of human beings would end.

    c. Although death is a sign of God's judgment today, this judgment has been taken away from Christ: Humankind goes from *nonexistence*, to the experience of life, and then *back to nonexistence*.

2. Hoekema: Barth has a faulty position. (Hoekema, p. 81)

    a. Why does the Bible link sin and death together?

    b. Why did Christ have to die for our sins?

    c. Why did Christ need to rise again *from among the dead*?

d. Why do the Scriptures teach that both faithful and unfaithful *must rise from the dead?*

C. Death is the result of the <u>sin of humankind</u>: The biblical evidence.

1. The definitive text:
   Gen. 2:16-17 – And the Lord God commanded the man, saying, "You may surely eat of every tree of the garden, [17] but of the tree of the knowledge of good and evil you shall not eat, for in the day that you eat of it you shall surely die."

   a. "Immediate execution of the sentence:" Was it an act of *common grace,* or did God judge all humankind *spiritually* that day they ate of the tree?

   b. Includes both *physical* and *spiritual* death.

   c. Physical death in the world is directly linked to the sin, rebellion of humankind.

2. The wages of sin is *death.*
   Romans 6:22-23 – But now that you have been set free from sin and have become slaves of God, the fruit you get leads to sanctification and its end, eternal life. [23] For the wages of sin is death, but the free gift of God is eternal life in Christ Jesus our Lord.

3. The soul that sins *shall die.*

   a. Ezekiel 18:4 – Behold, all souls are mine; the soul of the father as well as the soul of the son is mine: the soul who sins shall die.

b. Ezekiel 18:20 – The soul who sins shall die. The son shall not suffer for the iniquity of the father, nor the father suffer for the iniquity of the son. The righteousness of the righteous shall be upon himself, and the wickedness of the wicked shall be upon himself.

4. Through Adam, sin entered into the world, and with it, death.

   a. Through Adam, sin entered into the world.
      Romans 5:12 – Therefore, just as sin came into the world through one man, and death through sin, and so death spread to all men because all sinned.

   b. Through Adam, death entered this realm.
      1 Cor. 15:20-22 – But in fact Christ has been raised from the dead, the firstfruits of those who have fallen asleep. [21] For as by a man came death, by a man has come also the resurrection of the dead. [22] For as in Adam all die, so also in Christ shall all be made alive.

5. The progression of sin leads to death.
   James 1:13-14 – Let no one say when he is tempted, "I am being tempted by God," for God cannot be tempted with evil, and he himself tempts no one. [14] But each person is tempted when he is lured and enticed by his own desire. [15] Then desire when it has conceived gives birth to sin, and sin when it is fully grown brings forth death.

6. The body of all people, including believers, eventually will die (unless prevented by the Rapture of Christ. (cf. 1 Thess. 4.14-17)
   Romans 8:10-11 – But if Christ is in you, although the body is dead because of sin, the Spirit is life because of righteousness. [11] If the Spirit of him who raised Jesus from the dead dwells in you, he who raised Christ Jesus

from the dead will also give life to your mortal bodies through his Spirit who dwells in you.

D. The biblical relationship between physical death and redemption:

1. Christ came into the world to conquer and destroy death and he who holds its power over humankind.
   Hebrews 2:14-15 – Since therefore the children share in flesh and blood, he himself likewise partook of the same things, that through death he might destroy the one who has the power of death, that is, the devil, [15] and deliver all those who through fear of death were subject to lifelong slavery.

2. The prophecy is that the coming Redeemer would swallow up death forever.

   a. Isaiah 25:8 – He will swallow up death forever; and the Lord God will wipe away tears from all faces, and the reproach of his people he will take away from all the earth, for the Lord has spoken.

   b. Hosea 13:14 – Shall I ransom them from the power of Sheol? Shall I redeem them from Death? O Death, where are your plagues? O Sheol, where is your sting? Compassion is hidden from my eyes.

   c. 1 Cor. 15:54-55 – When the perishable puts on the imperishable, and the mortal puts on immortality, then shall come to pass the saying that is written: "Death is swallowed up in victory." [55] "O death, where is your victory? O death, where is your sting?"

3. Through his death, Christ received dominion over death and its effects.

a. Death has no dominion over him.
   Romans 6:9 – We know that Christ being raised from the dead will never die again; death no longer has dominion over him.

b. Being loosed from its power, he can now deliver those who are subject to it.
   Acts 2:24-28 – God raised him up, loosing the pangs of death, because it was not possible for him to be held by it. [25] For David says concerning him, " 'I saw the Lord always before me, for he is at my right hand that I may not be shaken; [26] therefore my heart was glad, and my tongue rejoiced; my flesh also will dwell in hope. [27] For you will not abandon my soul to Hades, or let your Holy One see corruption. [28] You have made known to me the paths of life; you will make me full of gladness with your presence.'

c. Christ's life is indestructible.
   Hebrews 7:16 – who has become a priest, not on the basis of a legal requirement concerning bodily descent, but by the power of an indestructible life.

d. His ministry is effective, for death cannot impede it.
   Hebrews 7:25 – Consequently, he is able to save to the uttermost those who draw near to God through him, since he always lives to make intercession for them.

4. Believers are not only redeemed from the power and effects of *sin*, but also from the power of *death*.

   a. Christ has abolished death, and brought life and immortality to light through the Good News.
      2 Tim. 1:8-10 – Therefore do not be ashamed of the testimony about our Lord, nor of me his prisoner, but share in suffering for the gospel by the power of God, [9] who saved us and called us to a holy

calling, not because of our works but because of his own purpose and grace, which he gave us in Christ Jesus before the ages began, [10] and which now has been manifested through the appearing of our Savior Christ Jesus, who abolished death and brought life and immortality to light through the gospel.

b. Christ holds the keys to both death and the grave (Hades).
Rev. 1:17-18 – When I saw him, I fell at his feet as though dead. But he laid his right hand on me, saying, "Fear not, I am the first and the last, [18] and the living one. I died, and behold I am alive forevermore, and I have the keys of Death and Hades.

c. In the coming city of God, death will be abolished forever.
Rev. 21:3-4 – And I heard a loud voice from the throne saying, "Behold, the dwelling place of God is with man. He will dwell with them, and they will be his people, and God himself will be with them as their God. [4] He will wipe away every tear from their eyes, and death shall be no more, neither shall there be mourning nor crying nor pain anymore, for the former things have passed away."

E. Why, then, do believers still die?

1. Our death is *not* a satisfaction for sins committed. Jesus has once for all paid the price for sins committed.
Hebrews 10:12-13 – But when Christ had offered for all time a single sacrifice for sins, he sat down at the right hand of God, [13] waiting from that time until his enemies should be made a footstool for his feet.

2. Our death releases us from the domain and power of sin in this world.

a. Our death will be the end of struggle with sin.
      Romans 6:7-8 – For one who has died has been set free from sin. [8] Now if we have died with Christ, we believe that we will also live with him.

   b. The burden of our fallen earthly body will be over.
      Romans 8:22-23 – For we know that the whole creation has been groaning together in the pains of childbirth until now. [23] And not only the creation, but we ourselves, who have the firstfruits of the Spirit, groan inwardly as we wait eagerly for adoption as sons, the redemption of our bodies.

   c. We enter into another realm altogether.
      Hebrews 12:22-23 – But you have come to Mount Zion and to the city of the living God, the heavenly Jerusalem, and to innumerable angels in festal gathering, [23] and to the assembly of the firstborn who are enrolled in heaven, and to God, the judge of all, and to the spirits of the righteous made perfect.

3. Through our death, we "enter into the full riches of eternal life only after we have passed through the portal of death." (Hoekema, p. 85)

   a. Phil. 1:21-23 – For to me to live is Christ, and to die is gain. [22] If I am to live in the flesh, that means fruitful labor for me. Yet which I shall choose I cannot tell. [23] I am hard pressed between the two. My desire is to depart and be with Christ, for that is far better.

   b. To be absent from this body, is to be transported into the very presence of the Lord.
      2 Cor. 5:6-8 – So we are always of good courage. We know that while we are at home in the body we are away from the Lord, [7] for we walk by faith, not by sight. [8] Yes, we are of good courage, and we would

rather be away from the body and at home with the Lord.

F. Summary

Death is the "last enemy" (1 Cor 15.26), which at the consummation will be "swallowed up" in Christ's final victory (1 Cor 15.55–57; but cf. 2 Tim 1.10). Here again the personification of death is evident, with Paul in 1 Corinthians 15.25–26 listing death as one of the enemies of Psalm 110.1, and in 1 Corinthians 15.54–55 taunting the power of death (cf. Is 25.7; Hos 13.14), which in the OT is sometimes characterized as a cosmic power. The reign of death exceeds humankind and encompasses the cosmos, which longs for its freedom from bondage to decay.

Gerald F. Hawthorne, R. P. Martin, and D. G. Reid,
The Dictionary of Paul and his Letters. (electronic ed.).
Logos Library Systems. Downers Grove, Ill. : InterVarsity Press, 1997.

II. Immortality

The notion of the immortality of the soul (i.e., that human beings in and of themselves possess their own inherent indestructible power for never-ending existence) is not spoken of as the Greeks of old did. Rather, it is best to say that human beings are immortal (not just their soul), and that rather than by our own existence actually continue on according to God's own power either for everlasting judgment or everlasting life, all of which is sustained by him and his power alone. The body of believers will be transformed by the power of Christ at his Second Coming, who will transform our lowly bodies so they can be conformed to his glorious body, because he can now as Lord subdue all things to himself.

2 Tim. 1:8-10 Therefore do not be ashamed of the testimony about our Lord, nor of me his prisoner, but share in suffering for the gospel by the power of God, [9] who saved us and called us to a holy calling, not because of our works but because of his own purpose and grace, which he gave us in Christ Jesus before the ages began, [10] and which now has been manifested through the appearing of our Savior Christ Jesus, who abolished death and brought life and immortality to light through the gospel

A. The concept of immortality in Western philosophy:

1. Immanuel Kant (1724-1804)
   The three great truths of "natural theology":

   a. The Existence of God.

   b. The Importance of virtue.

   c. The Immortality of the soul (as a motive for reward).

2. Plato (427-347 B.C.)

   a. Body and soul are two distinct substances. The *thinking soul* has a divine essence, while the body is composed of *physical matter*, and inferior substance.

   b. The *rational soul* (the *nous*), is immortal. It came down "from the heavens" and existed before our birth, and enters the body, dwelling in the head.

   c. At death, the body disintegrates, and the *nous* returns to the heavens *if, while on earth, one's life was honorable and integrious*. If not, it appears again in another human being or even an animal (but it is not destroyed).

3. Greek philosophy:
   The soul is based upon *rationalistic metaphysics*. The rational being is the higher, superior reality over the corporeal, or physical, reality.

B. The OT is distinct from Platonic and Kantian notions:

1. These views are completely contrary to the Israelite view of death and immortality, and such views cannot be found in the Old Testament.

2. According to the OT understanding of death and immortality, the *whole man* dies . . .

    a. Whenever *the spirit* expires. (Psalm 146:4; Eccles. 12:7)

    b. Whenever the soul goes out of a person. (Gen. 35:18; 2 Samuel 1:9; 1 Kings 17:21; Jonah 4:3)

    c. According to the OT notion of death, when one's body dies, the person returns to a state of death and belongs to the nether-world.

3. The OT speaks of the death of a person's *soul*.
Gen. 37:21; Num. 23:10; Deut. 22:21; Judges 16:30; Job 36:14; Psalm 78:50

4. One is defiled by even coming into contact with a dead body.
Lev. 19:28; Lev. 21:11; Lev. 22:4; Num. 5:2; Num. 6:6; Num. 9:6; Num. 19:10ff; Deut. 14:1; Haggai 2:13

5. The OT view of death is not, however, that a person is destroyed or completely annihilated. Rather, in Sheol they are separated or deprived from "all that makes for life on earth".

    a. Sheol contrasts with the "land of the living" in every way. (e.g., Job 28:13; Proverbs 15:24; Ezekiel 26:20; Ezekiel 32:23)

b. Sheol is considered an abode of darkness and the shadow of death. (Job 10:21-22; Psalm 88:12; Psalm 143:3)

c. Sheol is regarded as a place of destruction. (Job 26:6; Job 28:22; Job 31:12; Psalm 88:11; Proverbs 27:20)

d. Sheol is characterized as having no order. (Job 10:22)

e. Sheol is described as a place of silence, of oblivion. (Job 3:13, 17-18; Psalm 94:17; Psalm 115:17)

f. Neither God nor humankind are seen in Sheol. (Isaiah 38:11)

g. In Sheol, God can no longer praised or thanked. (Psalm 6:5; Psalm 115:17)

h. God's perfections are no longer recognized or affirmed in Sheol. (Psalm 88:10-13; Isaiah 38:18-19)

i. In Sheol, the dead are no longer able to work, or take account of anything, or possess either knowledge or wisdom. (Eccles. 9:5-6, 10)

C. The NT progressive revelation: immortality, God, and humankind.

1. God alone possesses immortality in himself, as God.

    a. John 5:26 – For as the Father has life in himself, so he has granted the Son also to have life in himself.

b. Exod. 3:14 – God said to Moses, "I AM WHO I AM." And he said, "Say this to the people of Israel, 'I am has sent me to you.' "

c. Psalm 36:9 – For with you is the fountain of life; in your light do we see light.

d. Psalm 90:2 – Before the mountains were brought forth, or ever you had formed the earth and the world, from everlasting to everlasting you are God.

e. Acts 17:25 – nor is he served by human hands, as though he needed anything, since he himself gives to all mankind life and breath and everything.

f. 1 Tim. 1:17 – To the King of ages, immortal, invisible, the only God, be honor and glory forever and ever. Amen.

g. 1 Tim. 6:16 – Who alone has immortality, who dwells in unapproachable light, whom no one has ever seen or can see. To him be honor and eternal dominion. Amen.

2. At the return of Christ, this mortal *shall put on* immortality.
1 Cor. 15:53-54 – For this perishable body must put on the imperishable, and this mortal body must put on immortality. [54] When the perishable puts on the imperishable, and the mortal puts on immortality, then shall come to pass the saying that is written: "Death is swallowed up in victory."

Three things this says about immortality:
(Hoekema, p. 88)

a. Immortality is here ascribed *only to believers*.

b. It is not a present possession, but a gift, a bestowal at the *Parousia*.

c. Immortality is not a just a characteristic of the soul, but of the *whole person*.

3. The term "immortality of the soul" is not used strictly in the NT language. However, *aphtharsia* ("immortality") is used seven times without reference to the soul in this sense. (Rom. 2.7; 2 Tim. 1.10; 1 Cor. 15.42, 50, 53-54)

4. The Bible does not teach the "inherent indestructibility" of the soul (i.e., human beings are created by God and their existence is entirely dependent upon his will and power).

5. Continued existence without God is never praised or sought in Scripture. Eternal life is directly related to one's relationship with God *in his kingdom*. Such persons are in eternal relationship with God and his people in God's recreated heaven and earth!

a. John 3:16-17 – For God so loved the world, that he gave his only Son, that whoever believes in him should not perish but have eternal life. [17] For God did not send his Son into the world to condemn the world, but in order that the world might be saved through him.

b. 1 Tim. 1:15-16 – The saying is trustworthy and deserving of full acceptance, that Christ Jesus came into the world to save sinners, of whom I am the foremost. [16] But I received mercy for this reason, that in me, as the foremost, Jesus Christ might display his perfect patience as an example to those who were to believe in him for eternal life.

    c. Romans 5:10 – For if while we were enemies we were reconciled to God by the death of his Son, much more, now that we are reconciled, shall we be saved by his life.

    d. Romans 8:32 – He who did not spare his own Son but gave him up for us all, how will he not also with him graciously give us all things?

6. Immortality is tied directly to the *resurrection of the body*. The notion of an unclothed soul living forever is a foreign concept in the NT.

    a. Christ has the power to transform our bodies to be conformed like his "glorious body."
Phil.. 3:20-21 – But our citizenship is in heaven, and from it we await a Savior, the Lord Jesus Christ, [21] who will transform our lowly body to be like his glorious body, by the power that enables him even to subject all things to himself.

    b. This mortality (embodied existence) will put on immortality (another kind of embodied existence).
1 Cor. 15:42-44 – So is it with the resurrection of the dead. What is sown is perishable; what is raised is imperishable. [43] It is sown in dishonor; it is raised in glory. It is sown in weakness; it is raised in power. [44] It is sown a natural body; it is raised a spiritual body. If there is a natural body, there is also a spiritual body.

    c. We will bear the image of the Second Adam.
1 Cor. 15:48-54 – As was the man of dust, so also are those who are of the dust, and as is the man of heaven, so also are those who are of heaven. [49] Just as we have borne the image of the man of dust, we shall also bear the image of the man of heaven. [50] I tell you this, brothers: flesh and blood cannot inherit the kingdom of God, nor does the perishable

inherit the imperishable. [51] Behold! I tell you a mystery. We shall not all sleep, but we shall all be changed, [52] in a moment, in the twinkling of an eye, at the last trumpet. For the trumpet will sound, and the dead will be raised imperishable, and we shall be changed. [53] For this perishable body must put on the imperishable, and this mortal body must put on immortality. [54] When the perishable puts on the imperishable, and the mortal puts on immortality, then shall come to pass the saying that is written: "Death is swallowed up in victory."

d. We will have a body just like his own.
1 John 3:2 – Beloved, we are God's children now, and what we will be has not yet appeared; but we know that when he appears we shall be like him, because we shall see him as he is.

III. The Intermediate State

'Hades' is the NT equivalent of Sheol (Matt. 11.23; 16.18; Luke 10.15; Acts 2.27, 31; Rev. 1.18; 6.8; 20.13f.), in most cases referring to death or the power of death. In Luke 16.23 it is the place of torment for the wicked after death, in accordance with some contemporary Jewish thinking, but it is doubtful whether this parabolic use of current ideas can be treated as teaching about the state of the dead. 1 Pet. 3.19 calls the dead who perished in the Flood 'the spirits in prison' (cf. 4.6). The NT hope for the Christian dead is concentrated on their participation in the resurrection (1 Thess. 4.13–18), and there is therefore little evidence of belief about the 'intermediate state'. Passages which indicate, or may indicate, that the Christian dead are with Christ are Luke 23.43; Rom. 8.38f.; 2 Cor. 5.8; Phil. 1.23; cf. Heb. 12.23. The difficult passage 2 Cor. 5.2–8 may mean that Paul conceives existence between death and resurrection as a bodiless existence in Christ's presence.

R. J. Bauckham. "Eschatology," *The New Bible Dictionary.*
D.R.W. Wood, and I. Howard Marshall. (3rd ed.)
Downers Grove, Ill.: InterVarsity Press, 1996.

A. The Historical Vision

1. Since Augustine (fourth century A.D.), "Christian theologians have taught that between death and resurrection the souls of men enjoy rest or suffer affliction while waiting either for the completion of their salvation or for the consummation of their damnation." Hoekema, p. 92.

2. Middle Ages: Purgatory

   a. Purgatory is a doctrine advocated by Roman Catholic and Greek Orthodox churches that confesses that during the period between death and resurrection, believers who died in a *state of grace* but *without Christian perfection* must experience purifying suffering of varying degrees and duration to atone for their sins and to prepare them for heaven.

   b. The biblical evidence for such a claim is based upon some of the following NT passages:

      (1) Luke 12:59 – I tell you, you will never get out until you have paid the very last penny.

      (2) 1 Cor. 3:15 – If anyone's work is burned up, he will suffer loss, though he himself will be saved, but only as through fire.

      (3) 1 Cor. 5:5 – You are to deliver this man to Satan for the destruction of the flesh, so that his spirit may be saved in the day of the Lord.

      (4) Jude 1:22-23 – And have mercy on those who doubt; [23] save others by snatching them out of the fire; to others show mercy with fear, hating even the garment stained by the flesh.

3. This doctrine of Purgatory has rightly been opposed for lack of biblical warrant.

   a. It ignores the plain biblical teaching of the transition of the believer from absence of the body to the presence of the Lord.
   cf. Luke 23.43; 2 Cor. 5.6–8; Phil. 1.23

   b. It ignores the testimony of the blessedness of the state of believers who have passed on. Rev. 14.13

   c. Above all, it undermines the sufficiency of Christ's single sacrifice to atone for "all sins completely and forever."

      (1) Hebrews 1:3 – He is the radiance of the glory of God and the exact imprint of his nature, and he upholds the universe by the word of his power. After making purification for sins, he sat down at the right hand of the Majesty on high.

      (2) Hebrews 9:26 – For then he would have had to suffer repeatedly since the foundation of the world. But as it is, he has appeared once for all at the end of the ages to put away sin by the sacrifice of himself.

      (3) Hebrews 10:12 – But when Christ had offered for all time a single sacrifice for sins, he sat down at the right hand of God [13] waiting from that time until his enemies should be made a footstool for his feet. [14] For by a single offering he has perfected for all time those who are being sanctified.

4. The Reformers rejected Purgatory.

    a. Calvin: more of a conscious state.
       Luther: less of a conscious state.

    b. Believers experience a state of blessedness and expectation.

    c. However, this blessedness is provisional and incomplete.
       (Hoekema, p. 92)

5. Recent criticism:

    a G. Van der Leeuw (1890-1950):
       After death, there is one eschatological perspective for believers – *the resurrection of the body.*

    b. Oscar Cullman:
       Between death and the resurrection, the disembodied spirit of believers (i.e., "inner man") is in a state of *sleep* in Christ's presence. This is called *psychopannychism*, the doctrine of "soul sleep".

       Cullmann, *Immortality of the Soul or Resurrection of the Dead?*, London, 1958, pp. 48–57)

    c. Paul Althaus (1888-1966):
       The doctrine of the intermediate state "*rips apart what belongs together: soul and body, the individual and the community, blessedness and final glory, the destiny of individuals and the destiny of the world.*"
       (Hoekema, p. 94.)

6. Biblical response: The NT argues that human beings are not annihilated, and that believers are not separated from the Lord.

B. OT evidence concerning the Intermediate State:

1. The two OT texts mentioning personal resurrection understand it as a faraway reality for those who have died.

    a. Isaiah 26:19 – Your dead shall live; their bodies shall rise. You who dwell in the dust, awake and sing for joy! For your dew is a dew of light, and the earth will give birth to the dead.

    b. Daniel 12:2 – And many of those who sleep in the dust of the earth shall awake, some to everlasting life, and some to shame and everlasting contempt.

2. This concept of a long distant prospective event was well-accepted in Judaism of Jesus' time, as seen in Martha's reaction to Jesus' statement of Lazarus' rising again from the dead (cf. John 11.24).

3. Some Jewish literature did explore various concepts of an intermediate state between death and resurrection, with those inhabiting Sheol/Hades existing in various and different compartments, either in paradise or in torment. (cf. Luke 16.23)

4. "Sheol is the OT manner of asserting that death does not terminate human existence." (George Eldon Ladd, in Hoekema, p. 95)

5. Sheol in the OT:

    a. It is the *realm of the dead.* Hoekema, p. 96 (cf. Gen. 37.35; 42.38)

    b. It is the *grave.* Hoekema, p. 96

(1) Psalm 9:17 – The wicked shall return to Sheol, all the nations that forget God.

(2) Psalm 16:10 – For you will not abandon my soul to Sheol, or let your holy one see corruption.

(3) Psalm 49:14 – Like sheep they are appointed for Sheol; Death shall be their shepherd, and the upright shall rule over them in the morning. Their form shall be consumed in Sheol, with no place to dwell.

(4) Psalm 55:15 – Let death steal over them; let them go down to Sheol alive; for evil is in their dwelling place and in their heart.

(5) Psalm 141:7 – As when one plows and breaks up the earth, so shall our bones be scattered at the mouth of Sheol.

(6) Proverbs 15:24 – The path of life leads upward for the prudent, that he may turn away from Sheol beneath.

c. Sheol is distinguished for those who are godly.

(1) Psalm 17:15 – As for me, I shall behold your face in righteousness; when I awake, I shall be satisfied with your likeness.

(2) Psalm 73:24 – You guide me with your counsel, and afterward you will receive me to glory.

(3) Psalm 49:15 – But God will ransom my soul from the power of Sheol, for he will receive me. Selah

(4) Psalm 16:10 – For you will not abandon my soul to Sheol, or let your holy one see corruption.

(5) Psalm 86:13 – For great is your steadfast love toward me; you have delivered my soul from the depths of Sheol.

(6) Psalm 89:48 – What man can live and never see death? Who can deliver his soul from the power of Sheol? Selah

C. The NT and the Intermediate State as they relate to Hades:

1. Christ has won the victory over Sheol/Hades. (cf. Ps. 16.7-11)
    Acts 2.31-32 -- he foresaw and spoke about the resurrection of the Christ, that he was not abandoned to Hades, nor did his flesh see corruption.

2. Christ has the keys of Hades.
    Rev. 1.17-18 -- When I saw him, I fell at his feet as though dead. But he laid his right hand on me, saying, "Fear not, I am the first and the last, 18 and the living one. I died, and behold I am alive forevermore, and I have the keys of Death and Hades.

3. Christ declares that the gates of Hades will not prevail against the church. Matt. 16.18 -- And I tell you, you are Peter, and on this rock[a] I will build my church, and the gates of hell[b] shall not prevail against it.

4. Hades is pictured as a place of torment and suffering for the ungodly. Luke 16.19-31, (i.e., the parable of the Rich Man and Lazarus.)

5. Hoekema's summary (p. 101) of the Intermediate State from the biblical use of Sheol/Hades:

    a. People do not go out of existence, but instead go to the realm of the dead.

    b. In this realm, the dead remain with death as their shepherd.

c. The ungodly will suffer torment, even before the resurrection of the body. Luke 16.19-31

d. The ungodly are held for the day of punishment. 2 Pet. 2.9

D. The New Testament and the "dead in Christ":

1. Jesus spoke to the penitent thief.
   Luke 23:42-43 – And he said, "Jesus, remember me when you come into your kingdom." [43] And he said to him, "Truly, I say to you, today you will be with me in Paradise."

   a. "Paradise" is used two other places:

      (1) 2 Cor. 12.4 (i.e., Paul caught up into Paradise)

      (2) Rev. 2.7 (i.e., the Tree of life in the Paradise of God)

   b. Christ's reference was to be "in heavenly bliss that very day."

2. Paul's desire was to depart and be with Christ.
   Phil. 1:21-23 – For to me to live is Christ, and to die is gain. [22] If I am to live in the flesh, that means fruitful labor for me. Yet which I shall choose I cannot tell. [23] I am hard pressed between the two. My desire is to depart and be with Christ, for that is far better.

   a. Death, physical departure, is seen here as "gain."

   b. Paul actually struggled with a desire to depart and "be with Christ."

c. This state or condition is, compared to the current state, "far better."

3. Paul was willing to be absent from the body, and to be present with the Lord.
2 Cor. 5:1-8 – For we know that if the earthly tent we live in is destroyed, we have a building from God, a house not made with hands, eternal in the heavens. [2] Here indeed we groan, and long to put on our heavenly dwelling, [3] so that by putting it on we may not be found naked. [4] For while we are still in this tent, we sigh with anxiety; not that we would be unclothed, but that we would be further clothed, so that what is mortal may be swallowed up by life. [5] He who has prepared us for this very thing is God, who has given us the Spirit as a guarantee. [6] So we are always of good courage. We know that while we are at home in the body we are away from the Lord, [7] for we walk by faith, not by sight. [8] Yes, we are of good courage, and we would rather be away from the body and at home with the Lord.

a. What is the nature of the building and the clothing? (cf. Hoekema, pp. 104-105)

(1) View One: "Building from God" is a kind of *intermediate body* between ours now and the resurrection.

(2) View Two: "Building from God" is the *resurrection body* we shall receive at the Parousia.

(3) View Three: "Building from God" describes "the *glorious existence* of the believer in heaven with Christ during the intermediate state."

(4) Hoekema's conclusion: View 1 is dismissed; both Views 2 and 3 are difficult.

b. Paul's plain words:

(1) While we are "at home in the body" we are "away from the Lord."

(2) We "would rather be away from the body" and "at home with the Lord."

4. Dr. Davis' appeal to mystery: Why must we have precise scientific knowledge of this?

   a. Paul couldn't specifically describe his experience.
   2 Cor. 12:2-3 – I know a man in Christ who fourteen years ago was caught up to the third heaven—whether in the body or out of the body I do not know, God knows. [3] And I know that this man was caught up into paradise—whether in the body or out of the body I do not know, God knows.

   b. We ought to walk by faith, not by sight.
   2 Cor. 5:6-8 – So we are always of good courage. We know that while we are at home in the body we are away from the Lord, [7] for we walk by faith, not by sight. [8] Yes, we are of good courage, and we would rather be away from the body and at home with the Lord.

   c. Let's desire what it was that Paul wanted. (He was neither suicidal nor psychotic!).
   Phil. 1.23 – I am hard pressed between the two. My desire is to depart and be with Christ, for that is far better.

E. Summary

....

The NT likewise seems to envisage an intermediate state: Christ promised immediate paradise to the crucified criminal; Paul sensed that death was but the door to Christ's presence; Hebrews evokes an unseen cloud of witnesses (Heb. 12.1); and John glimpsed the souls of martyrs longing for vindication (Rev. 6.9–10). This state is one of

rest and peace with God, and is presumably disembodied since it precedes resurrection as a spirit-animated body (1 Cor. 15.44). But no further details of it are given.

T. D. Alexander and B. S. Rosner.
The New Dictionary of Biblical Theology. (electronic ed.).
Downers Grove, Ill.: InterVarsity Press, 2001.

1. We are not to fear death as believers. To be absent from the body is to be present with the Lord. 2 Cor. 5.6-8

2. Those who have died in the Lord are the dead in Christ. We will see them again.
   1 Thess. 4:15-16 – For this we declare to you by a word from the Lord, that we who are alive, who are left until the coming of the Lord, will not precede those who have fallen asleep. [16] For the Lord himself will descend from heaven with a cry of command, with the voice of an archangel, and with the sound of the trumpet of God. And the dead in Christ will rise first.

3. Whether we *live or die,* we are the Lord's.
   Romans 14:7-9 – For none of us lives to himself, and none of us dies to himself. [8] If we live, we live to the Lord, and if we die, we die to the Lord. So then, whether we live or whether we die, we are the Lord's. [9] For to this end Christ died and lived again, that he might be Lord both of the dead and of the living.

4. Nothing, not even death, can separate us from the love of God in Christ Jesus our Lord.
   Romans 8:38-39 – For I am sure that neither death nor life, nor angels nor rulers, nor things present nor things to come, nor powers, [39] nor height nor depth, nor anything else in all creation, will be able to separate us from the love of God in Christ Jesus our Lord.

IV. Conclusion: On the "Outside of the World, the Wrong Side of the Door"

At present we are on the outside of the world, the wrong side of the door. We discern the freshness and purity of morning, but they do not make us fresh and pure. We cannot mingle with the splendors we see. But all of the leaves of the New Testament are rustling with the rumor that it will not always be so. Someday, God willing, we shall get in.

C. S. Lewis, *The Weight of Glory.*

Phil. 3:20-21 – But our citizenship is in heaven, and from it we await a Savior, the Lord Jesus Christ, [21] who will transform our lowly body to be like his glorious body, by the power that enables him even to subject all things to himself.

- Physical death must now be *viewed in the light of the resurrection of Jesus.*

- Immortality is the certain hope and future prospect of every true believer. *This mortal will surely put on immortality and be conformed to the glorious body of the risen Lord Jesus Christ.*

- The Intermediate State is mysterious and clear: to be absent from the body is to be *present with the Lord.*

The Bottom Line _____

Lesson Four
The Signs of the Times, the Rapture, and the Tribulation

....

The Expectation of the Second Coming of Jesus of Nazareth, the Risen Lord and King

The expectation of Christ's Second Advent is a most important aspect of New Testament eschatology–so much so, in fact, that the faith of the New Testament church is dominated by this expectation. Every book of the New Testament points us to the return of Christ and urges us to live in such a way as to be always ready for that return. This note is sounded repeatedly in the Gospels. We are taught that the Son of Man will come with his angels in the glory of his Father (Matt. 16.27); Jesus told the high priest that the latter would see the Son of Man sitting at the right hand of power and coming with the clouds of heaven (Mark 14.62). Frequently Jesus told his hearers to watch for his return, since he would be coming at an unexpected hour (Matt. 24.42, 44; Luke 12.40). He spoke of the blessedness of those servants whom he would find faithful at his coming (Luke 12.37, 43). After describing some of the signs which would precede his coming, the Lord said, "When these things begin to take place, look up and raise your heads, because your redemption is drawing near" (Luke 21. 28). And in his farewell discourse Jesus told his disciples that after he had left the earth, he would come again and take them to himself (John 14.23)."

Anthony A. Hoekema, *The Bible and the Future*. Grand Rapids: Eerdmans Publishing, 1979 (1994), p. 109.

....

I. The Signs of the Times

Matthew 16:2-3 – He answered them, "When it is evening, you say, 'It will be fair weather, for the sky is red.' [3] And in the morning, 'It will be stormy today, for the sky is red and threatening.' You know how to interpret the appearance of the sky, but you cannot interpret the signs of the times.

A. The Vocabulary of the Blessed Hope:

1. *Apokalypsis* (the Revelation):
   1 Cor. 1:7-8 – so that you are not lacking in any spiritual gift, as you wait for the revealing of our Lord Jesus Christ, [8] who will sustain you to the end, guiltless in the <u>day of our Lord</u> Jesus Christ.)

2. *Parousia* (the Coming – also translated "arrival" and "presence"):
   1 Thess. 4:15 – For this we declare to you by a word from the Lord, that we who are alive, who are left until the <u>coming of the Lord</u>, will not precede those who have fallen asleep.

3. *Epiphaneia* (the Manifestation):
   1 Tim. 6:13-15 – I charge you in the presence of God, who gives life to all things, and of Christ Jesus, who in his testimony before Pontius Pilate made the good confession, [14] to keep the commandment unstained and free from reproach until the <u>appearing of our Lord</u> Jesus Christ, [15] which he will display at the proper time—he who is the blessed and only Sovereign, the King of kings and Lord of lords.

B. The definition of the "Signs of the Times":

1. Greek: *ta semeia ton kariron*

2. *Kairos* refers to "a period of divine activity which should have brought the people to whom Jesus spoke (Pharisees and Sadducees) to a decision of faith in him, but which obviously had not done so." Hoekema, p. 129

3. Recent history in prophetic understanding establishes a difference between "realized" and "future" eschatology.

   a. Some have interpreted the idea of the signs as unnecessary, reading the events of resurrection and

Pentecost as the full consummation (spiritually speaking) of God's restored kingdom in the earth. These views are known in terms of "realized eschatology".

b. Others (typically conservative in doctrine) argue strongly for a yet-future realization of the prophetic vision of both Old and New Testaments, and therefore look for the Second Coming of Christ, and the accompanying signs connected with that coming, i.e., the "Already/Not Yet" biblical theology of Ladd (or "future eschatology").

4. Eschatology in recent biblical/theological studies history:

In recent years there has been an increased interest in eschatology. Some have defined it in such a way that it is almost all-inclusive, rather than merely a part of theology. Since the Christ-event was the introduction of the new age, much of the NT must be considered eschatology. Some have carried this so far as to suggest that the supposedly future events were already accomplished. Thus, the second coming of Christ took place at Pentecost. There is no future event to look forward to. This view is termed "realized eschatology." The theology of hope has extended this eschatological conception into all areas of theology, even into the doctrine of God. Thus, whereas the transcendence of God had been thought of as the God who has his being above or beyond us, these people think of him as lying before us. He is the God who is to be. His transcendence is thought of in relation to time, not to space. Conservatives have retained a more traditional conception of eschatology. There has been great interest in the predictive prophetic passages of Scripture, as indicated by the popularity of books like The Late Great Planet Earth (1973). Many have seen a correlation between current events in the Middle East and passages such as Daniel 9, Matthew 24, 25, 1 Thessalonians, and Revelation.

Millard Erickson, "Eschatology," *The Baker Encyclopedia of the Bible.*
Grand Rapids: Baker Book House, 1988.

C. Key texts on the Signs of the Times:

1. Jesus' engagement with the Pharisees and Sadducees:
   Matthew 16:1-4 – And the Pharisees and Sadducees came, and to test him they asked him to show them a sign from heaven. [2] He answered them, "When it is evening, you say, 'It will be fair weather, for the sky is red.' [3] And in the morning, 'It will be stormy today, for the sky is red and threatening.' You know how to interpret the appearance of the sky, but you cannot interpret the signs of the times. [4] An evil and adulterous generation seeks for a sign, but no sign will be given to it except the sign of Jonah." So he left them and departed.

   a. The signs of Jesus' coming as Messiah, those that were predicted by the prophets, were clear and able to be discerned by those of spiritual vision.

   b. A litany of Messianic signs was given by Jesus of Nazareth:
      Matthew 11:4-6 – And Jesus answered them, "Go and tell John what you hear and see: [5] the blind receive their sight and the lame walk, lepers are cleansed and the deaf hear, and the dead are raised up, and the poor have good news preached to them. [6] And blessed is the one who is not offended by me."

2. Notice the biblical nuance which perceives the "continuous looking for signs" as a *sign of hardheartedness!*

   a. Matthew 12:39-40 – But he answered them, "An evil and adulterous generation seeks for a sign, but no sign will be given to it except the sign of the prophet Jonah. [40] For just as Jonah was three days and three nights in the belly of the great fish, so will the Son of Man be three days and three nights in the heart of the earth.

b. Mark 8:12 – And he sighed deeply in his spirit and said, "Why does this generation seek a sign? Truly, I say to you, no sign will be given to this generation."

3. Also notice the significance of signs in preparing for the nearness and soon return of Messiah in glory. We must be careful not to read the meaning of signs too woodenly or boldly (i.e., being bitten by the "prophecy bug," which is interpreted as *using signs to map and measure the timing of Christ's coming*.)
Luke 17:22-25 – And he said to the disciples, "The days are coming when you will desire to see one of the days of the Son of Man, and you will not see it. [23] And they will say to you, 'Look, there!' or 'Look, here!' Do not go out or follow them. [24] For as the lightning flashes and lights up the sky from one side to the other, so will the Son of Man be in his day. [25] But first he must suffer many things and be rejected by this generation.

4. The general power of signs is to provide a context out of which to understand the *urgency of the hour* and the *need for hope and readiness on the part of those who embrace the coming*.
Luke 21:25-28 – "And there will be signs in sun and moon and stars, and on the earth distress of nations in perplexity because of the roaring of the sea and the waves, [26] people fainting with fear and with foreboding of what is coming on the world. For the powers of the heavens will be shaken. [27] And then they will see the Son of Man coming in a cloud with power and great glory. [28] Now when these things begin to take place, straighten up and raise your heads, because your redemption is drawing near."

D. Hoekema identifies *wrong ways* to view the Signs of the Times:

1. Wrong Way #1: Thinking of the Signs of the Times as referring <u>exclusively</u> to the end-time, as if they had to do only with the period immediately preceding the Parousia and had nothing to do with the centuries preceding the

Parousia.
Hoekema points out the following: (p. 130)

a. "Double fulfillment" principle: The prophetic word had meaning for the contemporary audience as well as the future generations to come.

b. Matthew 24, Mark 13, and Luke 21 all speak to issues and situations which would impact the contemporary generation that heard the words of Jesus *as well as* the actual conditions of the world at the Second Coming of Christ.

c. Case in point: Is the destruction of the Temple and the city of Jerusalem, connected to the actual Second Coming of Jesus?

  (1) Fulfillment One:
  Luke 21:20-24 – "But when you see Jerusalem surrounded by armies, then know that its desolation has come near. [21] Then let those who are in Judea flee to the mountains, and let those who are inside the city depart, and let not those who are out in the country enter it, [22] for these are days of vengeance, to fulfill all that is written. [23] Alas for women who are pregnant and for those who are nursing infants in those days! For there will be great distress upon the earth and wrath against this people. [24] They will fall by the edge of the sword and be led captive among all nations, and Jerusalem will be trampled underfoot by the Gentiles, until the times of the Gentiles are fulfilled.

  (2) Fulfillment Two:
  Luke 21:29-33 – And he told them a parable: "Look at the fig tree, and all the trees. [30] As soon as they come out in leaf, you see for yourselves and know that the summer is already near. [31] So also, when you see these things taking place, you know that the kingdom of God

is near. [32] Truly, I say to you, this generation will not pass away until all has taken place. [33] Heaven and earth will pass away, but my words will not pass away.

2. Wrong Way #2: Thinking of the Signs of the Times only in terms of abnormal, spectacular, or catastrophic events, i.e., as "spectacular interruptions of the normal course of history which irresistibly draw attention to themselves."
Hoekema points out the following: (p. 131)

   a. The decisive event of personal repentance and the gathering of believers into the church represents a real instance of the Kingdom of God. John 1.12-13; Matt. 18.20

   b. The Kingdom of God is not necessarily associated with the bizarre and catastrophic but also with the dynamic and the spiritual.
   Luke 17:20-21 – Being asked by the Pharisees when the kingdom of God would come, he answered them, "The kingdom of God is not coming with signs to be observed, [21] nor will they say, 'Look, here it is!' or 'There!' for behold, the kingdom of God is in the midst of you."

   c. This fact, however, does not suggest that the signs have no place in terms of preparing us for the coming of Christ.

3. Wrong Way #3: Thinking about the Signs of the Times in such a way as to "attempt to use them as a way of dating the exact time of Christ's return."
Hoekema points out the following: (p. 131)

   a. The exact time of Christ's return is not known by anyone here, nor the angels of God.
   Mark 13:32 – But concerning that day or that hour,

no one knows, not even the angels in heaven, nor the Son, but only the Father.
Matthew 24:36 – But concerning that day and hour no one knows, not even the angels of heaven, nor the Son, but the Father only.
Matthew 24:42 – Therefore, stay awake, for you do not know on what day your Lord is coming.
Matthew 25:13 – Watch therefore, for you know neither the day nor the hour.
Acts 1:7 – He said to them, "It is not for you to know times or seasons that the Father has fixed by his own authority.

b. "The signs of the times tell us about the certainty of the Second Coming, but do not divulge its precise date."

4. Wrong Way #4: Using the Signs of the Times to "construct an exact timetable of future happenings." Hoekema points out the following: (p. 131)

a. We need to discern the difference between *prophecy* and *history*.

b. We need also to be able to distinguish between *certainty of fulfillment* and the precise *nature of fulfillment*.

c. Example: The coming of the Holy Spirit at Pentecost.

(1) Prophecy:
Joel 2:28-32 – And it shall come to pass afterward, that I will pour out my Spirit on all flesh; your sons and your daughters shall prophesy, your old men shall dream dreams, and your young men shall see visions. [29] Even on the male and female servants in those days I will pour out my Spirit. [30] "And I will show wonders in the heavens and on the earth, blood

and fire and columns of smoke. [31] The sun shall be turned to darkness, and the moon to blood, before the great and awesome day of the Lord comes. [32] And it shall come to pass that everyone who calls on the name of the Lord shall be saved. For in Mount Zion and in Jerusalem there shall be those who escape, as the Lord has said, and among the survivors shall be those whom the Lord calls.

(2) Fulfillment:
Acts 2:1-4 – When the day of Pentecost arrived, they were all together in one place. [2] And suddenly there came from heaven a sound like a mighty rushing wind, and it filled the entire house where they were sitting. [3] And divided tongues as of fire appeared to them and rested on each one of them. [4] And they were all filled with the Holy Spirit and began to speak in other tongues as the Spirit gave them utterance.

E. Hoekema identifies *proper functions* of the Signs of the Times in NT eschatology:

1. The Signs of the Times point to what God has done in the past. (p. 133)

    a. "The signs of the times reveal that the great victory of Christ has been won, and that therefore the decisive change in history has occurred. They reveal that God is at work in the world, busy fulfilling his promises and bringing to realization the final consummation of redemption."
    Acts 2:34-36 – For David did not ascend into the heavens, but he himself says, 'The Lord said to my Lord, Sit at my right hand, [35] until I make your enemies your footstool.' [36] Let all the house of Israel therefore know for certain that God has made him both Lord and Christ, this Jesus whom you crucified.

b. The victory of *Christus Victor* has already been won and will soon be consummated. It is toward this consummation that the signs point.
Col. 2:15 – He disarmed the rulers and authorities and put them to open shame, by triumphing over them in him.

2. The Signs of the Times point forward to the end of history, and in particular, to the final consummation of all things at the return of Christ. (p. 134)

   a. They provide neither exact times nor absolute timetables, but rather the certainty of the end.

   b. Jesus's own word of promise: *the end will come.*
   Matthew 24:14 – And this gospel of the kingdom will be proclaimed throughout the whole world as a testimony to all nations, and then *the end will come.*

   c. *When* the nations will see Christ is not entirely clear, but *that* they will see Christ cannot be contested.
   Matthew 24:29-31 – Immediately after the tribulation of those days the sun will be darkened, and the moon will not give its light, and the stars will fall from heaven, and the powers of the heavens will be shaken. [30] Then will appear in heaven the sign of the Son of Man, and then all the tribes of the earth will mourn, and *they will see the Son of Man coming on the clouds of heaven with power and great glory.* [31] And he will send out his angels with a loud trumpet call, and they will gather his elect from the four winds, from one end of heaven to the other.

3. The Signs of the Times reveal the "antithesis in history" between God's reign and the kingdom of darkness. (p. 134)

   a. The universe throughout history is at war.
   Gen. 3.15 – "I will put enmity between you and

the woman, and between your offspring[a] and her offspring; he shall bruise your head, and you shall bruise his heel."

b. The parable of the Tares and the Wheat: Tares and wheat grow side by side in the same field until harvest time comes.
Matthew 13:29-30 – But he said, 'No, lest in gathering the weeds you root up the wheat along with them. [30] Let both grow together until the harvest, and at harvest time I will tell the reapers, Gather the weeds first and bind them in bundles to be burned, but gather the wheat into my barn.' "

4. Some Signs of the Times reveal the working of the Kingdom of God in the earth, while others show the damaging effects of the powers of evil in this age (e.g., missions and the preaching of the Gospel vs. molestation of an 18-month-old live on the Internet).

5. The Signs of the Times call for *decision*. (p. 135)

a. The signs can be discerned, and ought to be heeded.
Matthew 16:2-3 – He answered them, "When it is evening, you say, 'It will be fair weather, for the sky is red.' [3] And in the morning, 'It will be stormy today, for the sky is red and threatening.' You know how to interpret the appearance of the sky, but you cannot interpret the signs of the times.

b. Even signs of apostasy, falsehood, foolishness, and apathy need not discourage the one who is giving heed to the signs.
Luke 21:25-28 – "And there will be signs in sun and moon and stars, and on the earth distress of nations in perplexity because of the roaring of the sea and the waves, [26] people fainting with fear and with foreboding of what is coming on the world. For the powers of the heavens will be shaken. [27] And then

they will see the Son of Man coming in a cloud with power and great glory. [28] Now when these things begin to take place, straighten up and raise your heads, because your redemption is drawing near."

6. The Signs of the Times call for *constant watchfulness*. (p. 135)

a. Signs point to the fact of the coming, but not the timing of it. Matthew 24:38-42 – For as in those days before the flood they were eating and drinking, marrying and giving in marriage, until the day when Noah entered the ark, [39] and they were unaware until the flood came and swept them all away, so will be the coming of the Son of Man. [40] Then two men will be in the field; one will be taken and one left. [41] Two women will be grinding at the mill; one will be taken and one left. [42] Therefore, stay awake, for you do not know on what day your Lord is coming.

b. Having *some idea* of the signs can provide us with a *mind of preparation* to keep us ready and alert. Matthew 24:43-44 – But know this, that if the master of the house had known in what part of the night the thief was coming, he would have stayed awake and would not have let his house be broken into. [44] Therefore you also must be ready, for the Son of Man is coming at an hour you do not expect.

II. **General Characteristics and Categories of the Signs of the Times**

Categorization of the signs: "The signs of the time reveal both the grace of God and the judgment of God. The grace of God is manifested in the opportunity for salvation through Christ extended to mankind during the era between the first and second comings of Christ." Hoekema, p. 137.

A. Several signs give evidence of the invading grace of God in this age, and the "already present" nature of the Kingdom of God:

1. The indwelling of the Holy Spirit.

    a. Eph. 1:13-14 – In him you also, when you heard the word of truth, the gospel of your salvation, and believed in him, were sealed with the promised Holy Spirit, [14] who is the guarantee of our inheritance until we acquire possession of it, to the praise of his glory.

    b. Romans 8:15-17 – For you did not receive the spirit of slavery to fall back into fear, but you have received the Spirit of adoption as sons, by whom we cry, "Abba! Father!" [16] The Spirit himself bears witness with our spirit that we are children of God, [17] and if children, then heirs—heirs of God and fellow heirs with Christ, provided we suffer with him in order that we may also be glorified with him.

    c. Romans 8:23 – And not only the creation, but we ourselves, who have the firstfruits of the Spirit, groan inwardly as we wait eagerly for adoption as sons, the redemption of our bodies.

    d. 2 Cor. 1:22 – and who has also put his seal on us and given us his Spirit in our hearts as a guarantee.

    e. 2 Cor. 5:5 – He who has prepared us for this very thing is God, who has given us the Spirit as a guarantee.

2. The presence of the Church of Jesus Christ in the world, i.e., the calling of the Gentiles to full partnership in the Gospel.

Eph. 3:4-6 – When you read this, you can perceive my insight into the mystery of Christ, [5] which was not made known to the sons of men in other generations as it has now been revealed to his holy apostles and prophets by the Spirit. [6] This mystery is that the Gentiles are fellow heirs, members of the same body, and partakers of the promise in Christ Jesus through the gospel.

3. The spreading of the Gospel to the nation.

   a. The gospel will be preached to all nations before the end comes. Matthew 24:13-14 – But the one who endures to the end will be saved. [14] And this gospel of the kingdom will be proclaimed throughout the whole world as a testimony to all nations, and then the end will come.

   b. The Great Commission reveals the linkage between mission and the Second Coming of Christ. Matthew 28:19-20 – Go therefore and make disciples of all nations, baptizing them in the name of the Father and of the Son and of the Holy Spirit, [20] teaching them to observe all that I have commanded you. And behold, I am with you always, to the end of the age.

   c. This sign looks backward and forward. It looks *backward to the death and resurrection of Jesus Christ* as the Good News. It looks *forward to the Parousia*, assuring us that when the gospel has been given as a testimony to the nations, *after these things* the end will come.

It is important to note that this sign does not enable us to set a precise date for Christ's Second Coming. Who can be sure when the gospel will have been preached as a testimony to all nations? To give a concrete example, no one would be inclined to deny that the gospel of the kingdom has become a testimony, in the sense described above, to the United States of America. But who can tell whether the gospel has by this time become a testimony to every nation of the North and South American continents? Into how many languages and dialects must the Bible, or parts of the Bible, be translated before that goal will have been reached? How many members of a nation must be evangelized before one can say that the gospel is a testimony to that nation? What, in fact, constitutes a nation? We must humbly admit that only God will know when this sign will have been completely fulfilled."

Anthony Hoekema, The Bible and the Future, p. 139

4. The "salvation of the fullness of Israel":

  a. Israel serves as "God's timepiece."
     Matthew 10:23 – When they persecute you in one town, flee to the next, for truly, I say to you, you will not have gone through all the towns of Israel before the Son of Man comes.

     (1) Romans 9-11 reveals the significance of the nation of Israel, and its role in discerning the times related to the return of Christ.

     (2) Does it refer to the nation of Israel *as a totality,* to a spiritualized *Israel* (meaning the elect), or those *elect Jews from the nation of Israel?* (Hoekema, pp. 138-146)

     (3) Hoekema's view: "The salvation of all Israel, therefore, does not take place exclusively at the end-time, but takes place throughout the era between Christ's first and second coming–in fact, from the time of the call of Abraham." (p. 145)

     (4) Romans 11:25-29 – Lest you be wise in your own conceits, I want you to understand this mystery, brothers: a partial hardening has come upon Israel, until the fullness of the Gentiles has come in. [26] And in this way all Israel will be saved, as it is written, "The Deliverer will

come from Zion, he will banish ungodliness from Jacob"; [27] "and this will be my covenant with them when I take away their sins."[28] As regards the gospel, they are enemies of God for your sake. But as regards election, they are beloved for the sake of their forefathers. [29] For the gifts and the calling of God are irrevocable.

B. Several signs give evidence of the resistance of the kingdom of darkness against the advance of the Kingdom of God in this world in this age:

1. The coming tribulation. (cf. Matt. 24.3-51; Mark 13.3-37; Luke 21.5-36)

   a. Double fulfillment principle: The prophecies concerning the destruction of Jerusalem juxtaposed to prophecies of the return of Christ.

   b. Should we interpret these matters in regard to Jerusalem and Judea with "strict literalness?"

   c. The principle of historical-grammatical interpretation: In interpreting the text, understand the usages of literature, making no blunders either of history or of grammar and syntax.

2. The growing apostasy in the church: the "falling away" of many from the faith of the Gospel.

   a. Many will fall away.
   Matthew 24:10-13 – And then many will fall away and betray one another and hate one another. [11] And many false prophets will arise and lead many astray. [12] And because lawlessness will be increased, the love of many will grow cold. [13] But the one who endures to the end will be saved.

b. False Christs will arise.
Matthew 24:24-27 – For false christs and false prophets will arise and perform great signs and wonders, so as to lead astray, if possible, even the elect. [25] See, I have told you beforehand. [26] So, if they say to you, 'Look, he is in the wilderness,' do not go out. If they say, 'Look, he is in the inner rooms,' do not believe it. [27] For as the lightning comes from the east and shines as far as the west, so will be the coming of the Son of Man.

c. Some fell away during the times of the apostles.
Heb. 6.4-6 – For it is impossible, in the case of those who have once been enlightened, who have tasted the heavenly gift, and have shared in the Holy Spirit, [5] and have tasted the goodness of the word of God and the powers of the age to come, [6] and then have fallen away, to restore them again to repentance, since they are crucifying once again the Son of God to their own harm and holding him up to contempt.

d. It is prophesied that some will enter their previous conditions of defilements.
2 Pet. 2.20-21 – For if, after they have escaped the defilements of the world through the knowledge of our Lord and Savior Jesus Christ, they are again entangled in them and overcome, the last state has become worse for them than the first. [21] For it would have been better for them never to have known the way of righteousness than after knowing it to turn back from the holy commandment delivered to them.

e. Some will "go out from us" who are not "of us."
1 John 2.19 – They went out from us, but they were not of us; for if they had been of us, they would have continued with us. But they went out, that it might become plain that they all are not of us.

f. The Spirit testifies of those who will "depart from the faith."
    1 Tim. 4:1-2 – Now the Spirit expressly says that in later times some will depart from the faith by devoting themselves to deceitful spirits and teachings of demons, [2] through the insincerity of liars whose consciences are seared.

g. What is ahead in the last days?
    2 Tim. 3:1-2 – But understand this, that in the last days there will come times of difficulty. [2] For people will be lovers of self, lovers of money, proud, arrogant, abusive, disobedient to their parents, ungrateful, unholy.

h. Note "the time is coming."
    2 Tim. 4:3-4 – For the time is coming when people will not endure sound teaching, but having itching ears they will accumulate for themselves teachers to suit their own passions, [4] and will turn away from listening to the truth and wander off into myths.

i. A critical text:
    2 Thess. 2:3 – Let no one deceive you in any way. For that day will not come, unless the rebellion comes first, and the man of lawlessness is revealed, the son of destruction.

j. Excursus: *Can a true believer fall away and depart from the faith?*

    (1) If yes, they cannot be brought back again!
    Hebrews 10:26-27 – For if we go on sinning deliberately after receiving the knowledge of the truth, there no longer remains a sacrifice for sins, [27] but a fearful expectation of judgment, and a fury of fire that will consume the adversaries.

    (2) NO, THEY CANNOT FALL!
    John 10.27-29 – My sheep hear my voice, and

I know them, and they follow me. [28] I give them eternal life, and they will never perish, and no one will snatch them out of my hand. [29] My Father, who has given them to me,[a] is greater than all, and no one is able to snatch them out of the Father's hand.
1 Pet. 1.3-5 – Blessed be the God and Father of our Lord Jesus Christ! According to his great mercy, he has caused us to be born again to a living hope through the resurrection of Jesus Christ from the dead, [4] to an inheritance that is imperishable, undefiled, and unfading, kept in heaven for you, [5] who by God's power are being guarded through faith for a salvation ready to be revealed in the last time.

3. The anticipated appearance of the "man of sin," i.e., the Antichrist:

   a. OT antecedents of the Antichrist: Daniel's little horn and the coming man of sin.
   Daniel 7:24-27 – As for the ten horns, out of this kingdom ten kings shall arise, and another shall arise after them; he shall be different from the former ones, and shall put down three kings. [25] He shall speak words against the Most High, and shall wear out the saints of the Most High, and shall think to change the times and the law; and they shall be given into his hand for a time, times, and half a time. [26] But the court shall sit in judgment, and his dominion shall be taken away, to be consumed and destroyed to the end. [27] And the kingdom and the dominion and the greatness of the kingdoms under the whole heaven shall be given to the people of the saints of the Most High; their kingdom shall be an everlasting kingdom, and all dominions shall serve and obey them. (See also Dan. 11.36; 12.11)

   b. Antiochus Epiphanes, the Syrian ruler who in 168 B.C. (Cf. 1 Macc. 1.29ff) oppressed the Jews and overthrew their laws. (Hoekema, p. 154)

c. Jesus' reference to the *bdelygma eremoseos* (i.e., the desolating sacrilege, or "abomination that makes desolate").
Matthew 24:15-16 – "So when you see the abomination of desolation spoken of by the prophet Daniel, standing in the holy place (let the reader understand), [16] then let those who are in Judea flee to the mountains. (Cf. Mark 13.14)

4. Characteristics of the coming Antichrist:
2 Thess. 2.3-10 – Let no one deceive you in any way. For that day will not come, unless the rebellion comes first, and the man of lawlessness is revealed, the son of destruction, [4] who opposes and exalts himself against every so-called god or object of worship, so that he takes his seat in the temple of God, proclaiming himself to be God. [5] Do you not remember that when I was still with you I told you these things? [6] And you know what is restraining him now so that he may be revealed in his time. [7] For the mystery of lawlessness is already at work. Only he who now restrains it will do so until he is out of the way. [8] And then the lawless one will be revealed, whom the Lord Jesus will kill with the breath of his mouth and bring to nothing by the appearance of his coming. [9] The coming of the lawless one is by the activity of Satan with all power and false signs and wonders, [10] and with all wicked deception for those who are perishing, because they refused to love the truth and so be saved.

   a. He is a *person*. (v 3)

   b. He is an *apostate*. (v 3)

   c. He is *blasphemous*. (v 4)

   d. He is *persuasive*, in terms of miraculous signs. (v 9)

e. He will only be revealed when *he who restrains it* is removed. (v 6)

f. He is *animated* by the activity of *the evil one*. (v 9)

g. He will *deceive many* who refuse to hear the truth. (v 10)

5. Central features of the Antichrist:

   a. He opposes any and all deities that interfere with his own worship. (2 Thess. 2:3-4)

   b. He will be destroyed at the coming of Christ. (2 Thess. 2:8)

6. The spirit of Antichrist and the coming apostasy:

   a. The spirit of Antichrist was already present during the time of the apostles.
   1 John 4:1-3 – Beloved, do not believe every spirit, but test the spirits to see whether they are from God, for many false prophets have gone out into the world. [2] By this you know the Spirit of God: every spirit that confesses that Jesus Christ has come in the flesh is from God, [3] and every spirit that does not confess Jesus is not from God. This is the spirit of the antichrist, which you heard was coming and now is in the world already.

   b. *Antichristos* is only found in John's epistles (see 1 John 2.18, 22; 4.3; 2 John 7), to be interpreted as both a *rival* to Christ, and an *opponent* of Christ. (Hoekema, p 15)

C. Signs indicating the horrifying manifestation of the coming judgment and wrath of Almighty God:

All of these signs have their OT antecedents and are associated with the judgments of the end both specifically and generically (in terms of God's wrath against sin).

1. There will be emergence of wars and the rumors of wars.
   Matthew 24:6-8 – And you will hear of wars and rumors of wars. See that you are not alarmed, for this must take place, but the end is not yet. [7] For nation will rise against nation, and kingdom against kingdom, and there will be famines and earthquakes in various places. [8] All these are but the beginning of the birth pains.

2. Natural disasters and calamities will increase (earthquakes, famines, etc.).
   Mark 13.7-8 – And when you hear of wars and rumors of wars, do not be alarmed. This must take place, but the end is not yet. [8] For nation will rise against nation, and kingdom against kingdom. There will be earthquakes in various places; there will be famines. These are but the beginning of the birth pains.

   Luke 21.9-11 – And when you hear of wars and tumults, do not be terrified, for these things must first take place, but the end will not be at once." [10] Then he said to them, "Nation will rise against nation, and kingdom against kingdom. [11] There will be great earthquakes, and in various places famines and pestilences. And there will be terrors and great signs from heaven.

   a. Note the place of natural disasters in the association with the divine judgment of God. (e.g., Judg. 5.4-5; Ps. 18.7; 68.8; Isa. 24.19; 29.6; 64.1; Jer. 15.2; Ezek. 5.16-17; 14.13)

   b. The book of Revelation reveals God's control of creation in the dispensing of his divine judgments on humankind for its greed, idolatry, blasphemy, and iniquity.

3. There will be an increase in hardness of hearts to believe a lie instead of the truth of God's coming reign in the person of Jesus of Nazareth. Notice especially Paul's view:
2 Thess. 2:9-11 – The coming of the lawless one is by the activity of Satan with all power and false signs and wonders, [10] and with all wicked deception for those who are perishing, because they refused to love the truth and so be saved. [11] Therefore God sends them a strong delusion, so that they may believe what is false.

III. The Rapture and the Tribulation

The Bible speaks of a time of great anguish or tribulation, which will come upon the earth, exceeding anything that has ever occurred before. Some, identifying this with the 70th week of Daniel 9:24–27, believe it will be of seven years duration. Some believe the church will be present to experience this, the Lord not returning until the end of the period. These are termed posttribulationists.

Others, known as pretribulationists, believe that the Lord's second coming will be in two stages, or phases—that, in addition to his public second coming, Christ will come for his church, to remove them from the world, or "rapture" them, before the great tribulation.

Still others, known as midtribulationists, believe that the church will be present for the first half of the seven years but will be removed before the severe part of the tribulation begins.

Millard J. Erickson., "Eschatology," *The Baker Encyclopedia of the Bible.* (electronic ed.) Grand Rapids: Baker Book House, 1988.

Daniel 9:25-27 – Know therefore and understand that from the going out of the word to restore and build Jerusalem to the coming of an anointed one, a prince, there shall be seven weeks. Then for sixty-two weeks it shall be built again with squares and moat, but in a troubled time. [26] And after the sixty-two weeks, an anointed one shall be cut off and shall have nothing. And the people of the prince who is to come shall destroy the city and the sanctuary. Its end shall come with a flood, and to the end there shall be war. Desolations are decreed. [27] And he shall make a strong covenant with many for one week, and for half of the week he shall put an end to sacrifice and offering. And on the wing of abominations shall come one who makes desolate, until the decreed end is poured out on the desolator."

A. Rapture, Tribulation, Revelation: An overview of modern-day Pretribulationism.

1. The Second Coming of Christ is divided into two major sequences, separated by the Great Tribulation. These events are the Rapture (on the one hand), and the Revelation (on the other).

2. The Rapture is the term given to the "catching up of the Church to meet the Lord in the air," as mentioned in 1 Thessalonians.
1 Thess. 4:15-18 – For this we declare to you by a word from the Lord, that we who are alive, who are left until the coming of the Lord, will not precede those who have fallen asleep. [16] For the Lord himself will descend from heaven with a cry of command, with the voice of an archangel, and with the sound of the trumpet of God. And the dead in Christ will rise first. [17] Then we who are alive, who are left, will be caught up together with them in the clouds to meet the Lord in the air, and so we will always be with the Lord. [18] Therefore encourage one another with these words.

3. In many evangelical circles (as exemplified in the *Left Behind* series) the Rapture is pictured as a different event than the Revelation of Jesus Christ which occurs at the end of the Tribulation.

4. At the Rapture, Christ comes in the air *for his saints* (John 14.3), and "during the interval of the seven-year Tribulation, the saints are with the Lord in the air receiving their rewards at the *bema* of Christ." (Ladd, p. 62)

5. The Tribulation is divided into three distinct periods:

   a. The period of *preparation,* involving the continuation of the professing church after the Rapture, the revival of Israel, and the awakening of a revived Roman empire.

   b. The period of *peace,* when a dictator, i.e., "the Prince that shall come" (Dan. 9.26-27) who makes a covenant with Israel for a seven-year period.

   c. The period of *persecution,* when the Antichrist in the midst of the seven-year period (Rev. 11.2; 13.5; cf. Dan. 7.25; 9.27; 12.11-12) abruptly reverses his covenant with Israel, demands to be worshiped, and becomes the persecutor of God's people (i.e., the time of Jacob's trouble, Jer. 30.7 or "the Great Tribulation," cf. Dan. 12.1; Matt. 24.21; Rev. 7.14).

6. At the Revelation, Christ comes to earth in full glory *with* his saints.
   1 Thess. 3.13 – and may the Lord make you increase and abound in love for one another and for all, as we do for you, [13] so that he may establish your hearts blameless in holiness before our God and Father, at the coming of our Lord Jesus with all his saints.
   (Ladd, p. 62: He must come *for them* before he can come *with them.*)

7. Since the Rapture precedes the Tribulation (which precedes the Revelation), "it is assumed that it may occur at any moment; but the Revelation cannot occur until after the appearance of Antichrist and the Great Tribulation." *ibid.*

8. "The coming of Christ for the Rapture of the Church will be a secret coming and will be invisible to any except the Church; while the Revelation will be a

glorious outshining which will be evident to all the world." *ibid*.

B. Ladd's critique: The *Apokalypse*, the *Parousia*, and the *Epiphanes* are all the same event, and represent the one and the same *glorious return of Jesus Christ*.

1. The language of the New Testament does not give any hint of a "secret" coming.

2. This glorious return is the blessed hope of Christians, not the Rapture.

C. Biblical arguments for the Rapture:

1. The Rapture is nowhere dated in the prophecies of the OT, i.e., the dramatic removal of the church from the earth.

2. It is plainly taught in 1 Thess. 4.13-18 – But we do not want you to be uninformed, brothers, about those who are asleep, that you may not grieve as others do who have no hope. [14] For since we believe that Jesus died and rose again, even so, through Jesus, God will bring with him those who have fallen asleep. [15] For this we declare to you by a word from the Lord,[a] that we who are alive, who are left until the coming of the Lord, will not precede those who have fallen asleep. [16] For the Lord himself will descend from heaven with a cry of command, with the voice of an archangel, and with the sound of the trumpet of God. And the dead in Christ will rise first. [17] Then we who are alive, who are left, will be caught up together with them in the clouds to meet the Lord in the air, and so we will always be with the Lord. [18] Therefore encourage one another with these words.

Note: *This was given as a teaching to provide comfort to the sorrowing, not simply as preparation for an upcoming time for unprecedented horror and persecution.*

3. God has not appointed us for wrath, but for salvation.

    a. Galatians 3:13 – Christ redeemed us from the curse of the law by becoming a curse for us—for it is written, "Cursed is everyone who is hanged on a tree"

    b. 1 Thess. 5:9 – For God has not destined us for wrath, but to obtain salvation through our Lord Jesus Christ.

    c. 1 Thess. 1:9-10 – For they themselves report concerning us the kind of reception we had among you, and how you turned to God from idols to serve the living and true God, [10] and to wait for his Son from heaven, whom he raised from the dead, Jesus who delivers us from the wrath to come.

4. Christ has promised to spare us from the wrath which is about to happen upon the earth.
Rev. 3:10-11 – Because you have kept my word about patient endurance, I will keep you from the hour of trial that is coming on the whole world, to try those who dwell on the earth. [11] I am coming soon. Hold fast what you have, so that no one may seize your crown.

5. Christians see the coming of Jesus as a blessed hope, not as a destructive persecution of the elect.

    a. A blessed hope.
    Titus 2:13-14 – waiting for *our blessed hope*, the appearing of the glory of our great God and Savior Jesus Christ, [14] who gave himself for us to redeem us from all lawlessness and to purify for himself a

people for his own possession who are zealous for good works.

  b. Not looking forward to bone-crushing persecution.
Matthew 24:21-22 – For then there will be great tribulation, such as has not been from the beginning of the world until now, no, and never will be. [22] And if those days had not been cut short, no human being would be saved. But for the sake of the elect those days will be cut short.

6. God knows how to keep his holy ones safe even in the midst of trial.
2 Peter 2:9 – then the Lord knows how to rescue the godly from trials, and to keep the unrighteous under punishment until the day of judgment.

D. Various positions relative to the Rapture, Tribulation, and Revelation:

1. All of the events of the end (the Rapture, Tribulation, and the *Parousia*) occur *before The Millennium,* the thousand-year period of Jesus' reign on the earth.
Rev. 20:4 – Then I saw thrones, and seated on them were those to whom the authority to judge was committed. Also I saw the souls of those who had been beheaded for the testimony of Jesus and for the word of God, and who had not worshiped the beast or its image and had not received its mark on their foreheads or their hands. They came to life and reigned with Christ for a thousand years.

2. Positions relative to the Rapture are based on *where the Rapture takes place relative to the Tribulation.*

3. Pre-tribulationism: Christ's coming is divided into two phases.

a. The first is at the resurrection of the believing dead and translation of Christians who are alive at the "Rapture." This occurs before the "great tribulation" of Matthew 24, a period of unparalleled terror and judgment on the earth. While the world experiences God' judgment during the tribulation, the church will be judged and issued rewards for its faithfulness.

b. At the end of this seven years, Christ will return with a resurrection of those saints who died during the tribulation.

c. The heart of this view is Christ's intent to deliver the church from the tribulation, based in this view upon God's purpose, as Paul suggests in 1 Thess. 5.10 – "For God has not destined us for wrath, but to obtain salvation through our Lord Jesus Christ."

4. Post-tribulationism: This view holds that the coming of Christ for his people takes place *at the end* of the tribulation.

    a. This view rejects a "rapture" notion of Christ's coming, and believes the church will be present through the Great Tribulation.

    b. Post-tribulationism makes a difference between *God's wrath* and the *tribulation*. All Christians suffer *tribulation and persecution* for their allegiance to Jesus of Nazareth, whereas God's wrath is *God's judgment on the wicked*.
    John 3.36 – Whoever believes in the Son has eternal life, but whoever rejects the Son will not see life, for God's wrath remains on him.

5. Mid-tribulationism: This view seeks to resolve the conflict between pre-and post-tribulational views.

a. It asserts that the church will experience the less-severe first-half of the tribulation, and then be removed for the second half, where God pours out his wrath on the earth.

b. The church in this view, then, experiences tribulation, but avoids the wrath of God.

E. Views of The Millennium:

1. Premillennialism: Jesus will rule as Lord and Christ in a literal earthly reign for 1,000 years after his return.

   a. Called "chialism" (Greek for 1,000), this view was the dominant view of the church's first three centuries, and grew in popularity in conservative circles in the 19th century.

   b. The key passage for this view is a literal interpretation of Rev. 20:4-6 which speaks of a literal 1,000-year reign, and two resurrections: one before for the righteous, and the second after, for the wicked. The 1,000-year period occurs after the Great Tribulation, where Christ will come and establish a time of peace and justice.
   Rev. 20.4-6 – Then I saw thrones, and seated on them were those to whom the authority to judge was committed. Also I saw the souls of those who had been beheaded for the testimony of Jesus and for the word of God, and those who had not worshiped the beast or its image and had not received its mark on their foreheads or their hands. They came to life and reigned with Christ for a thousand years. [5] The rest of the dead did not come to life until the thousand years were ended. This is the first resurrection. [6] Blessed and holy is the one who shares in the first resurrection! Over such the second death has no power, but they will be priests of God

and of Christ, and they will reign with him for a thousand years.

2. Amillennialism: There will be *no literal millennium*, and no earthly reign of Christ.

   a. The great and final judgment comes after His second coming, and the eternal states of the believing and unbelieving commence at that time.

   b. Amillennialists interpret Revelation to be a symbolic book, and hold that such a view is simpler than either post- or pre-mil views. They take the mention of a millennium, and many other items in Revelation, as a largely symbolic reference.

3. Postmillennialism: The preaching of Jesus and the justice of the Kingdom will be so successful that the world will be converted, and the reign of Christ will be complete and universal.

   a. Appealing to verses like Isaiah 45.22-25, this view has been most popular at times when the church has been succeeding in political or social transformation.

   b. With the world wars of the 20th century and mass devastation and injustice of modern times, however, this view has lost much support and has not proved to be convincing to many in the Church.

F. Defining our Terms: Tribulation, The Tribulation, and the Great Tribulation.

1. *Tribulation (generic)*: That which every Christian believer endures by virtue of being connected and identified with the person of Jesus Christ.

a. John 16:33 – I have said these things to you, that in me you may have peace. In the world you will have tribulation. But take heart; I have overcome the world.

b. 2 Tim. 3:12 – Indeed, all who desire to live a godly life in Christ Jesus will be persecuted.

2. <u>The</u> *Tribulation*: This is the specific period of end times associated with the seventieth week of Daniel 9, a "week" of the prophet's reckoning to equal seven years. It represents the final "week" of a "seventy-week" period (490 years) which summarizes Daniel's prophecy on Israel's future.

   Dan. 9.24-27 – "Seventy weeks are decreed about your people and your holy city, to finish the transgression, to put an end to sin, and to atone for iniquity, to bring in everlasting righteousness, to seal both vision and prophet, and to anoint a most holy place. [25] Know therefore and understand that from the going out of the word to restore and build Jerusalem to the coming of an anointed one, a prince, there shall be seven weeks. Then for sixty-two weeks it shall be built again with squares and moat, but in a troubled time. [26] And after the sixty-two weeks, an anointed one shall be cut off and shall have nothing. And the people of the prince who is to come shall destroy the city and the sanctuary. Its end shall come with a flood, and to the end there shall be war. Desolations are decreed. [27] And he shall make a strong covenant with many for one week, and for half of the week he shall put an end to sacrifice and offering. And on the wing of abominations shall come one who makes desolate, until the decreed end is poured out on the desolator."

   a. Sixty-nine weeks (or 483 years) were concluded with the death of Jesus of Nazareth, who is the Christ. (Dan. 9.26).

b. An unusually long time gap has occurred between the 69th and 70th week, which is the future time of Jacob's trouble, or The Tribulation period.
Jeremiah 30.7 – Alas! That day is so great there is none like it; it is a time of distress for Jacob; yet he shall be saved out of it.

c. This prophetic burden in detailing the events of The Tribulation focused on the history and destiny of Israel, which remained a central focus even of Jesus' own explanation of it in Matthew 24-25.

d. According to many conservative expositors of Scripture, the character and description of The Tribulation coincide with the events highlighted in Revelation 6–19, i.e., the dramatic, consecutive series of seals, trumpets, and bowl judgments upon the world, consummating in the triumphant return of Christ to earth. (cf. Rev. 19.11–21).

3. *The Great Tribulation:* That period of time in the midst of the Tribulation where the "Prince that is to come" (Dan. 9, or the Antichrist) breaks his covenant with Israel, and persecutes the people of God with great ferocity and viciousness.
Matthew 24:21-22 – For then there will be great tribulation, such as has not been from the beginning of the world until now, no, and never will be. [22] And if those days had not been cut short, no human being would be saved. But for the sake of the elect those days will be cut short.

G. The Nature and Purpose of the Tribulation:

1. It is an outpouring of the wrath of God upon the earth, and all those who rejected his grace in Christ. (1 Thess. 1.10; Rev. 6.16, 17; 11.18; 14.19; 15.1; 16.1, 19)

2. It is a time of retribution and punishment upon the nations. (Isa. 24.20–21; Isa. 26.21; Jer. 25.32–33; 2 Thess. 2.12)

3. It is called the time of "Jacob's trouble," i.e., a period of tribulation for the people of Israel. (Jer. 30.7; Dan. 12.1)

4. It is described as a time of great destruction. (Joel 1.15; 1 Thess. 5.3)

5. It will be accompanied by great desolation. (Zeph. 1.14, 15)

6. At its heart, the period of the tribulation is a time of God's divine judgment. (Rev. 14.7; 16.5; 19.2).

7. It will greatly impact the people of Israel, leading to its conversion and divine deliverance. (Jer. 30.7; Ezek. 20.37; Dan. 12.1; Zech. 13.8–9)

IV. Conclusion: "You'd Better Get Ready, Jesus is Coming Again, Calling All Peoples of All Nations . . ." West Angeles Church of God in Christ

Properly understood and applied, eschatology has a powerful positive significance for Christians. It is to be a source of comfort (1 Thess. 4:18), of encouragement (1 Cor 15:58), of challenge to watchfulness and faithful service, and the assurance of reward (Mt 25:14–30). Because the time is limited, Christians are to use faithfully the opportunities that are theirs. Because of the certainty of our Lord's return, we are to be filled with hope and courage.

Millard J. Erickson., "Eschatology," *The Baker Encyclopedia of the Bible*. (electronic ed.) Grand Rapids: Baker Book House, 1988.

1 Cor. 15:57-58 – But thanks be to God, who gives us the victory through our Lord Jesus Christ. [58] Therefore, my

Lesson Four: The Signs of the Times, the Rapture, and the Tribulation ■ 121

beloved brothers, be steadfast, immovable, always abounding in the work of the Lord, knowing that in the Lord your labor is not in vain.

- With so many various theories and inquiries, it is important to remember that eschatology was never meant to be a bone of contention or "divisive force" among the body of Christ. Rather, eschatology is to be the "atmosphere we breathe," the literal worldview which animates and gives meaning to all we do, say, and pursue.

- We are to be neither overly affected nor tolerant of splits between us regarding differences in opinion such as tribulational issues or specific timetables of occurrences. Our differences regarding our views and various time views should not eclipse the *main point: all believers everywhere are to be aware and responsive to* the "signs of the times," and be watchful for the appearing of the Lord.

- What is more significant than speculating on the precise timing of the events preceding Christ's return is our *constant state of sober watchfulness,* and our *aggressive, joyful labor in the Gospel.* We must work while it is day, for night is coming when no person can work.
John 9:4-5 – We must work the works of him who sent me while it is day; night is coming, when no one can work. [5] As long as I am in the world, I am the light of the world.

The Bottom Line: _____

Lesson Five
The Second Coming and the Need to Watch

....

The Hope of the Second Coming Helps Us Prepare To Be A Big Shot in the World to Come

William Kelly was an outstanding student of the Bible whose scholarship and spirituality made him a real power for God in Great Britain at the close of the 19th century. Mr. Kelly helped a young relative prepare for Trinity College in Dublin, and in this way came to the attention of the professors there. They urged him to take up work at the college and thus distinguish himself. When Mr. Kelly showed a complete lack of enthusiasm, they were nonplused. One of them asked in exasperation, "But Mr. Kelly, aren't you interested in making a name for yourself in the world?" To which Mr. Kelly adroitly replied, "*Which* world, gentlemen?"

....

I. **The Theme of the Second Coming of Jesus Christ**

The wisest among us never forget the time is short and theirs is about almost up. . . . If your whole life was a day, then if you are 15, it's 8:51 a.m. If you are 20, it's 11:08 a.m. If you are 25, it's 12:25 p.m. If you are 30, it's 1:25 p.m. If you are 35, it's 2:59 p.m. If you are 40, it's 4:16 p.m. If you are 45, it's 5:43 p.m. If you are 50, it's 6:50 p.m. If you are 55, it's 8:08 p.m. If you are 60, it's 10:11 p.m. If you are 70, it's approaching midnight. If you're over 70, . . .

Titus 2:11-14 – For the grace of God has appeared, bringing salvation for all people, [12] training us to renounce ungodliness and worldly passions, and to live self-controlled, upright, and godly lives in the present age, [13] waiting for our blessed hope, the appearing of the glory of our great God and Savior Jesus Christ, [14] who gave himself for us to redeem us from all lawlessness and to purify for himself a people for his own possession who are zealous for good works.

A. A Recapitulation: *The Second Coming of our Lord Jesus Christ may be considered one of the central affirmations of the entire*

Scripture, and certainly of the New Testament apostolic witness to the Kingdom of God

1. It is posited that one out of every 30 verses in the Bible mention this doctrine.

2. For every *single mention* of the First Advent of Messiah into the world, there are *eight renderings* to the Second Coming (or Advent) of Christ.

3. Texts related to the Second Coming are mentioned in 318 references in Scripture, in 216 chapters of the Bible.

4. Entire books of the NT are devoted to dealing with its content (e.g., 1 and 2 Thessalonians), along with entire chapters focused on the particulars surrounding the Second Coming of our Lord (e.g., Matthew 24; Mark 13; Luke 21, etc.).

5. The OT prophets, although they tended to merge the two comings in their prophetic utterances, devote entire sections of their writings to the theme of the Second Coming of Messiah, and its meaning for the people of God and the created order.

B. Jesus of Nazareth taught consistently and witnessed boldly about the certainty and quality of his Second Advent.

1. In Jesus' extended prophetic declaration on his coming, he spoke clearly about the power and grandeur of his return to complete his work in the world.
Matthew 24:29-31 – Immediately after the tribulation of those days the sun will be darkened, and the moon will not give its light, and the stars will fall from heaven, and the powers of the heavens will be shaken. [30] Then will appear in heaven the sign of the Son of Man, and then all the tribes of the earth will mourn, and they will see

the Son of Man coming on the clouds of heaven with power and great glory. [31] And he will send out his angels with a loud trumpet call, and they will gather his elect from the four winds, from one end of heaven to the other.

2. The cares of this life, Jesus taught, can so weigh you down and blind you that his day comes suddenly on us unawares, like an animal in a trap.
Luke 21:34-36 – "But watch yourselves lest your hearts be weighed down with dissipation and drunkenness and cares of this life, and that day come upon you suddenly like a trap. [35] For it will come upon all who dwell on the face of the whole earth. [36] But stay awake at all times, praying that you may have strength to escape all these things that are going to take place, and to stand before the Son of Man."

3. In his most intimate setting, before his Passion and Death, our Lord Jesus spoke words of comfort of his return to his apostles, reminding them of his intent to come back for them.
John 14:3 – And if I go and prepare a place for you, I will come again and will take you to myself, that where I am you may be also.

C. The angels of the Ascension bore testimony that Jesus would in fact appear again a second time.

1. At the Ascension of the Lord Jesus:
Acts 1:10-11 – And while they were gazing into heaven as he went, behold, two men stood by them in white robes, 11 and said, "Men of Galilee, why do you stand looking into heaven? This Jesus, who was taken up from you into heaven, will come in the same way as you saw him go into heaven."

2. The messages of the Cross, the Resurrection, and the Return are anchored in the rich testimony of the Lord,

the angels, the prophets, and the apostles.
Hebrews 2:1-4 – Therefore we must pay much closer attention to what we have heard, lest we drift away from it. [2] For since the message declared by angels proved to be reliable and every transgression or disobedience received a just retribution, [3] how shall we escape if we neglect such a great salvation? It was declared at first by the Lord, and it was attested to us by those who heard, [4] while God also bore witness by signs and wonders and various miracles and by gifts of the Holy Spirit distributed according to his will.

D. The apostles, who were eyewitnesses of the glory and majesty of the Risen Lord, testified constantly of the truth of Christ's second appearing.

1. It was the message of hope and comfort in the face of those who died in Christ.
   1 Thess. 4:16-17 – For the Lord himself will descend from heaven with a cry of command, with the voice of an archangel, and with the sound of the trumpet of God. And the dead in Christ will rise first. [17] Then we who are alive, who are left, will be caught up together with them in the clouds to meet the Lord in the air, and so we will always be with the Lord.

2. For those who eagerly await his coming, he comes not to deal with sin but to save his own, to bring them to himself.
   Hebrews 9:28 – so Christ, having been offered once to bear the sins of many, will appear a second time, not to deal with sin but to save those who are eagerly waiting for him.

3. We are exhorted to live in such a manner as not to be ashamed of him when he appears.
   1 John 2:28 – And now, little children, abide in him, so that when he appears we may have confidence and not shrink from him in shame at his coming.

4. The apostolic witness of the Second Coming emphasizes his coming to judge the ungodly.
   Jude 1:14-15 – It was also about these that Enoch, the seventh from Adam, prophesied, saying, "Behold, the Lord came with ten thousands of his holy ones, [15] to execute judgment on all and to convict all the ungodly of all their deeds of ungodliness that they have committed in such an ungodly way, and of all the harsh things that ungodly sinners have spoken against him."

E. What is meant by the Second Coming:
   A personal, visible, and decisive coming of the glorified Jesus to consummate his work in the universe that he started in his Incarnation, his sacrifice on the Cross, his Resurrection, and his Ascension.

   1. It will be a *personal coming* of Jesus of Nazareth glorified, immortal, and charged with putting down all evil and his enemies in the universe.

      a. John 14:2-3 – In my Father's house are many rooms. If it were not so, would I have told you that I go to prepare a place for you? [3] And if I go and prepare a place for you, I will come again and will take you to myself, that where I am you may be also.

      b. John 17:24 – Father, I desire that they also, whom you have given me, may be with me where I am, to see my glory that you have given me because you loved me before the foundation of the world.

   2. It will be a *visible coming* of Jesus of Nazareth glorified, immortal before the sight of all the nations, coming with his saints.

      a. Matthew 24:30 – Then will appear in heaven the sign of the Son of Man, and then all the tribes of the earth will mourn, and they will see the Son of Man coming on the clouds of heaven with power and great glory.

b. Matthew 26:64 – Jesus said to him, "You have said so. But I tell you, from now on you will see the Son of Man seated at the right hand of Power and coming on the clouds of heaven."

3. It will be a *decisive coming* of Jesus of Nazareth glorified and immortal, who will once and for all put an end to the enemies of God, the effects of the curse, and the evil which is shot through the universe.

a. His Second Coming will put all enemies under his feet.
1 Cor. 15:24-25 – Then comes the end, when he delivers the kingdom to God the Father after destroying every rule and every authority and power. [25] For he must reign until he has put all his enemies under his feet.

b. His Second Coming will end the effects of the curse upon creation.
Romans 8:18-19 – For I consider that the sufferings of this present time are not worth comparing with the glory that is to be revealed to us. [19] For the creation waits with eager longing for the revealing of the sons of God.

c. His Second Coming will end the ancient evil that has tortured God's creation.
Rev. 12:7-12 – Now war arose in heaven, Michael and his angels fighting against the dragon. And the dragon and his angels fought back, [8] but he was defeated and there was no longer any place for them in heaven. [9] And the great dragon was thrown down, that ancient serpent, who is called the devil and Satan, the deceiver of the whole world— he was thrown down to the earth, and his angels were

thrown down with him. [10] And I heard a loud voice in heaven, saying, "Now the salvation and the power and the kingdom of our God and the authority of his Christ have come, for the accuser of our brothers has been thrown down, who accuses them day and night before our God. [11] And they have conquered him by the blood of the Lamb and by the word of their testimony, for they loved not their lives even unto death. [12] Therefore, rejoice, O heavens and you who dwell in them! But woe to you, O earth and sea, for the devil has come down to you in great wrath, because he knows that his time is short!"

F. Wrong views concerning the Second Coming of Christ:

1. Wrong View #1: Equating the Second Coming with Christ's coming at his death.
   Hebrews 9:27-28 – And just as it is appointed for man to die once, and after that comes judgment, [28] so Christ, having been offered once to bear the sins of many, will appear a second time, not to deal with sin but to save those who are eagerly waiting for him.

2. Wrong View #2: Equating the Second Coming with the coming of the Holy Spirit at Pentecost.
   Acts 1:10-11 – And while they were gazing into heaven as he went, behold, two men stood by them in white robes, [11] and said, "Men of Galilee, why do you stand looking into heaven? This Jesus, who was taken up from you into heaven, will come in the same way as you saw him go into heaven."

3. Wrong View #3: Equating the Second Coming with the destruction of Jerusalem under Titus in A.D. 70.

4. Wrong View #4: Spiritualizing the Second Coming of Christ in some kind of existential way (e.g., Rudolph Bultmann and the demythologization project).

II. **The Purpose of the Second Coming of Jesus Christ**

"In Revelation 21:6, God says the water of life comes 'without cost.' So does everything else in heaven, including your condo. That means no down payment, no realtor fees, no closing cost, no mortgage payments, no property tax, no utility bills, and no fear of foreclosure." Baker suggests, as well, that since there is no sin, there will be no hospitals. Since there is no death, there will be no cemeteries. Also, since there is no sin, there will be no regret.

Don Baker, "Heaven", Moody Bible Institute Founder's Week Messages, 1984 p. 211.

1 Peter 1:3 – Blessed be the God and Father of our Lord Jesus Christ! According to his great mercy, he has caused us to be born again to a living hope through the resurrection of Jesus Christ from the dead.

A. *The Second Coming and the Church:* The hope of eternal glory.

1. The translation into immortality.
1 Cor. 15:20-24 – But in fact Christ has been raised from the dead, the firstfruits of those who have fallen asleep. [21] For as by a man came death, by a man has come also the resurrection of the dead. [22] For as in Adam all die, so also in Christ shall all be made alive. [23] But each in his own order: Christ the firstfruits, then at his coming those who belong to Christ. [24] Then comes the end, when he delivers the kingdom to God the Father after destroying every rule and every authority and power.

2. The Marriage Supper of the Lamb.
Rev. 19:5-9 – And from the throne came a voice saying, "Praise our God, all you his servants, you who fear him, small and great." [6] Then I heard what seemed to be the voice of a great multitude, like the roar of many waters and like the sound of mighty peals of thunder, crying out, "Hallelujah! For the Lord our God the Almighty reigns. [7] Let us rejoice and exult and give him the glory, for the marriage of the Lamb has come, and his Bride has made herself ready; [8] it was granted her to clothe herself with fine linen, bright and pure"—

for the fine linen is the righteous deeds of the saints. [9] And the angel said to me, "Write this: Blessed are those who are invited to the marriage supper of the Lamb." And he said to me, "These are the true words of God."

3. To be in the presence of the Lord forever.
1 Thess. 4:16-17 – For the Lord himself will descend from heaven with a cry of command, with the voice of an archangel, and with the sound of the trumpet of God. And the dead in Christ will rise first. [17] Then we who are alive, who are left, will be caught up together with them in the clouds to meet the Lord in the air, and so we will always be with the Lord.

B. *The Second Coming and Nations:* The divine judgment of the living nations.

1. The "sheep" and the "goats" of Matthew 25.
Matthew 25:31-34 – "When the Son of Man comes in his glory, and all the angels with him, then he will sit on his glorious throne. [32] Before him will be gathered all the nations, and he will separate people one from another as a shepherd separates the sheep from the goats. [33] And he will place the sheep on his right, but the goats on the left. [34] Then the King will say to those on his right, 'Come, you who are blessed by my Father, inherit the kingdom prepared for you from the foundation of the world.

2. The battle of Armageddon, at the end of the Great Tribulation.
Joel 3:9-16 – Proclaim this among the nations: Consecrate for war; stir up the mighty men. Let all the men of war draw near; let them come up. [10] Beat your plowshares into swords, and your pruning hooks into spears; let the weak say, "I am a warrior." [11] Hasten and come, all you surrounding nations, and gather yourselves there. Bring down your warriors, O Lord. [12] Let the nations stir themselves up and come up to the Valley of Jehoshaphat; for there I will sit to judge all

the surrounding nations. [13] Put in the sickle, for the harvest is ripe. Go in, tread, for the winepress is full. The vats overflow, for their evil is great. [14] Multitudes, multitudes, in the valley of decision! For the day of the Lord is near in the valley of decision. [15] The sun and the moon are darkened, and the stars withdraw their shining. [16] The Lord roars from Zion, and utters his voice from Jerusalem, and the heavens and the earth quake. But the Lord is a refuge to his people, a stronghold to the people of Israel.

3. The judgment of the nations.
Rev. 16:14-16– For they are demonic spirits, performing signs, who go abroad to the kings of the whole world, to assemble them for battle on the great day of God the Almighty. [15] ("Behold, I am coming like a thief! Blessed is the one who stays awake, keeping his garments on, that he may not go about naked and be seen exposed!") [16] And they assembled them at the place that in Hebrew is called Armageddon.

4. Subduing the peoples under the feet of Messiah.
Rev. 19:11-19 – Then I saw heaven opened, and behold, a white horse! The one sitting on it is called Faithful and True, and in righteousness he judges and makes war. [12] His eyes are like a flame of fire, and on his head are many diadems, and he has a name written that no one knows but himself. [13] He is clothed in a robe dipped in blood, and the name by which he is called is The Word of God. [14] And the armies of heaven, arrayed in fine linen, white and pure, were following him on white horses. [15] From his mouth comes a sharp sword with which to strike down the nations, and he will rule them with a rod of iron. He will tread the winepress of the fury of the wrath of God the Almighty. [16] On his robe and on his thigh he has a name written, King of kings and Lord of lords. [17] Then I saw an angel standing in the sun, and with a loud voice he called to all the birds that fly directly overhead, "Come, gather for the great supper of God, [18] to eat the flesh of kings, the flesh of captains, the flesh of mighty men, the flesh of horses and their riders, and the flesh of all men, both free and

slave, both small and great." [19] And I saw the beast and the kings of the earth with their armies gathered to make war against him who was sitting on the horse and against his army.

C. *The Second Coming and the Jews:* The conversion of the Jews.

1. The deliverance and salvation of "all Israel."
   Romans 11:25-29 – Lest you be wise in your own conceits, I want you to understand this mystery, brothers: a partial hardening has come upon Israel, until the fullness of the Gentiles has come in. [26] And in this way all Israel will be saved, as it is written, "The Deliverer will come from Zion, he will banish ungodliness from Jacob"; [27] "and this will be my covenant with them when I take away their sins."[28] As regards the gospel, they are enemies of God for your sake. But as regards election, they are beloved for the sake of their forefathers. [29] For the gifts and the calling of God are irrevocable.

2. The recognition of Jesus of Nazareth as their long-awaited Messiah.
   Rev. 1:7-8 – Behold, he is coming with the clouds, and every eye will see him, even those who pierced him, and all tribes of the earth will wail on account of him. Even so. Amen. [8] "I am the Alpha and the Omega," says the Lord God, "who is and who was and who is to come, the Almighty."

3. Restoration to the land of God's promise. Isaiah 11.11; chapter 60

4. The restoration of the worship of Yahweh in Messiah. Ezekiel 40-48

5. The permanence of the promise never again to be removed from the land.

a. Ezekiel 34:28 – They shall no more be a prey to the nations, nor shall the beasts of the land devour them. They shall dwell securely, and none shall make them afraid.

b. Amos 9:15 – I will plant them on their land, and they shall never again be uprooted out of the land that I have given them," says the Lord your God.

D. *The Second Coming and the Enemy of God's people:* The judgment of the Antichrist.

1. The brightness of the coming of Christ, and the destruction of the Antichrist.
   2 Thess. 2:7-10 – For the mystery of lawlessness is already at work. Only he who now restrains it will do so until he is out of the way. [8] And then the lawless one will be revealed, whom the Lord Jesus will kill with the breath of his mouth and bring to nothing by the appearance of his coming. [9] The coming of the lawless one is by the activity of Satan with all power and false signs and wonders, [10] and with all wicked deception for those who are perishing, because they refused to love the truth and so be saved.

2. The destruction of the evil rebellion at Armageddon. (cf. Rev. 16, 19)
   Rev. 19.20 -- And the beast was captured, and with it the false prophet who in its presence had done the signs by which he deceived those who had received the mark of the beast and those who worshiped its image. These two were thrown alive into the lake of fire that burns with sulfur.

3. The consignment of Satan to the abyss for a thousand-year period.
   Rev. 20:1-3 – Then I saw an angel coming down from heaven, holding in his hand the key to the bottomless pit and a great chain. [2] And he seized the dragon, that

ancient serpent, who is the devil and Satan, and bound him for a thousand years, [3] and threw him into the pit, and shut it and sealed it over him, so that he might not deceive the nations any longer, until the thousand years were ended. After that he must be released for a little while.

E. *The Second Coming and the Millennial Reign of Christ:* The reign of God in the earth.

1. The Millennium: The thousand-year reign of the glorified Christ with his saints upon the earth.
   Rev. 20:4-5 – Then I saw thrones, and seated on them were those to whom the authority to judge was committed. Also I saw the souls of those who had been beheaded for the testimony of Jesus and for the word of God, and who had not worshiped the beast or its image and had not received its mark on their foreheads or their hands. They came to life and reigned with Christ for a thousand years. [5] The rest of the dead did not come to life until the thousand years were ended. This is the first resurrection.

2. It begins with the coming of Christ with his saints at the end of the Great Tribulation, i.e., the close of the seventieth week of Daniel.

3. It is preceded by the destruction of the Antichrist and the binding of Satan (i.e., the arbiters of evil on the earth).

4. Jesus of Nazareth, glorified and immortal, is the King of the realm, accompanied by his apostles and the church.

   a. The apostolic rule (over the "twelve tribes" of Israel?). Isaiah 66; Matt. 19.28

b. The reign of the church. Luke 19.11-19; Heb. 2.6-7; 2 Tim. 2.12

5. Jerusalem (old or new?) will be the capital city of the kingdom, with pilgrimages being made to the Holy City. Isaiah 2:2-4 – It shall come to pass in the latter days that the mountain of the house of the Lord shall be established as the highest of the mountains, and shall be lifted up above the hills; and all the nations shall flow to it, [3] and many peoples shall come, and say: "Come, let us go up to the mountain of the Lord, to the house of the God of Jacob, that he may teach us his ways and that we may walk in his paths." For out of Zion shall go the law, and the word of the Lord from Jerusalem. [4] He shall judge between the nations, and shall decide disputes for many peoples; and they shall beat their swords into plowshares, and their spears into pruning hooks; nation shall not lift up sword against nation, neither shall they learn war anymore.

6. The reign will be one of righteousness and justice, equity and peace shall abound, with abundance, rest, and glory. Isa 11.4; Ps. 98.9

7. The earth will be refreshed and renovated. Rom. 8.19-21; Isa. 65.17; Isa. 35

F. The end of The Millennium.

1. Apostasy and rebellion are once more and finally unleashed on the world.
Rev. 20.7-8 -- And when the thousand years are ended, Satan will be released from his prison [8] and will come out to deceive the nations that are at the four corners of the earth, Gog and Magog, to gather them for battle; their number is like the sand of the sea.

2. Satan, the instigator of rebellion against the reigning Lord, is finally destroyed.

3. The Great White Throne dispenses justice to all souls not written in the Lamb's book of life.
Rev. 20.11-15 -- Then I saw a great white throne and him who was seated on it. From his presence earth and sky fled away, and no place was found for them. [12] And I saw the dead, great and small, standing before the throne, and books were opened. Then another book was opened, which is the book of life. And the dead were judged by what was written in the books, according to what they had done. [13] And the sea gave up the dead who were in it, Death and Hades gave up the dead who were in them, and they were judged, each one of them, according to what they had done. [14] Then Death and Hades were thrown into the lake of fire. This is the second death, the lake of fire. [15] And if anyone's name was not found written in the book of life, he was thrown into the lake of fire.

4. A new heaven and new earth are manifest. (cf. Rev. 21, 22)
Rev. 21.1 -- Then I saw a new heaven and a new earth, for the first heaven and the first earth had passed away, and the sea was no more.

5. The New Jerusalem and the final state of humankind is revealed.
Rev. 22:1-6 – Then the angel showed me the river of the water of life, bright as crystal, flowing from the throne of God and of the Lamb [2] through the middle of the street of the city; also, on either side of the river, the tree of life with its twelve kinds of fruit, yielding its fruit each month. The leaves of the tree were for the healing of the nations. [3] No longer will there be anything accursed, but the throne of God and of the Lamb will be in it, and his servants will worship him. [4] They will see his face, and his name will be on their foreheads. [5] And night will be no more. They will need no light of lamp or sun, for the Lord God will be their light, and they will reign forever and ever. [6] And he said to me,

"These words are trustworthy and true. And the Lord, the God of the spirits of the prophets, has sent his angel to show his servants what must soon take place. "

G. The final work of the Son: Delivering the Kingdom to the Father in order that God may become all in all.
1 Cor. 15:24-28 – Then comes the end, when he delivers the kingdom to God the Father after destroying every rule and every authority and power. [25] For he must reign until he has put all his enemies under his feet. [26] The last enemy to be destroyed is death. [27] For " God has put all things in subjection under his feet." But when it says, "all things are put in subjection," it is plain that he is excepted who put all things in subjection under him. [28] When all things are subjected to him, then the Son himself will also be subjected to him who put all things in subjection under him, that God may be all in all.

III. The Nature of the Second Coming of Jesus Christ

Jesus is commander-in-chief of the armies of God, and is calling men and women, boys and girls from all over the globe to join Him in the Father's kingdom. He is empowering them to minister in His Name throughout the earth, and foretell of the coming of the Kingdom that soon will dawn within the earth in fullness. A Thousand years are like a day to the Lord; we are in the Last times, and this world as we know it, will be replaced with a kingdom of Justice and Peace where Jesus will reign where'er the sun in its courses run. To be ignorant of what Jesus is doing and shall soon do is to be ill-prepared to meet the challenges of a world which increasingly grows less impressed with the hope of glory, and more impressed with the glory of gain. Tragic indeed is the Christian who has lost his or her love for the appearing of the great God and our Savior, Jesus Christ.

Matthew 26:64 – Jesus said to him, "You have said so. But I tell you, from now on you will see the Son of Man seated at the right hand of Power and coming on the clouds of heaven.

Mark 8:38 – For whoever is ashamed of me and of my words in this adulterous and sinful generation, of him will the Son of Man also be ashamed when he comes in the glory of his Father with the holy angels.

A. For Jesus and the Apostles, the Second Coming of Jesus was *certain, definite, and absolutely sure.*

1. Certain and definite.
   Rev. 22:12-13 – "Behold, I am coming soon, bringing my recompense with me, to repay everyone for what he has done. [13] I am the Alpha and the Omega, the first and the last, the beginning and the end."

2. Absolutely sure.
   Rev. 22:7 – "And behold, I am coming soon. Blessed is the one who keeps the words of the prophecy of this book."

3. Attested by angelic witness.
   Acts 1:10-11 – And while they were gazing into heaven as he went, behold, two men stood by them in white robes, [11] and said, "Men of Galilee, why do you stand looking into heaven? This Jesus, who was taken up from you into heaven, will come in the same way as you saw him go into heaven."

B. Jesus' Second Coming is also *imminent.* That is, it could occur at any time.

1. There appears to be nothing in the teaching of the Word that hinders the coming of Christ and the introduction of the day of the Lord at any time.

2. It is best to understand the Second Coming of Jesus as "a great whole." As one commentator has put it, it will be a "series of events" associated with the consummation of all things under the reign of Jesus Christ.

3. From a biblical point of view, nothing seems to hinder the catching away of the saints and the Day of the Lord.

a. 2 Tim. 4:6-8 – For I am already being poured out as a drink offering, and the time of my departure has come. [7] I have fought the good fight, I have finished the race, I have kept the faith. [8] Henceforth there is laid up for me the crown of righteousness, which the Lord, the righteous judge, will award to me on that Day, and not only to me but also to all who have loved his appearing.

b. Titus 2:13 – waiting for our blessed hope, the appearing of the glory of our great God and Savior Jesus Christ.

c. 2 Peter 3:12-14 – waiting for and hastening the coming of the day of God, because of which the heavens will be set on fire and dissolved, and the heavenly bodies will melt as they burn! [13] But according to his promise we are waiting for new heavens and a new earth in which righteousness dwells. [14] Therefore, beloved, since you are waiting for these, be diligent to be found by him without spot or blemish, and at peace.

4. Objections to the imminence of the Lord:

   a. What of the preaching of the Gospel to all nations (Matt. 24.14)? *Who is to determine when and in what respect that all the nations have received the preaching of the Gospel to the nations?*

   b. What of Peter, James, and John being told they would not taste death until they had seen the coming of the Son of Man and his kingdom (cf. Matt. 16.28; Mark 9.1; Luke 9.27)?
   Could this have been fulfilled at the Transfiguration (cf. Matthew 17 with 2 Peter 1.16-18)

   c. What of the disciples being told that they would not have gone through all the cities of Israel until the

Son of Man come (cf. Matt. 10.23)?
Could it be that under the preaching ministry of the two witnesses of Revelation 11 that this will be fulfilled?

d. What of Jesus saying that this generation will not pass till all the things of Matthew 24 being fulfilled (cf. Matt. 24.34; Luke 21.32; Mark 13.30)?
Could the term "generation" here refer to the Jewish "race" (i.e., the same Greek term is used in Matt. 11.16; 16.4; Mark 8.38; Luke 7.31; 16.8; 17.25; Phil. 2.15)?

C. The Second Coming of Jesus Christ will be *personal*.

1. He comes for his own, after preparing a place for them. John 14.1-6

2. The Lord himself will descend from heaven with a shout. 1 Thess. 4.16

3. No proxies, substitutes, or messengers will come to consummate God's kingdom. Jesus will come himself, personally.

D. The Second Coming of Jesus Christ will be a *literal, corporeal return to earth*.

1. The testimony of the angels at the Ascension. Acts 1.11

2. A literal, real coming – not spiritualized, symbolic, or abstract.

3. Neither a spiritual nor psychic coming, but a literal physical (i.e., corporeal) coming.

E. The Second Coming of Jesus Christ will be *visible to all.*

1. He will appear in the sky, and be seen coming on the clouds of the sky, "with power and great glory. Matt. 24.30

2. Grace and mercy will be poured out on the Jews as they behold Jesus of Nazareth as their true Messiah.
    Zech. 12:10 – And I will pour out on the house of David and the inhabitants of Jerusalem a spirit of grace and pleas for mercy, so that, when they look on me, on him whom they have pierced, they shall mourn for him, as one mourns for an only child, and weep bitterly over him, as one weeps over a firstborn.

3. All the earth will wail because of him.
    Rev. 1:7 – Behold, he is coming with the clouds, and every eye will see him, even those who pierced him, and all tribes of the earth will wail on account of him. Even so. Amen.

F. The Second Coming of Jesus Christ will be *utterly magnificent, full of splendor and glory.*

1. The Synoptic gospels (i.e., Matthew, Mark, and Luke) imagine the Second Coming as magnificent and glorious in every way.

2. He comes on the clouds with great power and glory. (Matt. 24.30; Mark13.26; Luke21.27)

3. He will come heralded by the archangel's trumpet blast. (1 Thess. 4.16)

4. He will be accompanied by the angels of heaven. (Matt. 24.31)

5. His coming is associated with and accompanied by his taking His kingly throne, judging and reigning over the nations. (Matt.25.31-46).

G. The Second Coming of Jesus Christ will be *completely unexpected, and catch millions unawares.*

1. It will come swiftly, like a thief in the night, with many being completely unaware of his return.
1 Thess. 5.2 -- For you yourselves are fully aware that the day of the Lord will come like a thief in the night.

2. The parable of the ten virgins in Matt 25 suggests the unlikely timing of his coming, and the tendency for the time to be missed unless one is aware of it and looking for the coming of this truth.

3. Peter suggests in 2 Pet. 3.3-4 that his delayed coming may cause some to scoff, and they may even come to believe that his return is *fictitious*, a made-up sham with no basis in fact.

4. Jesus, however, says it will come with surprise like in the days of Noah, and the time of Lot.
Luke 17:26-30 – Just as it was in the days of Noah, so will it be in the days of the Son of Man. [27] They were eating and drinking and marrying and being given in marriage, until the day when Noah entered the ark, and the flood came and destroyed them all. [28] Likewise, just as it was in the days of Lot—they were eating and drinking, buying and selling, planting and building, [29] but on the day when Lot went out from Sodom, fire and sulfur rained from heaven and destroyed them all— [30] so will it be on the day when the Son of Man is revealed.

5. The nature of the Second Coming will be powerfully immediate. It will be swift, unexpected, and come with great surprise.

H. Finally, the Second Coming of Jesus Christ will be a *unified event with a series of distinct happenings included with it.*

1. Ladd's entire argument questions a kind of dual coming: one phase in secret, a "coming <u>for</u> the saints," and a second phase in public (after the seven-year tribulation period), a "coming <u>with</u> the saints". (cf. Hoekema pp. 165-166)

2. "The idea that after meeting the Lord in the air we shall be with him for seven years in heaven and later for a thousand years in the air above the earth is pure inference and nothing more. Everlasting oneness with Christ in glory is the clear teaching of [1Thess. 4.16-17], and not a pretribulational rapture." (Hoekema, p. 168.)

3. Hoekema understands the phrase "bring with Jesus" in 1 Thess. 4.14 as "the believing dead" who are now with Christ (as Paul teaches elsewhere, see Phil. 1.23 and 2 Cor. 5.8). When Christ returns, he will bring these believing dead with him from heaven. (Hoekema, p. 169)

    a. 1 Thess. 3.13 – so that he may establish your hearts blameless in holiness before our God and Father, at the coming of our Lord Jesus with all his saints.

    b. 1 Thess. 4.14 – For since we believe that Jesus died and rose again, even so, through Jesus, God will bring with him those who have fallen asleep.

4. Summary of Hoekema's argument against the pretribulational rapture:

    a. NT words do not support such a view. (p. 165)

b. Texts on the Great Tribulation do not hint at the Church being removed from the earth before the tribulation begins. (p. 166)

c. 1 Thess. 4.16-7 does not teach a pretribulational rapture. (p. 167-68)

d. Christ's coming with his people need not suggest a pretribulational rapture. (p. 169)

e. Describing the Great Tribulation as an outpouring of God's wrath does not advocate a pretribulational rapture. (p. 170)

5. As we have said before, texts like 1 Thess.4.16, 2 Thess. 2.8, and Matt.24.27 associate the term "parousia" to a powerful, single, and unified public event.

6. Saints await the one blessed hope, the appearing of the glory of our Great God and Savior Jesus Christ. (Titus. 2.13)

7. Dr. Davis' response: *There is no reason, however, to see the Second Coming as a unified event made up of different stages, manifestations, and time fulfillments which, on the surface appear to be a single event but are, in fact, a series of events all connected under the rubric of a single unified event.*

a. The "Christ event," is a term used to summarize all the various happenings associated with the First Coming of Christ, including his birth, infancy, adolescence, manhood, ministry, passion, death, resurrection, and ascension.

b. *Could not the Second Coming represent a unified event which, like the First Coming, involves an interrelated and interconnected web of events all associated with his return to earth?*

IV. The Need to Watch

The Second Coming of our Lord Jesus Christ is a call to readiness and awareness, to be sober and alert, always aware of the ever-present possibility that any day, our Lord can appear and the final chapter of the prophetic novel of God may be written on the pages of this world's history. To be watchful means that in every facet of our lives, that we breathe the air of this world and the atmosphere of eternity simultaneously, aware that we have been called to eternal glory, and spending every minute bit of energy, all mammon, and each minute conscious that at any time, the manifestation of the Messiah could occur.

How differently would you have lived today if you had suspected that today might have been the day when our Lord Jesus would appear?

2 John 1:8 – Watch yourselves, so that you may not lose what we have worked for, but may win a full reward.

A. The reasons for watching:

1. The imminent nature of the Second Coming demands it. Matthew 24:42-44 – Therefore, stay awake, for you do not know on what day your Lord is coming. [43] But know this, that if the master of the house had known in what part of the night the thief was coming, he would have stayed awake and would not have let his house be broken into. [44] Therefore you also must be ready, for the Son of Man is coming at an hour you do not expect.

2. The fickleness of human faithfulness demands it. Mark 13:33-37 – Be on guard, keep awake. For you do not know when the time will come. [34] It is like a man going on a journey, when he leaves home and

puts his servants in charge, each with his work, and commands the doorkeeper to stay awake. [35] Therefore stay awake—for you do not know when the master of the house will come, in the evening, or at midnight, or when the cock crows, or in the morning— [36] lest he come suddenly and find you asleep. [37] And what I say to you I say to all: Stay awake.

3. The power needed to fight the forces of the night upon us calls for it.
Romans 13:11-14 – Besides this you know the time, that the hour has come for you to wake from sleep. For salvation is nearer to us now than when we first believed. [12] The night is far gone; the day is at hand. So then let us cast off the works of darkness and put on the armor of light. [13] Let us walk properly as in the daytime, not in orgies and drunkenness, not in sexual immorality and sensuality, not in quarreling and jealousy. [14] But put on the Lord Jesus Christ, and make no provision for the flesh, to gratify its desires.

B. The nature of watching:

1. Living in the day. Romans 13.11-14;
1 John 2:8 – At the same time, it is a new commandment that I am writing to you, which is true in him and in you, because the darkness is passing away and the true light is already shining.

2. Working while it is day, because the sun is going down on this age.
John 9:4-5 – We must work the works of him who sent me while it is day; night is coming, when no one can work. [5] As long as I am in the world, I am the light of the world."

3. Following Jesus, and not being taken unawares by the events of the night.

a. John 8:12 – Again Jesus spoke to them, saying, "I am the light of the world. Whoever follows me will not walk in darkness, but will have the light of life."

b. John 12:35 – So Jesus said to them, "The light is among you for a little while longer. Walk while you have the light, lest darkness overtake you. The one who walks in the darkness does not know where he is going.

4. Making the absolute best use of our time in light of Kingdom values.

   a. Eph. 5:16 – making the best use of the time, because the days are evil.

   b. Col. 4:5 – Conduct yourselves wisely toward outsiders, making the best use of the time.

5. Staying sober and refusing to become intoxicated with the wine of the world's greed, pride, and lust, and all the things associated with it.
1 Thess. 5:4-9 – But you are not in darkness, brothers, for that day to surprise you like a thief. [5] For you are all children of light, children of the day. We are not of the night or of the darkness. [6] So then let us not sleep, as others do, but let us keep awake and be sober. [7] For those who sleep, sleep at night, and those who get drunk, are drunk at night. [8] But since we belong to the day, let us be sober, having put on the breastplate of faith and love, and for a helmet the hope of salvation. [9] For God has not destined us for wrath, but to obtain salvation through our Lord Jesus Christ.

C. Images of the souls who are simply not ready:

1. **Sleepiness:** *Numbness and ignorance of the critical hour we are living in.*
   Mark 13:35-37 – Therefore stay awake—for you do not know when the master of the house will come, in the evening, or at midnight, or when the cock crows, or in the morning— [36] lest he come suddenly and find you asleep. [37] And what I say to you I say to all: Stay awake."

2. **Desertion of the Kingdom fight due to distraction:** *Searching after things that cannot last and foregoing the things that can.*
   2 Tim. 4:10 – For Demas, in love with this present world, has deserted me and gone to Thessalonica. Crescens has gone to Galatia, Titus to Dalmatia.

3. **"Drunkenness and dissipation:"** *Wanton immorality and sinfulness can blunt all spiritual fervor for Christ and his soon-and-coming Kingdom.*
   Luke 21:34-36 – "But watch yourselves lest your hearts be weighed down with dissipation and drunkenness and cares of this life, and that day come upon you suddenly like a trap. [35] For it will come upon all who dwell on the face of the whole earth. [36] But stay awake at all times, praying that you may have strength to escape all these things that are going to take place, and to stand before the Son of Man."

4. **Worldliness:** *Turning one's back on the true treasure tomorrow for fleeting pleasure today.*

   a. Turning back to the world.,
      Luke 9:61-62 – Yet another said, "I will follow you, Lord, but let me first say farewell to those at my home." [62] Jesus said to him, "No one who puts his hand to the plow and looks back is fit for the kingdom of God."

b. No one can serve two armies.
   Luke 16:13 – No servant can serve two masters, for either he will hate the one and love the other, or he will be devoted to the one and despise the other. You cannot serve God and money.

c. The nostalgic look back after setting off toward deliverance.
   Luke 17:32 – Remember Lot's wife.

d. Money-love as the cancer of biblical faith.
   1 Tim. 6:10 – For the love of money is a root of all kinds of evils. It is through this craving that some have wandered away from the faith and pierced themselves with many pangs.

e. We are exhorted not to love the world.
   1 John 2:15-16 – Do not love the world or the things in the world. If anyone loves the world, the love of the Father is not in him. [16] For all that is in the world— the desires of the flesh and the desires of the eyes and pride in possessions—is not from the Father but is from the world.

5. **Selfishness and waste:** *Gathering up fame and fortune in a dying world and ignoring eternal investments in the world to come.*
   Matthew 6:19-21 – Do not lay up for yourselves treasures on earth, where moth and rust destroy and where thieves break in and steal, [20] but lay up for yourselves treasures in heaven, where neither moth nor rust destroys and where thieves do not break in and steal. [21] For where your treasure is, there your heart will be also.

6. **Fruitlessness:** *Living for purposes less noble and fulfilling than the fruit to be borne through the Gospel of Jesus Christ.*,
   Phil.. 2:21 – They all seek their own interests, not those of Jesus Christ.

D. The tragedy of not being ready: *undisciplined, uninspired, unfruitful.*

1. *Shrinking back in shame before him* when he appears.
   1 John 2:28 – And now, little children, abide in him, so that when he appears we may have confidence and not shrink from him in shame at his coming.

2. *Losing one's reward* (forfeiting one's crown).

   a. Rev. 3:11 – I am coming soon. Hold fast what you have, so that no one may seize your crown.

   b. Rev. 2:10 – Do not fear what you are about to suffer. Behold, the devil is about to throw some of you into prison, that you may be tested, and for ten days you will have tribulation. Be faithful unto death, and I will give you the crown of life.

   c. 1 Cor. 9:27 – But I discipline my body and keep it under control, lest after preaching to others I myself should be disqualified.

   d. Galatians 4:11 – I am afraid I may have labored over you in vain.

   e. Phil.. 3:16 – Only let us hold true to what we have attained.

   f. Hebrews 10:35 – Therefore do not throw away your confidence, which has a great reward.

   g. 2 John 1:8 – Watch yourselves, so that you may not lose what we have worked for, but may win a full reward.

3. *Failing to strive* to be established blameless in the presence of our Lord Jesus.

   a. 1 Thess. 3:13 – so that he may establish your hearts blameless in holiness before our God and Father, at the coming of our Lord Jesus with all his saints.

   b. 1 Thess. 5:23 – Now may the God of peace himself sanctify you completely, and may your whole spirit and soul and body be kept blameless at the coming of our Lord Jesus Christ.

E. The benefits of watching and being ready.

   1. *Readiness.*
   Matthew 24:42 – Therefore, stay awake, for you do not know on what day your Lord is coming.

   2. *Steadfastness.*
   1 Cor. 15:58 – Therefore, my beloved brothers, be steadfast, immovable, always abounding in the work of the Lord, knowing that in the Lord your labor is not in vain.

   3. *Vigilance.*
   Rev. 3:11 – I am coming soon. Hold fast what you have, so that no one may seize your crown.

The Hope of Jesus Makes Ready for the Rapture or for Death

In Catherine Marshall's book about her husband Peter, she cites a touching story of a young terminally ill son asking his mother what death was like, if it hurt.

"Kenneth," she said, "you remember when you were a tiny boy how you used to play so hard all day that when night came you would be too tired even to undress, and you would tumble into mother's bed and fall asleep? That was not your bed – it was not where you belonged.

"And you would only stay there a little while. In the morning, much to your surprise, you would wake up and find yourself in your own bed in your own room.

"You were there because someone had loved you and taken care of you. Your father had come – with big strong arms – and carried you away.

"Kenneth, death is just like that. We just wake up some morning to find ourselves in the other room–*our own room where we belong*–because the Lord Jesus loved us."

The lad's shining, trusting face looking up into hers told her that the point had gone home and that there would be no more fear – only love and trust in his little heart as he went to meet the Father in Heaven.

He never questioned again.

And several weeks later he fell asleep just as she had said.

– Catherine Marshall, *A Man Called Peter*

IV. Watching, Fighting, Praying: The Posture of A Christian Who Stands Ready for His Appearing

Fix your eyes on an object that does not move...

A farmer of a small but prosperous farm decided it was time to instruct his son on plowing a straight furrow with a horse drawn plow. In the time-honored tradition that he learned, he told the boy to fix his eyes on some object at the other end of the field, keep his attention on that, and plow straight for it. The boy started plowing, and his father went about his chores. When he returned after several hours to check on the boy's progress, he was shocked to find instead of straight rows something that looked like a question mark. The boy had obeyed his father's instructions. He had fixed his eyes on something at the other side of the field–*a cow.* Unfortunately, *the cow had moved!* Evidently, that father forgot to tell his son to look for *a stable object,* one that *wouldn't shift* or *move around.*

The Second Coming of Jesus Christ is a vision that will not shift or move around. It is an anchor for the soul. Let's pray that we may have strength to escape all the things going to take place, and to stand before the Son of Man.

Luke 21:34-36 – "But watch yourselves lest your hearts be weighed down with dissipation and drunkenness and cares of this life, and that day come upon you suddenly like a trap. [35] For it will come upon all who dwell on the face of the whole earth. [36] But stay awake at all times, praying that you may have strength to escape all these things that are going to take place, and to stand before the Son of Man."

- The Second Coming of our Lord Jesus must be at the center of our worship, celebration, preaching, and discipleship. It is the doctrine which provides us with the greatest incentive to sacrifice all we have and are in this world for the coming glory ahead.

- Rather than an abstract talking point or fodder for meaningless and unresolvable word fights about prophecy, the doctrine of the Second Coming is the center of the NT ethical vision. It is the reason why the apostles and saints of God lived with such intensity, fervency, and inspiration in their generation.

- An acute awareness and love of the Lord's appearing supplied the apostle Paul with vision, comfort, and motivation in all of his work as God's servant. A rediscovery of these truths can transform and inspire a new generation of urban Christians to attempt great things for God and suffer many things for the sake of Christ and his Gospel of the kingdom and his grace.

The Bottom Line: _____

Lesson Six
The Wrath of God during the Tribulation, and Millennial Views of Revelation 20

The Diamond of Grace Shines Clearer on the Black Velvet of the Judgment Ahead

Grace does not make everything right. Grace's trick is to show us that it is right for us to live; that it is truly good, wonderful even, for us to be breathing and feeling at the same time that everything clustering around us is wholly wretched. Grace is not a ticket to Fantasy Island; Fantasy Island is dreamy fiction. Grace is not a potion to charm life to our liking; charms are magic. Grace does not cure all our cancers, transform all our kids into winners, or send us all soaring into the high skies of sex and success. Grace is rather an amazing power to look earthy reality full in the face, see its sad and tragic edges, feel its cruel cuts, join in the primeval chorus against its outrageous unfairness, and yet feel in your deepest being that it is good and right for you to be alive on God's good earth. Grace is power, I say, to see life very clearly, admit it is sometimes all wrong, and still know that somehow, in the center of your life, "It's all right." This is one reason we call it amazing grace. Grace is the one word for all that God is for us in the form of Jesus Christ.

Lewis B. Smedes, *How Can It Be All Right When Everything Is Wrong?*
New York: Harper and Row, 1982, p. 3.

I. **The Wrath of God and the Tribulation**

Israel's God dwelt among them (Ex. 40.34–38; Lev. 26.11f; Num. 1.47–54), both to sanctify them and to destroy the evil from among them (e.g., Num. 11.1–3). This closeness between a people and their God was considered unique by Israel (Deut. 4.7f). His guidance was always with them and He blessed them with visible signs of His presence and leadership (Num. 9.15–23).

God's holiness had to be treated with meticulous respect. Therefore the Levites camped around the tabernacle of the testimony to protect the rest of Israel from the holy wrath of God (Num. 1.47–54). God's holiness demanded Israel's holiness and faithfulness if His presence was to continue (cf. Exod. 33). His holiness made the camp and the land holy, and Israel was to be careful not to defile the land or make it unclean (e.g., Num. 35.29–34). Uncleanness was to be cared for according to the instructions of Yahweh (e.g., Num. 19).

"God was the provider and preserver of Israel. Although He judged the people according to His word, He loved and preserved them according to His nature. Israel was cared for during the forty years of wanderings in the face of serious threats (cf. Ch. 26), surviving only by the grace of the One who was judging them."

G. W. Bromiley, The International Standard Bible Encyclopedia, Revised.
Grand Rapids: William B. Eerdmans Publishing, 1988; 2002.

Lev. 11:45 – For I am the Lord who brought you up out of the land of Egypt to be your God. You shall therefore be holy, for I am holy."

A. The Tribulation is a time of both judgment and preparation.

1. The Tribulation will bring harvest of the crop that God has sown, and burn the chaff that the enemy has sown. Matthew 13:27-30 – And the servants of the master of the house came and said to him, 'Master, did you not sow good seed in your field? How then does it have weeds?' [28] He said to them, 'An enemy has done this.' So the servants said to him, 'Then do you want us to go and gather them?' [29] But he said, 'No, lest in gathering the weeds you root up the wheat along with them. [30] Let both grow together until the harvest, and at harvest time I will tell the reapers, Gather the weeds first and bind them in bundles to be burned, but gather the wheat into my barn.' "

2. The Tribulation will make plain in full clarity the falseness and vileness of the devil's claim to power. Isaiah 14:12-15 – "How you are fallen from heaven, O Day Star, son of Dawn! How you are cut down to the ground, you who laid the nations low! [13] You said in your heart, 'I will ascend to heaven; above the stars of God I will set my throne on high; I will sit on the mount of assembly in the far reaches of the north; [14] I will ascend above the heights of the clouds; I will make

myself like the Most High.' [15] But you are brought down to Sheol, to the far reaches of the pit. (Cf. Rev. 20:1-3 Then I saw an angel coming down from heaven, holding in his hand the key to the bottomless pit and a great chain. [2] And he seized the dragon, that ancient serpent, who is the devil and Satan, and bound him for a thousand years, [3] and threw him into the pit, and shut it and sealed it over him, so that he might not deceive the nations any longer, until the thousand years were ended. After that he must be released for a little while.)

3. The Tribulation will result in a "great martyred multitude" and great living multitude for the reign of Christ. (cf. Matt. 25.32-34; Rev 7.9)
Rev 7.13-14 -- Then one of the elders addressed me, saying, "Who are these, clothed in white robes, and from where have they come?" [14] I said to him, "Sir, you know." And he said to me, "These are the ones coming out of the great tribulation. They have washed their robes and made them white in the blood of the Lamb.

4. The Tribulation will punish the Gentiles who rejected the Gospel of salvation in Jesus Christ. (cf. 2 Thess. 2.11-12; Rev. 19.15)
Romans 1:18 – For the wrath of God is revealed from heaven against all ungodliness and unrighteousness of men, who by their unrighteousness suppress the truth.

5. The Tribulation will purify Israel for its specific role in Christ's dominion. (cf. Ezek. 20.23, 38; Mal. 3.3)
Zech. 13:8-9 – In the whole land, declares the Lord, two thirds shall be cut off and perish, and one third shall be left alive. [9] And I will put this third into the fire, and refine them as one refines silver, and test them as gold is tested. They will call upon my name, and I will answer them. I will say, 'They are my people'; and they will say, 'The Lord is my God.' "

6. The Tribulation will impact, affect, and prepare creation and the earth itself for Christ's millennial reign, bring

about the redemption of nature. (cf. Rev. 16.20)
Romans 8:19-22 – For the creation waits with eager longing for the revealing of the sons of God. [20] For the creation was subjected to futility, not willingly, but because of him who subjected it, in hope [21] that the creation itself will be set free from its bondage to decay and obtain the freedom of the glory of the children of God. [22] For we know that the whole creation has been groaning together in the pains of childbirth until now.

7. The Tribulation will fulfill the OT promises to Israel.
Luke 1:30-33 – And the angel said to her, "Do not be afraid, Mary, for you have found favor with God. [31] And behold, you will conceive in your womb and bear a son, and you shall call his name Jesus. [32] He will be great and will be called the Son of the Most High. And the Lord God will give to him the throne of his father David, [33] and he will reign over the house of Jacob forever, and of his kingdom there will be no end."

8. The Tribulation will give a public display of Christ's glory to the nations of earth. (Rev. 19)
Rev. 1:5-7 – and from Jesus Christ the faithful witness, the firstborn of the dead, and the ruler of kings on earth. To him who loves us and has freed us from our sins by his blood [6] and made us a kingdom, priests to his God and Father, to him be glory and dominion forever and ever. Amen. [7] Behold, he is coming with the clouds, and every eye will see him, even those who pierced him, and all tribes of the earth will wail on account of him. Even so. Amen.

9. The Tribulation will answer the saints' prayer of "Thy kingdom come."
Matthew 6:9-10 – Pray then like this: "Our Father in heaven, hallowed be your name. [10] Your kingdom come, your will be done, on earth as it is in heaven.

10. The Tribulation will fulfill the promises to the church that saints will reign with Christ.

a. Rev. 3:21 – The one who conquers, I will grant him to sit with me on my throne, as I also conquered and sat down with my Father on his throne.

b. 1 Cor. 6:2-3 – Or do you not know that the saints will judge the world? And if the world is to be judged by you, are you incompetent to try trivial cases? [3] Do you not know that we are to judge angels? How much more, then, matters pertaining to this life!

c. 2 Tim. 2:12 – if we endure, we will also reign with him; if we deny him, he also will deny us.

d. Rev. 1:6 – and made us a kingdom, priests to his God and Father, to him be glory and dominion forever and ever. Amen.

e. Rev. 2:26-27 – The one who conquers and who keeps my works until the end, to him I will give authority over the nations, [27] and he will rule them with a rod of iron, as when earthen pots are broken in pieces, even as I myself have received authority from my Father.

B. The Wrath of God in Scripture.

1. Salvation is incomprehensible and makes no sense unless we understand it against the backdrop of being "saved from" and "saved by."

> "What are believers saved from? From their former position under the wrath of God, the dominion of sin, and the power of death (Rom. 1.18; 3.9; 5.21); from their natural condition of being mastered by the world, the flesh, and the devil (John 8.23-24; Rom. 8.7-8; 1 John 5.19); from the fears that a sinful life engenders (Rom. 8.15; 2 Tim. 1.7; Heb. 2.14-15),

and from the many vicious habits that were part of it (Eph. 4.17-24; 1 Thess. 4.3-8; Titus 2.11-3.6).

"How are believers saved from these things? Through Christ, and in Christ. The Father is as concerned to exalt the Son as he is to rescue the lost (John 5.19-23; Phil. 2.9-11; Col. 1.15-18; Heb. 1.4-14), and it is as true to say that the elect were appointed for Christ the beloved Son as it is to say that Christ was appointed for the beloved elect (Matt. 3.17; 17.5; Col. 1.13; 3.12; 1 Pet. 1.20; 1 John 4.9-10)."

J. I. Packer, Concise Theology: A Guide to Historic Christian Beliefs. Wheaton, Ill.: Tyndale House Publishing, 1995, c1993.

2. God's wrath comes in his own designated manner and timing.
   Rev. 11:15-18 – Then the seventh angel blew his trumpet, and there were loud voices in heaven, saying, "The kingdom of the world has become the kingdom of our Lord and of his Christ, and he shall reign forever and ever." [16] And the twenty-four elders who sit on their thrones before God fell on their faces and worshiped God, [17] saying, "We give thanks to you, Lord God Almighty, who is and who was, for you have taken your great power and begun to reign. [18] The nations raged, but your wrath came, and the time for the dead to be judged, and for rewarding your servants, the prophets and saints, and those who fear your name, both small and great, and for destroying the destroyers of the earth."

3. During the Tribulation, the worshiper of the beast and his image will drink the wine of God's wrath.
   Rev. 14:9-11 – And another angel, a third, followed them, saying with a loud voice, "If anyone worships the beast and its image and receives a mark on his forehead or on his hand, [10] he also will drink the wine of God's wrath, poured full strength into the cup of his anger, and he will be tormented with fire and sulfur in the presence of the holy angels and in the presence of the Lamb. [11] And the smoke of their torment goes up forever and ever, and they have no rest, day or night, these worshipers of the beast and its image, and whoever receives the mark of its name."

4. The imagery of the Tribulation highlights the vision of the winepress of the wrath of God.
   Rev. 14:18-19 – And another angel came out from the altar, the angel who has authority over the fire, and he called with a loud voice to the one who had the sharp sickle, "Put in your sickle and gather the clusters from the vine of the earth, for its grapes are ripe." [19] So the angel swung his sickle across the earth and gathered the grape harvest of the earth and threw it into the great winepress of the wrath of God.

5. The dynamic scene of heaven: golden bowls full of the wrath of God.
   Rev. 15:7-8 – And one of the four living creatures gave to the seven angels seven golden bowls full of the wrath of God who lives forever and ever, [8] and the sanctuary was filled with smoke from the glory of God and from his power, and no one could enter the sanctuary until the seven plagues of the seven angels were finished.

6. God's judgments are linked directly to the righteous display of his wrath.
   Rev. 16:5-6 – And I heard the angel in charge of the waters say, "Just are you, O Holy One, who is and who was, for you brought these judgments. [6] For they have shed the blood of saints and prophets, and you have given them blood to drink. It is what they deserve!"

C. Related texts in the NT on the wrath of God.

1. God's wrath will be revealed against every form of immorality, impurity, and idolatry.
   Col. 3:5-6 – Put to death therefore what is earthly in you: sexual immorality, impurity, passion, evil desire, and covetousness, which is idolatry. [6] On account of these the wrath of God is coming.

2. God's wrath is "revealed." It is unleashed and displayed in an open and clear manner upon those objects, events, and institutions which merit his righteous indignation.

   a. It is revealed against all forms of iniquity and sin. (cf. Col. 3.5-6)

   b. It is revealed against the "children of disobedience." Eph. 5:5-6 – For you may be sure of this, that everyone who is sexually immoral or impure, or who is covetous (that is, an idolater), has no inheritance in the kingdom of Christ and God. [6] Let no one deceive you with empty words, for because of these things the wrath of God comes upon the sons of disobedience.

   c. It is revealed in a thorough fashion.
   Num. 32:13 – And the Lord's anger was kindled against Israel, and he made them wander in the wilderness forty years, until all the generation that had done evil in the sight of the Lord was gone.

   d. It is revealed in the history of Israel. The righteousness of God demonstrated his justice and judgments.
   Psalm 78:31 – the anger of God rose against them, and he killed the strongest of them and laid low the young men of Israel.

   e. It is revealed against all ungodliness and unrighteousness.
   Romans 1:18 – For the wrath of God is revealed from heaven against all ungodliness and unrighteousness of men, who by their unrighteousness suppress the truth.

3. God's wrath in total: Being on the outside of the Golden City that is to come.
   Rev. 22:15 – Outside are the dogs and sorcerers and

the sexually immoral and murderers and idolaters, and everyone who loves and practices falsehood.

4. The great Tribulation is anticipatory of the wrath of God to come.

"Revelation pictures something that is taught nowhere else in the Bible: that at the same time as the great tribulation God will pass anticipatory judgments upon humanity. The seven trumpets and seven bowls are symbolic representations of these divine judgments or woes, which are poured out in the last climactic hour of the struggle between the Lamb and the dragon. These plagues cannot be identified, for the descriptions are highly symbolic. They are an anticipation of the wrath of God (16:1), which will be consummated with the return of Christ.

"Three aspects of the woes are to be noted. First, they are directed against those who bear the mark of the beast and worship its image (16:2). In the terrible hour people will have to stand on one side or the other. Martyrdom may await the followers of the Lamb, but the wrath of a holy God awaits those who submit to the beast. Second, the plagues have a merciful purpose. They are designed to drive people to their knees, as it were, in repentance before it is irrevocably too late. This merciful purpose in God's judgments is clearly suggested in such verses as 9:20; 16:9, 11, which reiterate that sinners, in spite of God's hand falling heavy in wrath upon them, do not repent and give God glory. Even the fearfulness of God's wrath in these last awful moments before the dawn of the new age has a merciful objective. Third, twelve thousand from each of the twelve tribes of Israel are marked with the protective seal of God (7:1-8). They suffer neither the plagues that He is about to pour out upon the beast and his followers (v 3; 9:4) nor His wrath. The seal of God or the mark of the beast will distinguish people in this last hour, whether they are on God's side or Satan's."

G. W. Bromiley, "Book of Revelation"
The International Standard Bible Encyclopedia, Revised. Grand Rapids: Eerdmans, 2002.

D. The Holiness of God: A lost doctrine in the church!

Why don't we preach it?

1. There is fear of being branded as a bigot and or xenophobic fanatic.

2. Morality is deemed to be out of fashion in many "seeker sensitive" contexts. It appears as if we have adopted a "holier-than-thou" attitude over against our neighbors and counterparts in larger society.

3. Conformity to the moral climate of our time. (Rodney King Moral Philosophy: "Can't we all just get along?")

4. Horrendous theology: Preach only the positive, pleasant, and prosperous issues associated with the person of God and his work in Christ. Ignore the dark, hard-to-hear-and-understand texts about his holiness and wrath.

5. Reductive understandings of biblical faith: Christianity has been reduced to moral decency, strengthening the nuclear family, opposing certain moral options and political affiliations, and living purposefully, albeit for suspiciously worldly-minded issues (i.e., a tendency exists to transform Christian faith into a kind of religious self-help approach to modern family life).

6. Shame and ambivalence in teaching the plain text of the Bible regarding the wrath of God and its ominous consequences for those who ignore God's warnings and provisions.

E. The Holiness of God: A missing jewel in evangelical teaching today!

Why can't we ignore it?

1. It is the very nature of the Lord as he is in himself.

a. Isaiah 6:3 – And one called to another and said: "Holy, holy, holy is the Lord of hosts; the whole earth is full of his glory!"

b. Rev. 4:8 – And the four living creatures, each of them with six wings, are full of eyes all around and within, and day and night they never cease to say, "Holy, holy, holy, is the Lord God Almighty, who was and is and is to come!"

c. Exod. 15:11 – Who is like you, O Lord, among the gods? Who is like you, majestic in holiness, awesome in glorious deeds, doing wonders?

d. Psalm 99:5 – Exalt the Lord our God; worship at his footstool! Holy is he!

e. Psalm 99:9 – Exalt the Lord our God, and worship at his holy mountain; for the Lord our God is holy!

f. Rev. 15:3-4 – And they sing the song of Moses, the servant of God, and the song of the Lamb, saying, "Great and amazing are your deeds, O Lord God the Almighty! Just and true are your ways, O King of the nations! [4] Who will not fear, O Lord, and glorify your name? For you alone are holy. All nations will come and worship you, for your righteous acts have been revealed."

2. It is the heart of the biblical ethic.
1 Peter 1:14-16 – As obedient children, do not be conformed to the passions of your former ignorance, [15] but as he who called you is holy, you also be holy in all your conduct, [16] since it is written, "You shall be holy, for I am holy."

3. The Gospel is incomprehensible without a clear articulation of what is at stake if, in fact, people resist and reject the love of God as offered in the person of Christ.
1 Thess. 1:9-10 – For they themselves report concerning us the kind of reception we had among you, and how you turned to God from idols to serve the living and true God, [10] and to wait for his Son from heaven, whom he raised from the dead, Jesus who delivers us from the wrath to come.

F. The Holiness of God: A lost doctrine in the church!

How should we approach it?

1. Tell the *truth*.
John 14.6 – Jesus said to him, "I am the way, and the truth, and the life. No one comes to the Father except through me.

2. Tell the *whole truth*.
John 8.31-32 – So Jesus said to the Jews who had believed him, "If you abide in my word, you are truly my disciples, 32 and you will know the truth, and the truth will set you free."

3. Tell *nothing but the truth*.
John 3:36 – Whoever believes in the Son has eternal life; whoever does not obey the Son shall not see life, but the wrath of God remains on him.

4. So, *may God help you!*
1 Tim. 4:10 – For to this end we toil and strive, because we have our hope set on the living God, who is the Savior of all people, especially of those who believe.

II. The Millennium

Biblical Visions of Joy

Biblical visions of the millennium go beyond description of the external situation and give us a picture of the inner state of the people as well. The result is a beatific vision-a picture of how the inhabitants of the land experience their blessed state. Above all, they are satisfied. God promises that in the coming age " my people shall be satisfied with my goodness " (Jer. 31.14, RSV; see also Jer. 50.19). Not only will God send "grain, wine, and oil," but his people "will be satisfied" (Joel 2.19, RSV). Again, "you shall eat in plenty and be satisfied, and praise the name of the Lord your God" (Joel 2.26, RSV). God promises to " satisfy your desire with good things" (Isa. 58.11, RSV). The voice of satisfied appetite runs strong in the millennial visions of the Bible. here people "come to the waters, . . . buy wine and milk without money and . . . eat what is good" (Isa. 55.1–2, RSV). It is no wonder that the OT millennial visions are filled with the vocabulary of joy, often expressed as a promise from God. "Then you shall see and be radiant, your heart shall thrill and rejoice" (Isa. 60.5, RSV). The people will say, "I will greatly rejoice in the Lord, my soul shall exult in my God" (Isa. 61.10, RSV). "Be glad," comes the prophetic voice, " and rejoice forever in that which I create; for behold, I create Jerusalem a rejoicing, and her people a joy " (Is 65.18, RSV). Even "the desert shall rejoice and blossom" (Isa. 35.1, RSV).

Leland Ryken, et al. *Dictionary of Biblical Imagery* (electronic ed.). Downers Grove, Il.: Inter Varsity Press, 2000, c1998.

Rev. 20:4-8 – Then I saw thrones, and seated on them were those to whom the authority to judge was committed. Also I saw the souls of those who had been beheaded for the testimony of Jesus and for the word of God, and who had not worshiped the beast or its image and had not received its mark on their foreheads or their hands. They came to life and reigned with Christ for a thousand years. [5] The rest of the dead did not come to life until the thousand years were ended. This is the first resurrection. [6] Blessed and holy is the one who shares in the first resurrection! Over such the second death has no power, but they will be priests of God and of Christ, and they will reign with him for a thousand years.

A. Definition: The term *Millennium* refers to the period of 1,000 years mentioned in Rev. 20.2–7 as it connects to the prophesied reign of the glorified Christ with saints over the earth. This vision of Christ's reign is directly connected to the messianic and Davidic kingdom promised of the "Anointed One of Yahweh" who would come and establish the reign of God on earth, as the prophets testified.

The three broad categories of doctrinal conviction regarding The Millennium refer to when Jesus will come in conjunction with it, and whether the language is to read literally or seen purely as symbolical. These views are normally set apart as:

> *Premillennialism* – Christ returns before the 1,000-year period.
>
> *Postmillennialism* – The present age of the Spirit and missions is the Millennium which will usher into our earth the Second Coming of Christ.
>
> *Amillennialism* – The 1,000-year period is symbolic and represents the age of the Church or some other spiritual reality, not a literal reign on the earth.

B. Types and antitypes of The Millennium in the Bible:

1. *The rest from works:* The Sabbath.
   Lev. 23.3 -- Six days shall work be done, but on the seventh day is a Sabbath of solemn rest, a holy convocation. You shall do no work. It is a Sabbath to the Lord in all your dwelling places. (cf. Exo. 20.8-11)

2. *The shalom of God among the earth:* The Jubilee Year.
   Lev. 25.10-11 -- And you shall consecrate the fiftieth year, and proclaim liberty throughout the land to all its inhabitants. It shall be a jubilee for you, when each of you shall return to his property and each of you shall return to his clan. 11 That fiftieth year shall be a jubilee for you; in it you shall neither sow nor reap what grows of itself nor gather the grapes from the undressed vines.

3. *The presence of God among people:* The Tabernacle.
   Exod. 25.8 -- And let them make me a sanctuary, that I may dwell in their midst. (cf. Exod. 29.42-46; 40.34)

4. *Celebrating the victory of God:* The Feast of Tabernacles. (Lev. 23.34-42)

5. *Enjoying the provision and peace:* Living in the Promised Land.
   Deut. 6.3 -- Hear therefore, O Israel, and be careful to do them, that it may go well with you, and that you may multiply greatly, as the Lord, the God of your fathers, has promised you, in a land flowing with milk and honey. (cf. Heb. 4.8-10)

6. The foreshadowing of the reign of Christ in the reign of Solomon:

   a. The breadth of Solomon's rule is a token of the vastness of Christ's kingdom.

      (1) Solomon:
      1 Kings 4:21 – Solomon ruled over all the kingdoms from the Euphrates to the land of the Philistines and to the border of Egypt. They brought tribute and served Solomon all the days of his life.

      (2) Messiah:
      Daniel 7:13-14 – I saw in the night visions, and behold, with the clouds of heaven there came one like a son of man, and he came to the Ancient of Days and was presented before him. [14] And to him was given dominion and glory and a kingdom, that all peoples, nations, and languages should serve him; his dominion is an everlasting dominion, which shall not pass away, and his kingdom one that shall not be destroyed.

b. The security of Solomon's rule is a token of the peace of Jesus' kingdom.

   (1) Solomon:
1 Kings 4:25 – And Judah and Israel lived in safety, from Dan even to Beersheba, every man under his vine and under his fig tree, all the days of Solomon.

   (2) Messiah:
Isaiah 11:9 – They shall not hurt or destroy in all my holy mountain; for the earth shall be full of the knowledge of the Lord as the waters cover the sea.

c. Solomon's great wisdom is a type of Jesus' remarkable wisdom and filling by the Holy Spirit.

   (1) Solomon:
1 Kings 4:29-34 – And God gave Solomon wisdom and understanding beyond measure, and breadth of mind like the sand on the seashore, [30] so that Solomon's wisdom surpassed the wisdom of all the people of the east and all the wisdom of Egypt. [31] For he was wiser than all other men, wiser than Ethan the Ezrahite, and Heman, Calcol, and Darda, the sons of Mahol, and his fame was in all the surrounding nations. [32] He also spoke 3,000 proverbs, and his songs were 1,005. [33] He spoke of trees, from the cedar that is in Lebanon to the hyssop that grows out of the wall. He spoke also of beasts, and of birds, and of reptiles, and of fish. [34] And people of all nations came to hear the wisdom of Solomon, and from all the kings of the earth, who had heard of his wisdom.

   (2) Messiah:
Isaiah 11:3-4 – And his delight shall be in the fear of the Lord. He shall not judge by what his eyes see, or decide disputes by what his ears hear, [4] but with righteousness he shall judge the poor, and decide with equity for the meek of

the earth; and he shall strike the earth with the rod of his mouth, and with the breath of his lips he shall kill the wicked.

d. Solomon's fame is a sign of Jesus' universal glory and honor.

(1) Solomon:
1 Kings 10:7 – but I did not believe the reports until I came and my own eyes had seen it. And behold, the half was not told me. Your wisdom and prosperity surpass the report that I heard.

(2) Messiah:
Isaiah 2:3-4 – and many peoples shall come, and say: "Come, let us go up to the mountain of the Lord, to the house of the God of Jacob, that he may teach us his ways and that we may walk in his paths." For out of Zion shall go the law, and the word of the Lord from Jerusalem. [4] He shall judge between the nations, and shall decide disputes for many peoples; and they shall beat their swords into plowshares, and their spears into pruning hooks; nation shall not lift up sword against nation, neither shall they learn war anymore.

e. The greatness of Solomon's riches is emblematic of Jesus' great wealth and glory to come.

(1) Solomon:
1 Kings 10:27 – And the king made silver as common in Jerusalem as stone, and he made cedar as plentiful as the sycamore of the Shephelah.

(2) Messiah:
Psalm 72:8-11 – May he have dominion from sea to sea, and from the River to the ends of the earth! [9] May desert tribes bow down before him and his enemies lick the dust! [10] May the kings of Tarshish and of the coastlands render

him tribute; may the kings of Sheba and Seba bring gifts! [11] May all kings fall down before him, all nations serve him!

C. View No. 1 of The Millennium: <u>Premillennialism</u> (chialiasm) in the early church (sometimes called "historic premillennialism")

1. Key authors and adherents:

   Papias of Hierapolis (c. 60- c. 130)
   Justin Martyr (c. 100- c. 165)
   Irenaeus (c. 130- c. 202)
   Tertullian (c. 155- c. 240)
   Victorinus of Pettau (died c. 304)
   Lactantius (c. 240- c. 320)

2. What their expectations were:

   a. They expected the personal coming of Christ in glory before the millennial reign, a 1,000-year reign on earth that would occur before the last judgment.

   b. They rooted their views on Rev. 20, as well as their understanding of Jewish apocalyptic expectation of a messianic kingdom that can be understood largely as a "restoration of paradise" upon the earth.

   c. The earth would be transformed to its Edenic glory, alongside abundant fruitfulness, renewed peace among the nations, the end of sin and sorrow, the transformation of the nature of the animals, and the joy of resurrected saints for a 1,000-year season of bliss before the final transformation of all things.

3. Its forcefulness in the Church:
   The materialistic nature of this kind of view was objectionable to the Fathers, including Augustine.

4. Comments:
Augustine's rejection deeply impacted this view, which virtually disappeared until its re-articulation in the 17th century.

D. View No. 2 of The Millennium: <u>Augustinian Amillennialism</u>

1. Key authors and adherents:

    Tyconius (a 4th century Donatist)
    Augustine (354-430)

2. What their expectations were:

    a. The millennial reign of Christ is to be understood not literally, but as a representation of the age of the church.

    b. This age of the church extends from the resurrection of Christ until his return to earth at the Parousia.

    c. The figure 1,000 is symbolic, not to be interpreted in terms of an actual time frame but in terms of its signification of the age of the Church.

    d. This view denies a future 1,000-year reign, but rather argues its meaning on both the present rule of Christ, as well as an other-worldly eschatological hope.

3. Its forcefulness in the Church:
This has been the prominent view of the Church through the medieval period down to the present time.

4. Comments:
The Protestant reformers adapted this view.

a. They took The Millennium to be an actual period of time (dated in various ways) during which the Gospel of Christ was taken throughout the world.

b. Satan's release at the end of this period (cf. Rev. 20.7) refers to the rise of the medieval papacy!

c. Christ's return is imminent, which will bring God's final judgment on all things, and see the dissolution of this world as we know it.

E. View No. 3 of The Millennium: <u>Joachimism and Protestant Postmillennialism</u>

1. Key author and adherents:
Joachim (a 12th century abbot), who inspired a new form of eschatological thought in the later 16th century.

2. What their expectations were:

a. Before history would come to an end, an age of the Spirit would appear.

b. This age of the Spirit would come equally as a period of peace and spiritual prosperity for the church on earth, and they identified this state with The Millennium of Rev. 20.

c. This view is post-millennial since it holds that The Millennium would be inaugurated by a spiritual intervention of Christ in the power of his Spirit. The coming of Jesus in bodily advent, therefore, does not precede The Millennium but follows after it.

3. Its forcefulness in the Church:

a. Those who held this view saw the Protestant Reformation as the dawning of a "new age of prosperity for the church."

b. Thomas Brightman (1562-1607): The Millennium would come into being after Spirit-led preaching of the gospel would convert the world, leading to Christ's rule spiritually over the world.

c. The 18th century was the age of postmillennialism. Wheaton College was a product of this thinking, with its focus on missions, revival, and missionary thinking.

4. Comments:
Liberal progressive thought, along with the world wars, seriously eroded the force and power of this view, since it is essentially anchored on a doctrine of progress. (cf. 1 Tim. 4)

F. View No. 4 of The Millennium: <u>Protestant Premillennialism</u> (including dispensational premillennialism)

1. Key authors and adherents:

   Early 17th century – Joseph Mede (1586-1638).
   Most dispensationalists, especially influenced by:
   John Nelson Darby (1800-1882)
   Lewis Sperry Chafer (1871-1952)
   John F. Walvoord (1910-2002)
   J. Dwight Pentecost (1915-2014)
   Charles Ryrie (1925-2016)

2. What their expectations were:

   a. Generally, premillennialists today hold that the personal advent of Christ and the bodily resurrection of the saints will come before the actual 1,000-year reign of Jesus on earth.

b. This view, which occurs in many subtle forms today, tend to focus on the difference between this present evil age and the description of The Millennium to come.

c. Postmillennialism tends to gain its momentum by basing it theological judgments on the observation of hopeful signs of an approaching millennium. Premillennialism understands the current world situation as getting progressively less open to God, even deeply pessimistic.

3. Its forcefulness in the Church:
Premillennialists all agree on a fundamental tenet of theology: No outward influence of the church or humankind can establish the reign of God on earth. Nothing short of the very personal coming of the Son of God in glory will suffice.

4. Comments:
Dispensationalism has tended to advance theories of the Second Coming which argue for a "secret rapture" which precedes Christ's coming, ending the Church age and commencing the OT fulfillment of the prophecies to Israel during the millennial reign.

G. View No. 5 of The Millennium: <u>Symbolic Amillennialism</u>

1. Key authors and adherents:

Those who hold the number "1,000" to be symbolic, but also interpret The Millennium as a discrete period of time.

2. What their expectations were:
   This is an explicitly modern view, which tends to be asserted every now and then.

   a. This view holds The Millennium is a symbol, not of a period at all, but of the complete achievement of Christ's kingdom and his total victory over evil at the Parousia.

   b. The Millennium, in this way, represents not a period of church history per se, but the entire work of Christ as Lord, ruling over the powers of the evil one at his return and rule.

3. Its forcefulness in the Church:
   Very limited effect on the church.

4. Comments:
   While the symbolism of Revelation allows for expanded meanings of the Revelation 20 text, there is no reason to arbitrarily dismiss the meaning of it as a literal 1,000-year period.

H. Significance of The Millennium for preaching and practice.

1. Preach these truths in order to calm fears of current saber rattling and restlessness about the fate and workings of the nations.
   2 Peter 3:8-14 – But do not overlook this one fact, beloved, that with the Lord one day is as a thousand years, and a thousand years as one day. [9] The Lord is not slow to fulfill his promise as some count slowness, but is patient toward you, not wishing that any should perish, but that all should reach repentance. [10] But the day of the Lord will come like a thief, and then the heavens will pass away with a roar, and the heavenly bodies will be burned up and dissolved, and the earth and the works that are done on it will be exposed. [11]

Since all these things are thus to be dissolved, what sort of people ought you to be in lives of holiness and godliness, [12] waiting for and hastening the coming of the day of God, because of which the heavens will be set on fire and dissolved, and the heavenly bodies will melt as they burn! [13] But according to his promise we are waiting for new heavens and a new earth in which righteousness dwells. [14] Therefore, beloved, since you are waiting for these, be diligent to be found by him without spot or blemish, and at peace.

2. Preach these truths to assure the saints that our Lord Jesus will in fact will return and reign over the earth, bringing justice and peace to it forever.

   a. Isaiah 65:17 – "For behold, I create new heavens and a new earth, and the former things shall not be remembered or come into mind.

   b. Isaiah 66:22 – "For as the new heavens and the new earth that I make shall remain before me, says the Lord, so shall your offspring and your name remain.

   c. Luke 1:30-33 – And the angel said to her, "Do not be afraid, Mary, for you have found favor with God. [31] And behold, you will conceive in your womb and bear a son, and you shall call his name Jesus. [32] He will be great and will be called the Son of the Most High. And the Lord God will give to him the throne of his father David, [33] and he will reign over the house of Jacob forever, and of his kingdom there will be no end."

3. Preach these truths because we are on the brink of a new order of peace, rooted in God's own transformation of this world into the glorious freedom of the children of God.

a. Our freedom to come:
   Romans 8:18-21 – For I consider that the sufferings of this present time are not worth comparing with the glory that is to be revealed to us. [19] For the creation waits with eager longing for the revealing of the sons of God. [20] For the creation was subjected to futility, not willingly, but because of him who subjected it, in hope [21] that the creation itself will be set free from its bondage to decay and obtain the freedom of the glory of the children of God.

b. Rev. 21:1-4 – Then I saw a new heaven and a new earth, for the first heaven and the first earth had passed away, and the sea was no more. [2] And I saw the holy city, new Jerusalem, coming down out of heaven from God, prepared as a bride adorned for her husband. [3] And I heard a loud voice from the throne saying, "Behold, the dwelling place of God is with man. He will dwell with them, and they will be his people, and God himself will be with them as their God. [4] He will wipe away every tear from their eyes, and death shall be no more, neither shall there be mourning nor crying nor pain anymore, for the former things have passed away."

Living Here and Now in the Power of the Resurrection, Fleeing the Wrath to Come

The great Easter truth is not that we are to live newly after death - that is not the great thing - but that we are to live here and now by the power of the resurrection; not so much that we are to live forever as that we are to, and may, live nobly now because we are to live forever."

– Phillips Brooks

III. Conclusion: Be humble, because you can't put the ocean in a hole . . .

Though he put all his mental faculties to the task, St. Augustine was having a difficult time resolving the question of the Trinity. One day as he walked along the shore, he noticed a little boy playing. The boy had used a seashell to dig a hole in the sand, and was going back and forth from the water to the hole, filling the shell with water, then pouring it into the hole. Augustine asked the boy what he was doing, and the youngster replied, "I am putting the ocean in this hole." Augustine laughed, then suddenly realized he was guilty of the same fallacious thinking. He said, "Standing on the shores of time, *I am trying to get into this finite mind things that are infinite!*

Seeking to understand the workings of the triune God on behalf of his holy character and righteous works is somewhat like trying to fill a hole with the ocean. We can know, however, that the Second Coming of Jesus Christ has a practical and frightening side concerning those things, people, situations, places, institutions, and practices that offend his perfect holiness and righteous will. The Tribulation will in fact bring a final and lasting end to those things that offend the glory of God's majesty, and with The Millennium, the righteous will of God will be manifest in the reign of Jesus Christ and his saints.

Psalm 72:18-19 – Blessed be the Lord, the God of Israel, who alone does wondrous things. [19] Blessed be his glorious name forever; may the whole earth be filled with his glory! Amen and Amen!

Jesus Shall Reign Where'er the Sun
A Hymn by Isaac Watts • Adapted from Psalm 72

Jesus shall reign where'er the sun, does his successive journeys run;
His kingdom stretch from shore to shore, Till moons shall wax and wane no more.

Behold the islands with their kings, and Europe her best tribute brings;
From north to south the princes meet, to pay their homage at His feet.

There Persia, glorious to behold, there India shines in eastern gold;
And barb'rous nations at His word submit, and bow, and own their Lord.

To Him shall endless prayer be made, and praises throng to crown His head;
His Name like sweet perfume shall rise with every morning sacrifice.

People and realms of every tongue dwell on His love with sweetest song;
And infant voices shall proclaim their early blessings on His Name.

Blessings abound wherever He reigns; the prisoner leaps to lose his chains;
The weary find eternal rest, and all the sons of want are blessed.

Where He displays His healing power, death and the curse are known no more:
In Him the tribes of Adam boast more blessings than their father lost.

Let every creature rise and bring peculiar honors to our King;
Angels descend with songs again, and earth repeat the loud amen!

Great God, whose universal sway the known and unknown worlds obey,
Now give the kingdom to Thy Son, extend His power, exalt His throne.

The scepter well becomes His hands; all Heav'n submits to His commands;
His justice shall avenge the poor, and pride and rage prevail no more.

With power He vindicates the just, and treads th'oppressor in the dust:
His worship and His fear shall last till hours, and years, and time be past.

As rain on meadows newly mown, so shall He send his influence down:
His grace on fainting souls distills, like heav'nly dew on thirsty hills.

The heathen lands, that lie beneath the shades of overspreading death,
Revive at His first dawning light; and deserts blossom at the sight.

The saints shall flourish in His days, dressed in the robes of joy and praise;
Peace, like a river, from His throne shall flow to nations yet unknown.

- The wrath of God will be demonstrated in the judgments that occur during the Great Tribulation, bringing a full and final satisfaction of God's righteous indignation on those things that offend his holiness.

- The Millennium of Christ will see our risen Lord righteous and glorified, ruling in the midst of a refreshed earth with his Church as his co-heir and co-regent, over the nations for 1,000 years. This is the privilege and blessing of all the saints.

- The teaching of the Tribulation and Millennium ought to enable us to preach the truth regarding God's holiness which will be demonstrated in both, in the former through judgments of wrath and in the latter through his righteous rule upon the refreshed earth. We should then flee the wrath to come, and pray that his Kingdom would come on earth as it is in heaven. These acts should be done fervently and simultaneously.

The Bottom Line _____

Lesson Seven
The Resurrection of the Dead, Final Judgment, and Eternal Punishment

Is It Safe Now For You to Die?

Dr. Maurice Rawlings, cardiologist and professor of medicine at the University of Tennessee College of Medicine in Chattanooga has reported extensively about him and his emergency room colleagues who have treated numerous "near death" medical cases of patients whose medical condition went into arrest, and they "came back" after intense resuscitation. He states in his writings how it is now standard that those who have near death experiences later speak of having experiences of light, lush green meadows, rows of smiling relatives, and tremendous peace. However, in his study, also reported in his book *Beyond Death's Door,* Dr. Rawlings's research obtained new information by interviewing patients immediately after resuscitation while they are still too shaken to deny where they have been.

Nearly 50% of the group of 300 he interviewed reported in their moments after "clinical death" lakes of fire and brimstone, devil-like figures, and other sights hailing from the darkness of "hell." He says that many who report such visions later change their story because most people are simply too ashamed to admit they have perhaps been in a preview sense to "hell," and will not even admit such experiences to their families. Concludes Dr. Rawlings, "Just listening to these patients has changed my whole life. There's a life after death, and if I don't know where I'm going, *it's not safe to die.*"

Maurice Rawlings, *Omni* Magazine. March 1985.

I. The Resurrection

Far more than merely the sense of reanimation of a person to renewed but (alas!) mortal existence again, the teaching of the Scriptures regarding resurrection affirms the heart of the matter: In the identification of the righteous with the person of Jesus Christ, those who have passed on will soon experience the power of eternal glorification and transformation, described as being "raised immortal" (cf. 1 Cor. 15:52), and "exalted" (Acts 2.32–33; 5.30–31). We who belong to Christ and yet have fallen asleep are about to be raised from the realm of the dead to a glorified, never-ending, exalted state of being in the very presence of God himself. Resurrection may be a moment, but its effects will be endless!

1 Cor. 15:42-44 – So is it with the resurrection of the dead. What is sown is perishable; what is raised is imperishable. [43] It is sown in dishonor; it is raised in glory. It is sown in weakness; it is raised in power. [44] It is sown a natural body; it is raised a spiritual body. If there is a natural body, there is also a spiritual body.

A. Here are key OT citations of a general resurrection, of belief that those who have died will be raised again:

1. In our flesh we shall see the Lord.
   Job 19:26 – And after my skin has been thus destroyed, yet in my flesh I shall see God.

2. The soul of God's anointed will not be abandoned to Sheol.
   Psalm 16:9-10 – Therefore my heart is glad, and my whole being rejoices; my flesh also dwells secure. [10] For you will not abandon my soul to Sheol, or let your holy one see corruption.

3. We will be satisfied with his likeness when we awake.
   Psalms 17:15 – As for me, I shall behold your face in righteousness; when I awake, I shall be satisfied with your likeness.

4. We will be ransomed from the power of Sheol.
   Psalms 49:15 – But God will ransom my soul from the power of Sheol, for he will receive me. Selah

5. Resurrection as being received into glory.
   Psalms 73:24 – You guide me with your counsel, and afterward you will receive me to glory.

6. Our bodies will rise.
   Isaiah 26:19 – Your dead shall live; their bodies shall rise. You who dwell in the dust, awake and sing for joy! For your dew is a dew of light, and the earth will give birth to the dead.

7. Messiah will see his offspring after he gives himself a ransom for their sin.
   Isaiah 53:10-12 – Yet it was the will of the Lord to crush him; he has put him to grief; when his soul makes an offering for sin, he shall see his offspring; he shall prolong his days; the will of the Lord shall prosper in his hand. [11] Out of the anguish of his soul he shall see and be satisfied; by his knowledge shall the righteous one, my servant, make many to be accounted righteous, and he shall bear their iniquities. [12] Therefore I will divide him a portion with the many, and he shall divide the spoil with the strong, because he poured out his soul to death and was numbered with the transgressors; yet he bore the sin of many, and makes intercession for the transgressors.

8. The righteous will stand at the "end of days."
   Daniel 12:13 – But go your way till the end. And you shall rest and shall stand in your allotted place at the end of the days."

B. Texts where resurrection terminology and typology affirms Israel's future restoration as a nation and as the people of God:

1. The valley of dead bones, and the "resurrection" of the bones into an army by the Spirit upon them. (Ezek. 37:1–14)

2. After *three days* the Lord will raise us up.
   Hosea 6:1-3 – Come, let us return to the Lord; for he has torn us, that he may heal us; he has struck us down, and he will bind us up. [2] After two days he will revive

us; on the third day he will raise us up, that we may live before him. [3]Let us know; let us press on to know the Lord; his going out is sure as the dawn; he will come to us as the showers, as the spring rains that water the earth.

3. Jesus and the allusion to Jonah in the belly of the great fish.
   Matthew 12:39-41 – But he answered them, "An evil and adulterous generation seeks for a sign, but no sign will be given to it except the sign of the prophet Jonah. [40] For just as Jonah was three days and three nights in the belly of the great fish, so will the Son of Man be three days and three nights in the heart of the earth. [41] The men of Nineveh will rise up at the judgment with this generation and condemn it, for they repented at the preaching of Jonah, and behold, something greater than Jonah is here.

C. Five types of resurrection referred to in the New Testament:

1. The physical restoration (reanimation) to life of select persons to a renewed, but mortal, life.

   a. The raising of the young man of Nain.
      Luke 7:14-15 – Then he came up and touched the bier, and the bearers stood still. And he said, "Young man, I say to you, arise." [15] And the dead man sat up and began to speak, and Jesus gave him to his mother.

   b. The raising of Lazarus.
      John 11:43-44 – When he had said these things, he cried out with a loud voice, "Lazarus, come out." [44] The man who had died came out, his hands and feet bound with linen strips, and his face wrapped with a cloth. Jesus said to them, "Unbind him, and let him go."

Lesson Seven: The Resurrection of the Dead, Final Judgment, and Eternal Punishment ■ 187

      c. Allusions to miracles of God in the OT.
Hebrews 11:35 – Women received back their dead by resurrection. Some were tortured, refusing to accept release, so that they might rise again to a better life.

2. The resurrection of Jesus Christ to immortality and divine glory.
Acts 2:22-24 – Men of Israel, hear these words: Jesus of Nazareth, a man attested to you by God with mighty works and wonders and signs that God did through him in your midst, as you yourselves know— [23] this Jesus, delivered up according to the definite plan and foreknowledge of God, you crucified and killed by the hands of lawless men. [24] God raised him up, loosing the pangs of death, because it was not possible for him to be held by it.

3. The spiritual "resurrection" of believers to new life through faith in Jesus Christ as Savior and Lord.
Colossians 2:12 – having been buried with him in baptism, in which you were also raised with him through faith in the powerful working of God, who raised him from the dead.

4. The coming and future resurrection of believers to eternal life, as members of the harvest of Christ.
1 Corinthians 15:42 – So is it with the resurrection of the dead. What is sown is perishable; what is raised is imperishable.

5. The future resurrection of unbelievers to judgment.

      a. Resurrection of life versus resurrection of judgment.
John 5:28-29 – Do not marvel at this, for an hour is coming when all who are in the tombs will hear his voice [29] and come out, those who have done good to the resurrection of life, and those who have done evil to the resurrection of judgment.

b. Paul's testimony about his resurrection faith.
Acts 24:15 – having a hope in God, which these men themselves accept, that there will be a resurrection of both the just and the unjust.

D. The Resurrection of Jesus serves as the ground for all biblical revelation on the resurrection.

1. The resurrection of the dead, and of Jesus in particular, represents the central doctrine in all Christian faith and belief.

   a. 1 Cor. 15:12-15 – Now if Christ is proclaimed as raised from the dead, how can some of you say that there is no resurrection of the dead? [13] But if there is no resurrection of the dead, then not even Christ has been raised. [14] And if Christ has not been raised, then our preaching is in vain and your faith is in vain. [15] We are even found to be misrepresenting God, because we testified about God that he raised Christ, whom he did not raise if it is true that the dead are not raised.

   b. Jesus did not simply teach the resurrection. He is in fact the Resurrection and the Life itself!
   John 11.25-26 – Jesus said to her, "I am the resurrection and the life. Whoever believes in me, though he die, yet shall he live, [26] and everyone who lives and believes in me shall never die. Do you believe this?"

2. The Resurrection of Jesus points to the key doctrine of spiritual identification in the NT: The union of believers with Christ.

   a. We are never again to be separated from him.
   Matt. 28.20 – teaching them to observe all that I

have commanded you. And behold, I am with you always, to the end of the age."

    b. His going away (in suffering and death) did not prevent him from coming to us again (in resurrected glory, and in the power of the Holy Spirit).
John 14:28 – You heard me say to you, 'I am going away, and I will come to you.' If you loved me, you would have rejoiced, because I am going to the Father, for the Father is greater than I.

    c. We are now united with Christ, alive together with him, raised and ascended to the throne in heavenly places in Christ Jesus.
Eph. 2:4-5 – But God, being rich in mercy, because of the great love with which he loved us, [5] even when we were dead in our trespasses, made us alive together with Christ—by grace you have been saved—

3. The Resurrection of Jesus supplies the members of the Church with power to accomplish the will of God in this realm ("mo' power!"), transcending mere history and turning it into daily appropriated power for living.

    a. To know the power of his resurrection is our aim, not as a doctrine, but a vital life changing reality in our lives.
Phil. 3:10 – that I may know him and the power of his resurrection, and may share his sufferings, becoming like him in his death.

    b. The Spirit of life in us now liberates us for a new life in Christ.
Romans 8:1-4 – There is therefore now no condemnation for those who are in Christ Jesus. [2] For the law of the Spirit of life has set you free in Christ Jesus from the law of sin and death. [3] For God has done what the law, weakened by the flesh,

could not do. By sending his own Son in the likeness of sinful flesh and for sin, he condemned sin in the flesh, [4] in order that the righteous requirement of the law might be fulfilled in us, who walk not according to the flesh but according to the Spirit.

4. The Resurrection of Jesus delivers us from the demonic rule of the present age, and inaugurates a new creation where the old has indeed passed away and the new life in the Kingdom of God has come (already, but not yet fully, revealed).

   a. We are delivered in Christ's power from the present evil age.
   Galatians 1:4 – who gave himself for our sins to deliver us from the present evil age, according to the will of our God and Father.

   b. Through his resurrection power we are delivered from the prince of the power of the air.
   Ephesians 2:2 – in which you once walked, following the course of this world, following the prince of the power of the air, the spirit that is now at work in the sons of disobedience.

   c. The resurrection will not simply make things new in the future age; rather, things are new today, right here, right now in him.
   2 Corinthians 5:17 – Therefore, if anyone is in Christ, he is a new creation. The old has passed away; behold, the new has come.

5. In the person of Jesus Christ, and through his Resurrection, the Age to Come has broken into this present age, with our Lord becoming the first-fruits of those who sleep, and the firstborn of the dead.

a. Christ is the firstfruits of the eschatological harvest of souls who are destined to live in the Age to Come.
1 Corinthians 15:20 – But in fact Christ has been raised from the dead, the firstfruits of those who have fallen asleep.

b. Christ's death is the firstborn from the dead, i.e., the first of all those destined to live forever in the new heavens and earth.
Colossians 1:18 – And he is the head of the body, the church. He is the beginning, the firstborn from the dead, that in everything he might be preeminent.

c. Jesus is the "firstborn" (preeminent one) from the dead.
Revelation 1:5-6 – and from Jesus Christ the faithful witness, the firstborn of the dead, and the ruler of kings on earth. To him who loves us and has freed us from our sins by his blood [6]and made us a kingdom, priests to his God and Father, to him be glory and dominion forever and ever. Amen.

d. Through his Resurrection, our faith is now referred to as a "living hope."
1 Peter 1:3 – Blessed be the God and Father of our Lord Jesus Christ! According to his great mercy, he has caused us to be born again to a living hope through the resurrection of Jesus Christ from the dead.

e. The Resurrection of Jesus serves therefore as the absolute proof of the coming consummation of the plan of God, the resurrection of the dead, the gift of the Holy Spirit, and promise of eternal life for those who believe.

f. Acts 4:1-2 – And as they were speaking to the people, the priests and the captain of the temple and the Sadducees came upon them, [2] greatly annoyed because they were teaching the people and proclaiming in Jesus the resurrection from the dead.

g. Romans 8:11 – If the Spirit of him who raised Jesus from the dead dwells in you, he who raised Christ Jesus from the dead will also give life to your mortal bodies through his Spirit who dwells in you.

6. Finally, the Resurrection of Jesus stirs up the longing of the Church for the Parousia, for the soon return of Christ at the end of this present fleeting age, where Christ will make these glorious promises real and concrete.

a. He will bring with him those who have fallen asleep.
1 Thess 4:14 – For since we believe that Jesus died and rose again, even so, through Jesus, God will bring with him those who have fallen asleep.

b. The Father will raise up those who have died and believe, even as he raised up our Lord Jesus from the dead.
2 Cor. 4:14 – knowing that he who raised the Lord Jesus will raise us also with Jesus and bring us with you into his presence.

E. Critical theological emphases associated with the Resurrection of Jesus:

1. Jesus' resurrection represents both the "pledge and the paradigm" of the forthcoming bodily resurrection of those clinging to Christ in faith.

a. He is the pledge (i.e., the guarantee upon which we depend for our own future transformation).

(1) The Father raised up Jesus and will raise us up by the same mighty power.

1 Corinthians 6:14 – And God raised the Lord and will also raise us up by his power.

(2) Christ is the pattern for an entirely new transformed humanity, the "Last Adam," as it were.
1 Corinthians 15:20-23 – But in fact Christ has been raised from the dead, the firstfruits of those who have fallen asleep. [21] For as by a man came death, by a man has come also the resurrection of the dead. [22] For as in Adam all die, so also in Christ shall all be made alive. [23] But each in his own order: Christ the firstfruits, then at his coming those who belong to Christ.

(3) Our new bodies will conform strictly to the glory of Christ, as they have conformed strictly to the weakness of Adam.
1 Corinthians 15:48-49 – As was the man of dust, so also are those who are of the dust, and as is the man of heaven, so also are those who are of heaven. [49] Just as we have borne the image of the man of dust, we shall also bear the image of the man of heaven.

b. He is the paradigm (i.e., our bodies will be transformed to resemble in every respect the glorified spiritual body of the risen Christ in glory).

(1) 1 John 3:2 – Beloved, we are God's children now, and what we will be has not yet appeared; but we know that when he appears we shall be like him, because we shall see him as he is.

(2) The Lord Jesus will transform our bodies to be conformed to his own glorious body.
Phil. 3:20-21 – But our citizenship is in heaven, and from it we await a Savior, the Lord Jesus Christ, [21] who will transform our lowly body to be like his glorious body, by the power that enables him even to subject all things to himself.

(3) God's purpose is to use Jesus as pattern of entirely new human community.

Romans 8:29 – For those whom he foreknew he also predestined to be conformed to the image of his Son, in order that he might be the firstborn among many brothers.

2. In a spiritual sense, we who believe are already both raised and ascended in Christ, sharing his victory over the world and sin through his risen life.

   a. We are said to have been resurrected and ascended with him.
   Ephesians 2:6 – and raised us up with him and seated us with him in the heavenly places in Christ Jesus.

   b. We were associated with his burial through baptism, and raised with him by faith.
   Colossians 2:12 – having been buried with him in baptism, in which you were also raised with him through faith in the powerful working of God, who raised him from the dead.

   c. Since we have been raised with Christ, we are to seek the things that are above.
   Colossians 3:1 – If then you have been raised with Christ, seek the things that are above, where Christ is, seated at the right hand of God.

   d. This victory is demonstrated in our identification with him in baptism and new life.

      (1) We are to consider ourselves so identified with Christ in his death that we reckon ourselves as those alive from the dead.
      Romans 6:10-11 – For the death he died he died to sin, once for all, but the life he lives he lives to God. [11] So you also must consider yourselves dead to sin and alive to God in Christ Jesus.

(2) As we were identified with his death, so we are now to walk in his new life.
Romans 6:4 – We were buried therefore with him by baptism into death, in order that, just as Christ was raised from the dead by the glory of the Father, we too might walk in newness of life.

3. The Holy Spirit, who raised our Lord from the dead, also will raise the bodies of believers who have passed on to new life as he who is called the "Spirit of life." (i.e., Rom. 8:2)

   a. He has sealed believers for the day of redemption.
   Ephesians 1:13-14 – In him you also, when you heard the word of truth, the gospel of your salvation, and believed in him, were sealed with the promised Holy Spirit, [14] who is the guarantee of our inheritance until we acquire possession of it, to the praise of his glory.

   b. He will raise our mortal bodies from the grave to immortality, even as he did the body of our Lord Jesus.
   Romans 8:11 – If the Spirit of him who raised Jesus from the dead dwells in you, he who raised Christ Jesus from the dead will also give life to your mortal bodies through his Spirit who dwells in you.

   c. It is he who imparts new resurrection life to all those who believe in Christ as Lord and Christ.
   2 Cor. 3:6 – who has made us sufficient to be ministers of a new covenant, not of the letter but of the Spirit. For the letter kills, but the Spirit gives life.

   d. He is the down payment as well as the primary power through which the Father will transform our bodies to the new resurrection glory.

(1) The Spirit indwelling us is our guarantee of the life to come.
2 Cor. 1:21-22 – And it is God who establishes us with you in Christ, and has anointed us, [22] and who has also put his seal on us and given us his Spirit in our hearts as a guarantee.

(2) 2 Corinthians 5:5 – He who has prepared us for this very thing is God, who has given us the Spirit as a guarantee.

(3) 2 Corinthians 13:4 – For he was crucified in weakness, but lives by the power of God. For we also are weak in him, but in dealing with you we will live with him by the power of God.

4. The resurrection of the new and transformed human race is interconnected to the transformation and refreshing of the entire universe at the revelation of the glorious freedom of the children of God.

   a. All creation awaits the glorification of God's saints. (Rom. 8:18–25)

   b. The resurrection is linked to the glorification of God as all-in-all in the ages to come. (1 Cor. 15:20–28)

   c. Our bodies will be transformed because the glorified Christ is now able to subject all things everywhere under his sovereign control and sway. (Phil. 3:20–21)

   d. "As at the fall, so in the restoration, what affects man affects all of creation." S. B. Ferguson.

   e. The resurrection of humankind is a part of a framework of transformation that will ultimately touch all creation. Our new glorified bodies will in fact be placed within a "new heaven and a new earth."

(1) We wait for a new creation where the righteousness of God dwells.
2 Peter 3:13 – But according to his promise we are waiting for new heavens and a new earth in which righteousness dwells.

(2) Revelation 21 provides us the vision of the new creation.
Revelation 21:1-5 – Then I saw a new heaven and a new earth, for the first heaven and the first earth had passed away, and the sea was no more. [2] And I saw the holy city, new Jerusalem, coming down out of heaven from God, prepared as a bride adorned for her husband. [3] And I heard a loud voice from the throne saying, "Behold, the dwelling place of God is with man. He will dwell with them, and they will be his people, and God himself will be with them as their God. [4] He will wipe away every tear from their eyes, and death shall be no more, neither shall there be mourning nor crying nor pain anymore, for the former things have passed away." [5] And he who was seated on the throne said, "Behold, I am making all things new." Also he said, "Write this down, for these words are trustworthy and true."

F. Characteristics of the resurrection body of believers:

1. The bodies of believers who are resurrected will be of God's own origin and design, the perfect product of his omniscient vision and animating power.

   a. 1 Corinthians 15:38 – But God gives it a body as he has chosen, and to each kind of seed its own body.

   b. 2 Corinthians 5:1-2 – For we know that if the tent, which is our earthly home, is destroyed, we have a building from God, a house not made with hands, eternal in the heavens. [2] For in this tent we groan, longing to put on our heavenly dwelling

2. They will be spiritual bodies, which does not mean that they will be actually made up of spirit. As one commentator puts it, they will be "animated and guided by the spirit" – fully responsive to the Spirit of God in such a way as to be forever free from sinful inclinations.

   a. 1 Corinthians 6:13-14 – "Food is meant for the stomach and the stomach for food"—and God will destroy both one and the other. The body is not meant for sexual immorality, but for the Lord, and the Lord for the body. [14] And God raised the Lord and will also raise us up by his power.

   b. 1 Corinthians 15:44-46 – It is sown a natural body; it is raised a spiritual body. If there is a natural body, there is also a spiritual body. [45] Thus it is written, "The first man Adam became a living being"; the last Adam became a life-giving spirit. [46] But it is not the spiritual that is first but the natural, and then the spiritual.

3. The resurrection body of believers will be incorruptible and imperishable, gloriously powerful and beautiful. 1 Cor. 15:42–43 – So is it with the resurrection of the dead. What is sown is perishable; what is raised is imperishable. 43 It is sown in dishonor; it is raised in glory. It is sown in weakness; it is raised in power.

4. The body of believers will be utterly free from the possibility or hint of either sickness, frailty, or decay. As one commentator puts it, this body is "of unparalleled beauty and endless energy; it is angel-like."

   a. Neither marry nor are given in marriage: a new state of human existence.

Mark 12:25 – For when they rise from the dead, they neither marry nor are given in marriage, but are like angels in heaven.

    b. Equal to the angels, children of the resurrection.
Luke 20:36 – for they cannot die anymore, because they are equal to angels and are sons of God, being sons of the resurrection.

5. They will be both deathless and appropriate to a new order of transformed glory, "perfectly suited to the ecology of heaven."

    a. The body we receive will be of a "heavenly kind."
1 Corinthians 15:40 – There are heavenly bodies and earthly bodies, but the glory of the heavenly is of one kind, and the glory of the earthly is of another.

    b. The body we receive will bear the image of the "man of heaven."
1 Corinthians 15:47-49 – The first man was from the earth, a man of dust; the second man is from heaven. [48] As was the man of dust, so also are those who are of the dust, and as is the man of heaven, so also are those who are of heaven. [49] Just as we have borne the image of the man of dust, we shall also bear the image of the man of heaven.

6. Above all, they will be perfectly conformed to the glorious body of our risen Lord, whose resurrection body is the pattern God will employ to define each one in his new order of human existence.

G. The resurrection of life and the resurrection of judgment.

1. In his teaching on the resurrection, Jesus distinguishes between two distinct resurrections.

John 5.28-29 – Do not marvel at this, for an hour is coming when all who are in the tombs will hear his voice [29] and come out, those who have done good to the **resurrection of life**, and those who have done evil to the **resurrection of judgment**.

   a. Acts 24:15 – having a hope in God, which these men themselves accept, that there will be a resurrection of both the just and the unjust.

   b. The first and the second resurrection:
Revelation 20:4-6 – Then I saw thrones, and seated on them were those to whom the authority to judge was committed. Also I saw the souls of those who had been beheaded for the testimony of Jesus and for the word of God, and who had not worshiped the beast or its image and had not received its mark on their foreheads or their hands. They came to life and reigned with Christ for a thousand years. [5] The rest of the dead did not come to life until the thousand years were ended. This is the first resurrection. [6] Blessed and holy is the one who shares in the first resurrection! Over such the second death has no power, but they will be priests of God and of Christ, and they will reign with him for a thousand years.

2. The scriptures teach that all human beings will be judged as to their works *as evidence of their faith in Christ* or *lack of faith in him.*

   a. The one who believes in the Son has life, and the one disobeying the Son receives the wrath of God.
John 3:36 – Whoever believes in the Son has eternal life; whoever does not obey the Son shall not see life, but the wrath of God remains on him.

   b. Jesus has been appointed by God to be judge of the living and the dead.
Acts 10:42 – And he commanded us to preach to the

people and to testify that he is the one appointed by God to be judge of the living and the dead.

    c. God will judge the secrets of all people by Christ Jesus in the final day.
Romans 2:16 – on that day when, according to my gospel, God judges the secrets of men by Christ Jesus.

    d. The Father will judge each one's deeds impartially through Jesus Christ.
1 Peter 1:17 – And if you call on him as Father who judges impartially according to each one's deeds, conduct yourselves with fear throughout the time of your exile,

    e. The Great White Throne judgment.
Revelation 20:11-13 – Then I saw a great white throne and him who was seated on it. From his presence earth and sky fled away, and no place was found for them. [12] And I saw the dead, great and small, standing before the throne, and books were opened. Then another book was opened, which is the book of life. And the dead were judged by what was written in the books, according to what they had done. [13] And the sea gave up the dead who were in it, Death and Hades gave up the dead who were in them, and they were judged, each one of them, according to what they had done.

3. In these judgments, two differing, distinct verdicts will be entered.

    a. Those appointed for eternal life will be judged relative to their service rendered to Christ.
1 Cor. 3.12-15 – Now if anyone builds on the foundation with gold, silver, precious stones, wood, hay, straw— [13] each one's work will become manifest, for the Day will disclose it, because it will be revealed by fire, and the fire will test what sort

of work each one has done. [14] If the work that anyone has built on the foundation survives, he will receive a reward. [15] If anyone's work is burned up, he will suffer loss, though he himself will be saved, but only as through fire.

    b. Those condemned to eternal perdition will be consigned to eternal punishment.
Matt. 25:46 – And these will go away into eternal punishment, but the righteous into eternal life.

    2 Thess. 1:8–9 – in flaming fire, inflicting vengeance on those who do not know God and on those who do not obey the gospel of our Lord Jesus. [9] They will suffer the punishment of eternal destruction, away from the presence of the Lord and from the glory of his might,

4. What will be the form of those who are "raised" in the resurrection unto judgment?
Answer: It is unclear in scripture what the nature of their reanimated bodies will be. Those who rejected the grace of God in Christ Jesus will be reanimated to appear before God, but the form and characteristic of their bodies is not disclosed in Scripture.

5. Excursus: What of the rich man in the parable of Jesus in Luke 16?

II. The Final Judgment

Before the Judgment Seat We All Must Stand

Before the Judgment Seat of Christ my service will be judged not by how much I have done, but by how much I could have done.

– A.W. Tozer

Romans 14:10-12 – Why do you pass judgment on your brother? Or you, why do you despise your brother? For we will all stand before the judgment seat of God; [11] for it is written, "As I live, says the Lord, every knee shall bow to me, and every tongue shall confess to God." [12] So then each of us will give an account of himself to God.

A. The Final Judgment as connected to the Parousia.

1. This judgment is yet to occur; it is a future judgment.

    a. It is associated with the totality of a person's life, after their death.

        (1) It is the appointment that all people must and will keep.
        Hebrews 9:27 – And just as it is appointed for man to die once, and after that comes judgment.

        (2) "Payday's comin' after while! (Can I get a witness!)"
        Matthew 16:27 – For the Son of Man is going to come with his angels in the glory of his Father, and then he will repay each person according to what he has done.

    b. This judgment is associated with the resurrection to life and the resurrection to judgment.
    John 5.28-29 – Do not marvel at this, for an hour is coming when all who are in the tombs will hear his voice [29] and come out, those who have done good to the resurrection of life, and those who have done evil to the resurrection of judgment.

    c. Christ has been appointed as judge by God who "has fixed a day" to judge the world in righteousness.
    Acts 17:31 – because he has fixed a day on which he will judge the world in righteousness by a man

whom he has appointed; and of this he has given assurance to all by raising him from the dead.

   d. The judgment is called "the day of wrath when God's righteous judgment will be revealed."
      Romans 2:5 – But because of your hard and impenitent heart you are storing up wrath for yourself on the day of wrath when God's righteous judgment will be revealed.

   e. The day will bring fear and a "fury of fire" for God's adversaries.
      Hebrews 10:26-27 – For if we go on sinning deliberately after receiving the knowledge of the truth, there no longer remains a sacrifice for sins, [27] but a fearful expectation of judgment, and a fury of fire that will consume the adversaries.

2. This judgment will be awesome in scope and impact.

   a. It is described as a "great and awesome" day.
      Malachi 4:5 – Behold, I will send you Elijah the prophet before the great and awesome day of the Lord comes."

   b. It will dramatically impact the universe and humankind.
      Malachi 3:2 – But who can endure the day of his coming, and who can stand when he appears? For he is like a refiner's fire and like fullers' soap.

   c. It will consummate the work begun on the Cross for the sake of God's elect.
      1 Thess. 5:23 – Now may the God of peace himself sanctify you completely, and may your whole spirit and soul and body be kept blameless at the coming of our Lord Jesus Christ.

d. It will be a day that utterly consumes those *on the wrong side of salvation*.
Malachi 4:1 – For behold, the day is coming, burning like an oven, when all the arrogant and all evildoers will be stubble. The day that is coming shall set them ablaze, says the Lord of hosts, so that it will leave them neither root nor branch.

3. The basis of the final judgment will be one's relationship to God in Jesus Christ.

   a. Those who believe inherit life. Those who disobey inherit wrath.
   John 3.36 – Whoever believes in the Son has eternal life; whoever does not obey the Son shall not see life, but the wrath of God remains on him.

   b. Only those who have the Son of God possess life.
   1 John 5.11-13 – And this is the testimony, that God gave us eternal life, and this life is in his Son. [12] Whoever has the Son has life; whoever does not have the Son of God does not have life.

4. It is a differentiated judgment, based on the subjects and character of the verdict demanded and required.

   a. Believers are judged on the basis of their deeds. This is judgment of rewards for service, not judgment of works for salvation.
   Eph. 2.8-9 – For by grace you have been saved through faith. And this is not your own doing; it is the gift of God, [9] not a result of works, so that no one may boast.

   b. Because no person is saved on the basis of their moral goodness or the righteousness accrued by their deeds in obedience to the Law, the judgment of believers is unto reward, not unto relationship with God.

1 Cor. 3.12-14 – Now if anyone builds on the foundation with gold, silver, precious stones, wood, hay, straw— [13] each one's work will become manifest, for the Day will disclose it, because it will be revealed by fire, and the fire will test what sort of work each one has done. [14] If the work that anyone has built on the foundation survives, he will receive a reward.

    c. Though a believer's works may burn, she herself will be saved, but only as one escaping through the flames. 1 Cor. 3.15 – If anyone's work is burned up, he will suffer loss, though he himself will be saved, but only as through fire.

B. The glorified Christ Jesus is the Judge.

    1. The glorified Christ is pictured in the future judgment as the King sitting upon his throne judging the nations. Matthew 25:31-33 – "When the Son of Man comes in his glory, and all the angels with him, then he will sit on his glorious throne. [32] Before him will be gathered all the nations, and he will separate people one from another as a shepherd separates the sheep from the goats. [33] And he will place the sheep on his right, but the goats on the left.

    2. All authority for the future judgments of the Church and the nations is given unto the risen Christ.
John 5.22 – For the Father judges no one, but has given all judgment to the Son,

    3. The judgment seat of Christ will be the place for the judgment of all persons, both saved and unsaved.
2 Corinthians 5:10 – For we must all appear before the judgment seat of Christ, so that each one may receive what is due for what he has done in the body, whether good or evil.

Lesson Seven: The Resurrection of the Dead, Final Judgment, and Eternal Punishment

4. The judgment of Jesus is directly connected to his appearing.
   2 Timothy 4:1-3 – I charge you in the presence of God and of Christ Jesus, who is to judge the living and the dead, and by his appearing and his kingdom: [2] preach the word; be ready in season and out of season; reprove, rebuke, and exhort, with complete patience and teaching.

5. His judgment appears to be proportionate to the measure of knowledge one had of God's will, i.e., the greater of knowledge of His will, the more responsibility one will bear in judgment.

   a. The hardness of heart of cities who refused to repent will result in the harsher judgment they will receive.
      Matthew 11:20-24 – Then he began to denounce the cities where most of his mighty works had been done, because they did not repent. [21] "Woe to you, Chorazin! Woe to you, Bethsaida! For if the mighty works done in you had been done in Tyre and Sidon, they would have repented long ago in sackcloth and ashes. [22] But I tell you, it will be more bearable on the day of judgment for Tyre and Sidon than for you. [23] And you, Capernaum, will you be exalted to heaven? You will be brought down to Hades. For if the mighty works done in you had been done in Sodom, it would have remained until this day. [24] But I tell you that it will be more tolerable on the day of judgment for the land of Sodom than for you."

   b. The word that Jesus has spoken to those who rejected the truth will be their judge in the end.
      John 12:48 – The one who rejects me and does not receive my words has a judge; the word that I have spoken will judge him on the last day.

   c. Those who possess the law (i.e., the Word of God) will be judged by the law of God.
      Romans 2:12 – For all who have sinned without the

law will also perish without the law, and all who have sinned under the law will be judged by the law.

6. Excursus: In what sense will believers actually share in the judgment with Christ?

   a. Jesus speaks of the disciples as judges of the Twelve Tribes of Israel in the new order. Is this symbolic or literal?

      (1) Matthew 19:28 – Jesus said to them, "Truly, I say to you, in the new world, when the Son of Man will sit on his glorious throne, you who have followed me will also sit on twelve thrones, judging the twelve tribes of Israel.

      (2) Luke 22:28-30 – You are those who have stayed with me in my trials, [29] and I assign to you, as my Father assigned to me, a kingdom, [30] that you may eat and drink at my table in my kingdom and sit on thrones judging the twelve tribes of Israel.

   b. Believers are said to judge angels.
   1 Cor. 6:2-3 – Or do you not know that the saints will judge the world? And if the world is to be judged by you, are you incompetent to try trivial cases? [3] Do you not know that we are to judge angels? How much more, then, matters pertaining to this life!

   c. God has said that believers will sit on thrones judging the world itself in the new age.

      (1) Even the one who overcomes at Laodecia will reign with him.
      Revelation 3:21 – The one who conquers, I will grant him to sit with me on my throne, as I also conquered and sat down with my Father on his throne.

(2) Those of the first resurrection reign with Christ for 1,000 years.
Revelation 20:4 – Then I saw thrones, and seated on them were those to whom the authority to judge was committed. Also I saw the souls of those who had been beheaded for the testimony of Jesus and for the word of God, and who had not worshiped the beast or its image and had not received its mark on their foreheads or their hands. They came to life and reigned with Christ for a thousand years.

C. Who will be judged in the Final Judgment?

1. All human beings, whether saved or not, will be judged by Christ, but with entirely different purposes and ends in mind.

    a. All will stand before the living Christ.
    Matt. 25.32 – Before him will be gathered all the nations, and he will separate people one from another as a shepherd separates the sheep from the goats.

    b. 2 Cor. 5.10 – For we must all appear before the judgment seat of Christ, so that each one may receive what is due for what he has done in the body, whether good or evil.

    c. Heb. 9.27 – And just as it is appointed for man to die once, and after that comes judgment,

2. All will be judged according to their deeds, whether good or bad (i.e., the concept of "repayment").

a. Jeremiah 17:10 – I the Lord search the heart and test the mind, to give every man according to his ways, according to the fruit of his deeds.

b. Matthew 16:27 – For the Son of Man is going to come with his angels in the glory of his Father, and then he will repay each person according to what he has done.

c. Isaiah 59:18 – According to their deeds, so will he repay, wrath to his adversaries, repayment to his enemies; to the coastlands he will render repayment.

d. Romans 2:6 – He will render to each one according to his works.

e. Rev. 20:13 – And the sea gave up the dead who were in it, Death and Hades gave up the dead who were in them, and they were judged, each one of them, according to what they had done.

3. Evil angels will be judged.
2 Pet. 2.4 – For if God did not spare angels when they sinned, but cast them into hell and committed them to chains of gloomy darkness to be kept until the judgment;

D. The special case: Judgment of believers.

1. The church of God will be judged.
1 Peter 4:17-19 – For it is time for judgment to begin at the household of God; and if it begins with us, what will be the outcome for those who do not obey the gospel of God? [18] And "If the righteous is scarcely saved, what will become of the ungodly and the sinner?" [19] Therefore let those who suffer according to God's will entrust their souls to a faithful Creator while doing good.

2. The Crowns that result from faithful service to Jesus Christ.

   a. The Incorruptible Crown: For faithful perseverance.
      1 Cor. 9:25 – Every athlete exercises self-control in all things. They do it to receive a perishable wreath, but we an imperishable.

   b. The Crown of Righteousness: For those longing for Christ's appearing.
      2 Tim. 4:8 – Henceforth there is laid up for me the crown of righteousness, which the Lord, the righteous judge, will award to me on that Day, and not only to me but also to all who have loved his appearing.

   c. The Crown of Life: For those who persevere under trial and love God.

      (1) James 1:12 – Blessed is the man who remains steadfast under trial, for when he has stood the test he will receive the crown of life, which God has promised to those who love him.

      (2) Rev. 2:10 – Do not fear what you are about to suffer. Behold, the devil is about to throw some of you into prison, that you may be tested, and for ten days you will have tribulation. Be faithful unto death, and I will give you the crown of life.

   d. The Crown of Glory: For God-honoring shepherding of God's flock.
      1 Peter 5:2-4 – shepherd the flock of God that is among you, exercising oversight, not under compulsion, but willingly, as God would have you; not for shameful gain, but eagerly; [3] not domineering over those in your charge, but being examples to the flock. [4] And when the chief Shepherd appears, you will receive the unfading crown of glory.

e. The Crown of Fruitfulness: For those who have borne fruit in Christ.
1 Thess. 2:19-20 – For what is our hope or joy or crown of boasting before our Lord Jesus at his coming? Is it not you? [20] For you are our glory and joy.

3. Word to the wise: *So live and serve that you neither lose nor forfeit your crown!*

   a. Rev. 3:11 – I am coming soon. Hold fast what you have, so that no one may seize your crown.

   b. Compete according to the rules of the game!
   2 Tim. 2:5 – An athlete is not crowned unless he competes according to the rules.

   c. Don't be caught naked at the Lord's banquet table.
   1 John 2:28 – And now, little children, abide in him, so that when he appears we may have confidence and not shrink from him in shame at his coming.

E. The character of the Final Judgment:

1. It will be totalistic. It represents the total and all-encompassing consummation of God's righteous judgment upon all those beings which either resisted or embraced his will.

2. It will be final.

   a. "Once passed, the judgment will be *permanent and irrevocable*." Millard Erickson.

b. Those who do not know God will be subject to God's unending judgment.

c. It is irreversible, as is evident in the story of the rich man and Lazarus in Luke 16.19-31.

d. It will be terrifying in consequence.
Matt. 25:41 – Then he will say to those on his left, 'Depart from me, you cursed, into the eternal fire prepared for the devil and his angels.'

3. It will determine the eternal state and reward of those involved, either to eternal punishment or eternal life
Matt. 25.46 – And these will go away into eternal punishment, but the righteous into eternal life."

Let's Deliver the Ignorant from The Dangerous Zone of Comfort

When a minister speaks at a funeral, he must seek to accomplish two objectives. He needs to "comfort the disturbed and disturb the comfortable." Those who are in touch with the reality of death and eternal life can feel very vulnerable so they need to experience a message of comfort. Those who are complacent about death and the reality of impending judgment desperately need to be unsettled from their dangerous zone of comfort.

Paul Powell, *Death From The Other Side*, 1995, p.12

III. Eternal Punishment

No Such Thing as a "Geep"

Some scientists at the Institute of Animal Physiology in Cambridge, England have added a new twist to Jesus' classification of sheep and goats. These lab-coat-clad intellectuals have through the wonders of technology crossed a *sheep* with a *goat* in test-tube experiments. They have dubbed their new hybrid animal a *"geep."*

San Antonio Express-News, 4-22-97, p.9E.

While it may be a new discovery in the laboratory, it appears to be nothing new in the church. The great judgment seat of Christ will separate the sheep from the goats; "geeps," unfortunately for some, will have no spot reserved for them.

Matthew 25:46 – And these will go away into eternal punishment, but the righteous into eternal life.

A. The final state of the wicked: Controversy and tension.

1. If our God is in fact the God of love and kindness displayed in the person and work of Jesus of Nazareth, how can we ascribe the idea to him that he will *eternally punish those who do not believe in his Son?*

2. Philosophical differences:

   a. The difference between contradictory and complementary ideas: *Merely because things look contradictory to us does not mean that they are. They can in fact be BOTH TRUE, revealing at a deeper level a unity beyond the first glance (i.e., the etymology of the word "respect," to "look again").*

   b. The difference between dialectic and dialogical thinking: *There is no need to view truth only as an Aristotelian syllogism (i.e., "either this or that"), but also as a Hebraic dialogical truth ("Both this and that").*

   c. The differences between rationalistic analysis and divine synthesis: *Only God can bring together the truth in his being which to us appears conflicting and mutually exclusive.*

B. Jesus' images of the final state of the wicked:

1. The image of "eternal fire."
   Matthew 25:41 – Then he will say to those on his left, 'Depart from me, you cursed, into the eternal fire prepared for the devil and his angels.'

2. The image of "fiery furnace."
   Matthew 13:42 – and throw them into the fiery furnace. In that place there will be weeping and gnashing of teeth.

3. The image of "outer darkness."
   Matthew 8:12 – while the sons of the kingdom will be thrown into the outer darkness. In that place there will be weeping and gnashing of teeth."

4. The place of "weeping and gnashing of teeth."
   Luke 13:28 – In that place there will be weeping and gnashing of teeth, when you see Abraham and Isaac and Jacob and all the prophets in the kingdom of God but you yourselves cast out.

5. The image of "eternal punishment."
   Matthew 25:46 – And these will go away into eternal punishment, but the righteous into eternal life.

6. The image of "Gehenna."
   (Translated "hell" in ESV). This term refers to a technical designation of the "valley of Hinnom," which in Hebrew commentary became a euphemism for the place of final punishment, for two reasons at least:

   a. The valley of Hinnom had been the source and seat of the worst kind of idolatrous worship of the Canaanite god Molech, to whom its worshipers actually sacrificed their own children by fire to it in its worship rituals. (2 Chron. 28:3; 2 Chron. 33:6)

b. King Josiah defiled the valley on account of these practices (recorded in 2 Kings 23.10), and it then became associated prophetically with judgment to be visited upon the people. (Jeremiah 7:32)

c. Gehenna was also the city's waste and carcass dump, where rubbish and offal were collected and burned outside the city, rendering the name connotatively with "extreme defilement."

d. Representative texts where Gehenna is translated "hell" in English:

(1) Matthew 10:28 – And do not fear those who kill the body but cannot kill the soul. Rather fear him who can destroy both soul and body in hell.

(2) Matthew 18:9 – And if your eye causes you to sin, tear it out and throw it away. It is better for you to enter life with one eye than with two eyes to be thrown into the hell of fire.

(3) Matthew 23:33 – You serpents, you brood of vipers, how are you to escape being sentenced to hell?

C. Other NT images of the final state:

1. The image of "torment."
Rev. 14.9-11 – And another angel, a third, followed them, saying with a loud voice, "If anyone worships the beast and its image and receives a mark on his forehead or on his hand, [10] he also will drink the wine of God's wrath, poured full strength into the cup of his anger, and he will be tormented with fire and sulfur in the presence of the holy angels and in the presence of the Lamb. [11] And the smoke of their torment goes up forever and ever, and they have no rest, day or night, these worshipers of the beast and its image, and whoever receives the mark of its name."

Lesson Seven: The Resurrection of the Dead, Final Judgment, and Eternal Punishment ■ 217

2. The image of "the bottomless pit."
   Rev. 9.1-2 – And the fifth angel blew his trumpet, and I saw a star fallen from heaven to earth, and he was given the key to the shaft of the bottomless pit.[a] 2 He opened the shaft of the bottomless pit, and from the shaft rose smoke like the smoke of a great furnace, and the sun and the air were darkened with the smoke from the shaft.
   Rev. 9.11 – They have as king over them the angel of the bottomless pit. His name in Hebrew is Abaddon, and in Greek he is called Apollyon.

3. The image of "the wrath of God."
   Rom. 2.5 – But because of your hard and impenitent heart you are storing up wrath for yourself on the day of wrath when God's righteous judgment will be revealed.

4. The image of "this condemnation."
   Jude 1:4 – For certain people have crept in unnoticed who long ago were designated for this condemnation, ungodly people, who pervert the grace of our God into sensuality and deny our only Master and Lord, Jesus Christ.

5. The image of "the second death."
   Rev. 21.8 – But as for the cowardly, the faithless, the detestable, as for murderers, the sexually immoral, sorcerers, idolaters, and all liars, their portion will be in the lake that burns with fire and sulfur, which is the second death.

6. The image of "eternal destruction and exclusion from the face of the Lord."
   2 Thessalonians 1:5-10 – This is evidence of the righteous judgment of God, that you may be considered worthy of the kingdom of God, for which you are also suffering— 6 since indeed God considers it just to repay with affliction those who afflict you, 7 and to grant relief to you who are afflicted as well as to us, when the Lord Jesus is revealed from heaven with his mighty angels [8] in flaming fire, inflicting vengeance on those who do not know God and on those who do not obey the gospel of

our Lord Jesus. [9] They will suffer the punishment of eternal destruction, away from the presence of the Lord and from the glory of his might, [10] when he comes on that day to be glorified in his saints, and to be marveled at among all who have believed, because our testimony to you was believed.

D. The most basic characteristic of hell: the absence of God.

1. The most powerful image of hell is the notion of *exclusion from the face of the Lord (the essence of "hell" and "punishment")*.

   a. Harking back to the original sin.
      Gen. 3:8 – And they heard the sound of the Lord God walking in the garden in the cool of the day, and the man and his wife hid themselves from the presence of the Lord God among the trees of the garden.

   b. Cain's mark of rebellion, murder, and idolatry.
      Gen. 4:16 – Then Cain went away from the presence of the Lord and settled in the land of Nod, east of Eden.

   c. The heart of the matter: joy in the presence of the Lord.
      Psalm 16:11 – You make known to me the path of life; in your presence there is fullness of joy; at your right hand are pleasures forevermore.

   d. The Judge's verdict on the ungodly.
      Matthew 7:23 – And then will I declare to them, 'I never knew you; depart from me, you workers of lawlessness.'

   e. The essence of the message of condemnation upon the lost.
      Matthew 25:41– Then he will say to those on his left,

'Depart from me, you cursed, into the eternal fire prepared for the devil and his angels.'

2. What does such an exclusion involve?

   a. It involves the absence of any sense of life, light, beauty, justice, or divine provision.

   b. It involves the experience of anguish, suffering, and conscious distress.

   c. It involves the unalterable destruction of one's moral and spiritual condition.

3. The essence of hell: *supreme, never-ending hopelessness and distress.*

4. The finality of the judgment is awesome.
   "When the verdict is rendered at the last judgment, the wicked will be assigned to their *final* state. To some, this seems contrary to reason, and even perhaps to Scripture. Here we encounter the concept of universalism, that is, the view that all will eventually be saved."

   Millard Erickson, Introducing Christian Doctrine, p. 411.

5. The case *for universalism:*

   a. All knees will bow, and all tongues will confess. Phil. 2.10-11 – so that at the name of Jesus every knee should bow, in heaven and on earth and under the earth, [11] and every tongue confess that Jesus Christ is Lord, to the glory of God the Father.

b. Christ died as the propitiation for the entire human population.
1 John 2.1-2 – My little children, I am writing these things to you so that you may not sin. But if anyone does sin, we have an advocate with the Father, Jesus Christ the righteous. [2] He is the propitiation for our sins, and not for ours only but also for the sins of the whole world.

c. All things have been reconciled to God in Christ.
Col. 1.19-20 – For in him all the fullness of God was pleased to dwell, 20 and through him to reconcile to himself all things, whether on earth or in heaven, making peace by the blood of his cross.

d. God will have mercy upon all.
Romans 11.32 – For God has consigned all to disobedience, that he may have mercy on all.

e. Other passages: Rom. 5.18; 11.32; 1 Cor. 15.22

6. The case *against universalism*:

a. The consignment of some to eternal punishment.
Matt. 25.46 – And these will go away into eternal punishment, but the righteous into eternal life.

b. Those who believe do not perish but receive life eternal.
John 3.16 – For God so loved the world, that he gave his only Son, that whoever believes in him should not perish but have eternal life.

c. There is a resurrection of the just, and those who are raised to judgment.
John 5.28-29 – Do not marvel at this, for an hour is coming when all who are in the tombs will hear his

voice [29] and come out, those who have done good to the resurrection of life, and those who have done evil to the resurrection of judgment.

  d. Why is there angst to preach, to win others, to know the burden of the apostles if salvation for all people is automatic and not tied to repentance and faith?

   (1) Romans 10:9-16 – because, if you confess with your mouth that Jesus is Lord and believe in your heart that God raised him from the dead, you will be saved. [10] For with the heart one believes and is justified, and with the mouth one confesses and is saved. [11] For the Scripture says, "Everyone who believes in him will not be put to shame." [12] For there is no distinction between Jew and Greek; the same Lord is Lord of all, bestowing his riches on all who call on him. [13] For "everyone who calls on the name of the Lord will be saved." [14] But how are they to call on him in whom they have not believed? And how are they to believe in him of whom they have never heard? And how are they to hear without someone preaching? [15] And how are they to preach unless they are sent? As it is written, "How beautiful are the feet of those who preach the good news!" [16] But they have not all obeyed the gospel. For Isaiah says, "Lord, who has believed what he has heard from us?"

   (2) Acts 26:17-18 – delivering you from your people and from the Gentiles— to whom I am sending you [18] to open their eyes, so that they may turn from darkness to light and from the power of Satan to God, that they may receive forgiveness of sins and a place among those who are sanctified by faith in me.

 E. The character of future punishment: Annihilationism and theories of the final state of the wicked.

1. Again, the future judgment is irreversible and eternal.

   "Once passed, the judgment will be permanent and irrevocable."

   Millard Erickson

2. It is important to note that the Bible gives the clear sense that *everyone will not be saved,* as well as the idea that *there will be no eternal punishment!*

3. Annihilationism:
   This school maintains that although some will not be saved, there remains only a single class of future existence.

   a. Those who are saved will experience unending life.

   b. Those who are not saved will be eliminated or annihilated, i.e., cease to exist.

   c. The root of the argument:

      (1) God is s a God of love and kindness.

      (2) God's mercy will temper his judgment.

      (3) No person, however sinful, deserves endless suffering and torture.

4. Forms of annihilationism:

   a. *Form 1:* The extinction of the evil person is a direct result of sin. Sin is essentially *self-destruction.*

   b. *Form 2:* God cannot and will not allow the sinful person to possess eternal life. The end of the wicked

is built into the very fabric of biblical thinking and argument.

5. The response to annihilationism: It appears to contradict the clear teaching of Scripture.

   a. The punishment of sinners in the final state is compared to "unquenchable fire."
      Mark 9.48 – where their worm does not die and the fire is not quenched.'

   b. Words like "eternal," "everlasting," and "forever" are used to refer to the future state of the wicked.

      (1) Isaiah 33:14 – The sinners in Zion are afraid; trembling has seized the godless: "Who among us can dwell with the consuming fire? Who among us can dwell with *everlasting burnings?*"

      (2) Jeremiah 17:4 – You shall loosen your hand from your heritage that I gave to you, and I will make you serve your enemies in a land that you do not know, for *in my anger a fire is kindled that shall burn forever.*"

      (3) Matthew 18:8 – And if your hand or your foot causes you to sin, cut it off and throw it away. It is better for you to enter life crippled or lame than with two hands or two feet to be thrown into *the eternal fire.*

      (4) Matthew 25:41 – Then he will say to those on his left, 'Depart from me, you cursed, into *the eternal fire prepared for the devil and his angels.*

      (5) Jude 1:7 – just as Sodom and Gomorrah and the surrounding cities, which likewise indulged in sexual immorality and pursued unnatural desire, serve as an example by undergoing a *punishment of eternal fire.*

c. The nature of the end corresponds to the state of endless . . .

    "contempt"   (Dan.12.2)
    "destruction"   (2 Thess. 1.9)
    "chains"   (Jude 6)
    "torment"   (Rev. 14.11; 20.10)
    "punishment"   (Matt. 25.46)

d. The question of the essence of God's holiness in himself:
How can God who is infinite in holiness be truly satisfied by a finite punishment?

e. The question of the essence of God's goodness and love:
How does the notion of endless suffering correspond to what we know of God as revealed in the humility and grace of Jesus of Nazareth?

6. The answer to this question:
The final state is merely giving to humankind what they have always wanted since the Fall – absolute non-interference from God forever.

a. God does not consign anyone to hell, but merely selects those whom he will for redemption: *All would go to hell if he chose not to save some!*

(1) Romans 8:28-30 – And we know that for those who love God all things work together for good, for those who are called according to his purpose. [29] For those whom he foreknew he also predestined to be conformed to the image of his Son, in order that he might be the firstborn among many brothers. [30] And those whom he predestined he also called, and those whom he called he also justified, and those whom he justified he also glorified.

(2) Romans 9:14-18 – What shall we say then? Is there injustice on God's part? By no means! [15] For he says to Moses, "I will have mercy on whom I have mercy, and I will have compassion on whom I have compassion." [16] So then it depends not on human will or exertion, but on God, who has mercy. [17] For the Scripture says to Pharaoh, "For this very purpose I have raised you up, that I might show my power in you, and that my name might be proclaimed in all the earth." [18] So then he has mercy on whomever he wills, and he hardens whomever he wills.

b. God's gracious provision and intervention is the operative cause of everyone accepting the grace of God in Christ.

(1) Matthew 11:25 – At that time Jesus declared, "I thank you, Father, Lord of heaven and earth, that you have hidden these things from the wise and understanding and revealed them to little children;

(2) John 1:12-13 – But to all who did receive him, who believed in his name, he gave the right to become children of God, [13] who were born, not of blood nor of the will of the flesh nor of the will of man, but of God.

c. The hardness of human hearts and the perversity of sin ensures that every person who rejects the grace of God in Christ are themselves responsible for their state, and not God himself.

7. What of those who have never heard of the Good news of God in Jesus Christ?

a. Those who knew more will be more accountable for what they knew and rejected.
Matt. 11.21-24 – "Woe to you, Chorazin! Woe to

you, Bethsaida! For if the mighty works done in you had been done in Tyre and Sidon, they would have repented long ago in sackcloth and ashes. [22] But I tell you, it will be more bearable on the day of judgment for Tyre and Sidon than for you. [23] And you, Capernaum, will you be exalted to heaven? You will be brought down to Hades. For if the mighty works done in you had been done in Sodom, it would have remained until this day. [24] But I tell you that it will be more tolerable on the day of judgment for the land of Sodom than for you."

b. The measure of punishment appears to be based upon the measure of knowledge, which determines the culpability before God.
Luke 12.47-48 – And that servant who knew his master's will but did not get ready or act according to his will, will receive a severe beating. [48] But the one who did not know, and did what deserved a beating, will receive a light beating. Everyone to whom much was given, of him much will be required, and from him to whom they entrusted much, they will demand the more.

c. This is the difference:
> *Objective* (the actual level of pain);
> *Subjective* (the awareness of the pain of the separation from God).

d. The heart of the matter:

The misery they will experience from having to live with their wicked self eternally will be proportionate to their degree of awareness of precisely what they were doing when they chose evil!"

Millard Erickson

IV. **Conclusion**

....

From Agent of Hell to Soldier of Christ

Luis Palau tells of a woman in Peru whose life was radically transformed by the power of Christ. Rosario was her name. She was a terrorist, a brute of a woman who was an expert in several martial arts. In her terrorist activities she had killed twelve policemen. When Luis conducted a crusade in Lima, she learned of it and, being incensed at the message of the gospel, made her way to the stadium to kill Luis. Inside the stadium, as she contemplated how to get to him, she began to listen to the message he preached on hell. She fell under conviction for her sins and embraced Christ as her Savior. *Ten years later,* Luis met this convert for the first time. She had by then assisted in the planting of five churches; was a vibrant, active witness and worker in the church; and had founded an orphanage that houses over one thousand children.

....

Rev. 22:12-15 – Behold, I am coming soon, bringing my recompense with me, to repay everyone for what he has done. [13] I am the Alpha and the Omega, the first and the last, the beginning and the end." [14] Blessed are those who wash their robes, so that they may have the right to the tree of life and that they may enter the city by the gates. [15] Outside are the dogs and sorcerers and the sexually immoral and murderers and idolaters, and everyone who loves and practices falsehood.

- This life is transitory; we ought to live our lives with eternity in mind.

- What lies ahead is infinitely more important than what we are facing today.

- The life to come cannot be adequately measured against the struggles of today.

- The essence of hell is exclusion from the presence and face of the loving God who gave us his Son as a sacrifice for sin.

The Bottom Line: _____

Lesson Eight
The Blessed Hope: The New Heavens and Earth and the Consummated Kingdom of God

....

*The Blessed Hope of "Thy Kingdom Come!"
Produces Intensity, Desire, Humility, and Certainty– At the Same Time!*

A sharp, dualistic separation between the present and future, as if the eschaton were a reality presently strange and completely unknowable, is definitely unbiblical. just as the Catechism relates the second petition of the Lord's Prayer to our continuous submission "more and more" to Word and Spirit (Q. 123), so also the eschatological preaching and promise always continue to function in the present as comfort and admonition. Naturally, this doxology is related to die eschaton, but it is by no means foreign to life in the present. The doxological is essentially linked with true faith and love. This song of praise is not a powerless recognition of and subjection to the power of Christ like the confession of the man with an unclean spirit: "1 know who you are, the Holy One of God" (Mark 1:24; cf. 3:11). No, it is a doxology in countless forms, replete with worship, gratitude, meekness, and praise. In our present earthly life, with its "not yet," this doxology comes when the word of Christ dwells in us richly as we sing "psalms and hymns and spiritual songs" with thankfulness in our hearts to God (Col. 3:16).

The doxology, as long as it is sung on the earth, continues to be overshadowed by the deficiencies that characterize this life, including religious egocentrism. But unless the powers of the age to come operate in this life (Fief). 6:5) , our perspective on the eschaton will fade, and the harmony of prayer, thankfulness and watchfulness will be disrupted (Col. 4:2f.) ." Eschatology then simply degenerates into a last chapter of dogmatics, an irrelevant futurism lacking any appeal, a future age with no word for the present. The doxology is silenced; and when that happens a great crisis in perseverance results, for only the doxology offers resistance against the pitfalls, temptations, and darkness that still lurk in the present dispensation of "not yet."

So, the whole of the eschatological expectation can finally be recapitulated in the well-known petition "Thy Kingdom come." If we understand it anywhere, we understand here that our prayers too are tested, tested for the seriousness with which they take their place in the Christian life. On this point the gospel is clear: the prayer "Thy Kingdom come" is unreal and worthless unless its meaning and its consequences are understood. Numerous questions in the area of eschatology remain to remind us that we still see only in a mirror, dimly (1 Cor. 13:12) . But none of these riddles threatens the clarity of the eschatological call, a challenge that can be heard and understood in this time of the "not yet." The way to that which is to be revealed has its beginnings in what is already revealed. This is the full meaning of the earthly pilgrimage to the future. This is the pilgrimage Paul describes to the Philippians: "Brethren, I not consider that I have made it my own; but one thing I do, forgetting what lies behind and straining forward to what lies ahead, I press on toward the goal for the prize of the upward call of God in Christ Jesus" (3.13f.). This expectation is profoundly affected by the "not yet," but it also recognizes itself to be on the way on which no one goes astray. It spells intensity, desire, humility, and certainty.

G. C. Berkouwer, The Return of Christ.
Grand Rapids: Eerdmans Publishing Company, 1972, pp. 450-452.

I. The Story of God: The King of Kings Shall Finally Reign!

All the sweep of redemptive history is divided into two ages separated by the Day of the Lord. The New Testament adds several important features to this [understanding]: the Day of the Lord will witness the coming of the Son of Man, the resurrection of the dead, and the judgment of men. This is emphasized by Paul when he speaks of the victorious reign of Christ. Speaking of the resurrection Paul says, "Christ the first fruits, then at his coming those who belong to Christ. Then comes the end, when he delivers the kingdom to God the Father after destroying every rule and every authority and power. For he must reign until he has put all his enemies under his feet. The last enemy to be destroyed is death" (I Cor. 15:23-26). Here we have what amounts to a definition of the Kingdom of God. *The Kingdom of God is the redemptive rule of God in Christ, destroying his enemies and by implication bringing to his people the blessing of his reign.*

"This makes several conclusions inescapable. The Kingdom of God is the work of God, not of men; nowhere do we find the idiom, much used in some circles, of building the Kingdom of God. To be sure, they may proclaim the work of the Kingdom (Matt. 24:14; Acts 8:12; 28:31), but the Kingdom is ever and always God's Kingdom, God's rule. Furthermore, it is clear that the Kingdom will not triumph in this age. This age remains evil until evil is purged out of his Kingdom by the Son of Man. Again, this shows why the Second Coming of Christ is essential to a biblical theology: apart from his victorious return, there will be no final victory over sin, Satan, and death. However, God's Kingdom is sure to come; all the promises of God remain unfulfilled apart from Christ's return. Finally, this theology of the Kingdom of God makes it clear that God's redemptive purpose is not merely a way of salvation for individual souls; it is a purpose for history. We have already tried to make this clear in the chapter on the Second Coming of Christ. Because God has already intervened in history, history has a purpose and a goal; rather we should say that "redemptive" history has a purpose and a goal: the Kingdom of God."

– George Eldon Ladd, The Last Things.
Grand Rapids: Eerdmans, 1978, pp. 107-108.

1 Corinthians 15:22-28 – For as in Adam all die, so also in Christ shall all be made alive. [23] But each in his own order: Christ the firstfruits, then at his coming those who belong to Christ. [24] Then comes the end, when he delivers the kingdom to God the Father after destroying every rule and every authority and power. [25] For he must reign until he has put all his enemies under his feet. [26] The last enemy to be destroyed is death. [27] For " God has put all things in subjection under his feet." But when it says, "all things are put in subjection," it is plain that he is excepted who put all things in subjection under him. [28] When all things are subjected to him, then the Son himself will also be subjected to him who put all things in subjection under him, that God may be all in all.

A. The risen and glorified Jesus of Nazareth is in truth *Christ the Lord*.

   1. To God alone belongs the Kingdom.

       a. Psalm 10:16 – The Lord is king forever and ever; the nations perish from his land.

       b. Psalm 24:1-2 – The earth is the Lord's and the fullness thereof, the world and those who dwell therein, [2] for he has founded it upon the seas and established it upon the rivers.

       c. Psalm 24:10 – Who is this King of glory? The Lord of hosts, he is the King of glory! Selah

       d. Psalm 47:7-8 – For God is the King of all the earth; sing praises with a psalm! [8] God reigns over the nations; God sits on his holy throne.

       e. Jeremiah 10:7 – Who would not fear you, O King of the nations? For this is your due; for among all the

wise ones of the nations and in all their kingdoms there is none like you.

2. God is King of the universe, of the nations, and of Israel!

   a. Isaiah 33:22 – For the Lord is our judge; the Lord is our lawgiver; the Lord is our king; he will save us.

   b. Isaiah 44:6 – Thus says the Lord, the King of Israel and his Redeemer, the Lord of hosts: "I am the first and I am the last; besides me there is no god."

3. The story will end with the entrance of the Kingdom of God in the earth, with the glorified Jesus ruling forever as Lord.

   a. He is the great Son of the Most High.
   Luke 1:32-33 – He will be great and will be called the Son of the Most High. And the Lord God will give to him the throne of his father David, [33] and he will reign over the house of Jacob forever, and of his kingdom there will be no end.

   b. He is the Savior, Messiah, the Lord.
   Luke 2:11 – For unto you is born this day in the city of David a Savior, who is Christ the Lord.

   c. He is David's Lord, whose enemies will finally cringe under his feet.
   Matt.22.41-45 – Now while the Pharisees were gathered together, Jesus asked them a question, [42] saying, "What do you think about the Christ? Whose son is he?" They said to him, "The son of David." [43] He said to them, "How is it then that David, in the Spirit, calls him Lord, saying, [44] " 'The Lord said to my Lord, Sit at my right hand, until I put

your enemies under your feet'? [45] If then David calls him Lord, how is he his son?"

4. The same Jesus who was crucified God has made both *kyrios* and *christos*.
Acts 2.36 – Let all the house of Israel therefore know for certain that God has made him both Lord and Christ, this Jesus whom you crucified.

B. All the promises regarding the "Son of David" will finally be fulfilled in the consummated Kingdom of God.

1. The prophetic cry of dying Jacob regarding Judah will come to pass.

    a. From Judah, the anointed One will come.
    Gen. 49:10 – The scepter shall not depart from Judah, nor the ruler's staff from between his feet, until tribute comes to him; and to him shall be the obedience of the peoples.

    b. The risen Jesus is identified as the Lion of the tribe of Judah, the Root of David.
    Rev. 5:5 – And one of the elders said to me, "Weep no more; behold, the Lion of the tribe of Judah, the Root of David, has conquered, so that he can open the scroll and its seven seals."

2. The star to come out of Jacob will have dominion forever.
Num. 24:17-19 – I see him, but not now; I behold him, but not near: a star shall come out of Jacob, and a scepter shall rise out of Israel; it shall crush the forehead of Moab and break down all the sons of Sheth. [18] Edom shall be dispossessed; Seir also, his enemies, shall be dispossessed. Israel is doing valiantly. [19] And one from Jacob shall exercise dominion and destroy the survivors of cities!"

3. The promise given to David will finally be fulfilled.
   2 Sam. 7.12-16 – When your days are fulfilled and you lie down with your fathers, I will raise up your offspring after you, who shall come from your body, and I will establish his kingdom. [13] He shall build a house for my name, and I will establish the throne of his kingdom forever. [14] I will be to him a father, and he shall be to me a son. When he commits iniquity, I will discipline him with the rod of men, with the stripes of the sons of men, [15] but my steadfast love will not depart from him, as I took it from Saul, whom I put away from before you. [16] And your house and your kingdom shall be made sure forever before me. Your throne shall be established forever.

4. The anointed seed of David to reign forever will be fulfilled in Christ's glorious and just reign.

   a. God swore oath to David.
      Psalm 89:20 – I have found David, my servant; with my holy oil I have anointed him.

   b. God committed to provide a King on the throne.
      Psalm 89:29 – I will establish his offspring forever and his throne as the days of the heavens.

   c. David's offspring would forever endure.
      Psalm 89:36-37 – His offspring shall endure forever, his throne as long as the sun before me. [37] Like the moon it shall be established forever, a faithful witness in the skies." Selah

   d. Peter spoke of David's prophetic insight.
      Acts 2:30-31 – Being therefore a prophet, and knowing that God had sworn with an oath to him that he would set one of his descendants on his throne, [31] he foresaw and spoke about the resurrection of the Christ, that he was not abandoned to Hades, nor did his flesh see corruption.

5. Even after the destruction of Jerusalem and the dethroning of the last King of Judah by Nebuchadnezzar in 585 B.C., God promised to restore David's fallen "house" (kingdom).
Amos 9:11 – In that day I will raise up the booth of David that is fallen and repair its breaches, and raise up its ruins and rebuild it as in the days of old.

6. Jesus is the Son of David of the flesh.

    a. Joseph was of the family of David. (Matt. 1.16; Luke 1.27)

    b. By inference, Mary was also of the family of David. (Matt. 1.1-17; Luke 3.23-38)

    c. Notice the word of Gabriel to Mary. (Luke 1.31-32)

    d. Jesus was referred to as the "son of David" on numerous occasions. (Matt. 12.23; Mark 10.47; cf. Zech. 9.9 with Matt. 21.5-9)

C. The "King of Kings" throughout this age has been proclaimed King and Lord in heaven.

1. Figuratively, Jesus has gone away to be invested with royal authority, and then to return to rule in power. (Luke 19.12)

2. The ascended Jesus now sits at the right hand of God while the Father makes a footstool for his feet out of his enemies.

a. Mark 16:19 – So then the Lord Jesus, after he had spoken to them, was taken up into heaven and sat down at the right hand of God.

b. Acts 2:32-36 – This Jesus God raised up, and of that we all are witnesses. [33] Being therefore exalted at the right hand of God and having received from the Father the promise of the Holy Spirit, he has poured out this that you yourselves are seeing and hearing. [34] For David did not ascend into the heavens, but he himself says, " 'The Lord said to my Lord, Sit at my right hand, until I make your enemies your footstool.' Let all the house of Israel therefore know for certain that God has made him both Lord and Christ, this Jesus whom you crucified."

3. God has established our Lord in heaven with absolute authority and power, both for this world and the next, in preparation for his reign to come.

   a. The ground of the Great Commission. (Matt. 28.18-20)

   b. The essence of his session in heaven. (Eph. 1.20-22)

   c. The necessary result of his humiliation upon the Cross, and the Father's subsequent glorification of him. (Phil. 2.9-11)

4. The coronation of Jesus Christ in the heavens is not presently and finally established on earth.
   Heb. 2.8 – Now in putting everything in subjection to him, he left nothing outside his control.

D. At the consummation of the Kingdom, our Lord Jesus will in fact take full possession of his Kingdom.

1. In the end, the kingdoms of this world will in fact become the Kingdom of our God and of our Lord Jesus. Revelation 11:15-18 – Then the seventh angel blew his trumpet, and there were loud voices in heaven, saying, "The kingdom of the world has become the kingdom of our Lord and of his Christ, and he shall reign forever and ever." [16] And the twenty-four elders who sit on their thrones before God fell on their faces and worshiped God, [17] saying, "We give thanks to you, Lord God Almighty, who is and who was, for you have taken your great power and begun to reign. [18] The nations raged, but your wrath came, and the time for the dead to be judged, and for rewarding your servants, the prophets and saints, and those who fear your name, both small and great, and for destroying the destroyers of the earth."

2. Dominion, glory, and a kingdom will be given to Christ Jesus over all the earth and its peoples.
Dan. 7.13-14 – I saw in the night visions, and behold, with the clouds of heaven there came one like a son of man, and he came to the Ancient of Days and was presented before him. [14] And to him was given dominion and glory and a kingdom, that all peoples, nations, and languages should serve him; his dominion is an everlasting dominion, which shall not pass away, and his kingdom one that shall not be destroyed.

3. The nations and the extremities of the earth will be given to Christ as his inheritance forever.
Ps. 2.5-8 – Then he will speak to them in his wrath, and terrify them in his fury, saying, [6] "As for me, I have set my King on Zion, my holy hill." [7] I will tell of the decree: The Lord said to me, "You are my Son; today I have begotten you. [8] Ask of me, and I will make the nations your heritage, and the ends of the earth your possession.

E. The majesty and glory of the coming Kingdom will boggle the mind and astound the heart!

1. His throne is forever, and the scepter of his kingdom is one of equity. All forms of oppression and injustice will end.
   Ps. 45.4-6 – In your majesty ride out victoriously for the cause of truth and meekness and righteousness; let your right hand teach you awesome deeds!
   [5] Your arrows are sharp in the heart of the king's enemies; the peoples fall under you. [6] Your throne, O God, is forever and ever. The scepter of your kingdom is a scepter of uprightness;

2. Of the increase of his government and peace there will be neither limit nor end, establishing his reign with absolute justice and righteousness.
   Isa. 9.6-7 – For to us a child is born, to us a son is given; and the government shall be upon[a] his shoulder, and his name shall be called Wonderful Counselor, Mighty God, Everlasting Father, Prince of Peace.
   [7] Of the increase of his government and of peace there will be no end, on the throne of David and over his kingdom, to establish it and to uphold it with justice and with righteousness from this time forth and forevermore. The zeal of the Lord of hosts will do this.

3. The Spirit of the Lord will rest upon him.
   Isaiah 11:2 – And the Spirit of the Lord shall rest upon him, the Spirit of wisdom and understanding, the Spirit of counsel and might, the Spirit of knowledge and the fear of the Lord.

4. His reign will be a banner for all peoples, and the nations will turn to him.
   Isaiah 11:10 – In that day the root of Jesse, who shall stand as a signal for the peoples—of him shall the nations inquire, and his resting place shall be glorious.

5. All people will see him glorified in his magnificence.

   a. Isaiah 33:17 – Your eyes will behold the king in his beauty; they will see a land that stretches afar.

b. Isaiah 33:22 – For the Lord is our judge; the Lord is our lawgiver; the Lord is our king; he will save us.

6. He will announce justice to the nations and will not fail until justice is established to the very ends of the earth.
Isaiah 42:1-4 – Behold my servant, whom I uphold, my chosen, in whom my soul delights; I have put my Spirit upon him; he will bring forth justice to the nations. [2] He will not cry aloud or lift up his voice or make it heard in the street; [3] a bruised reed he will not break, and a faintly burning wick he will not quench; he will faithfully bring forth justice. [4] He will not grow faint or be discouraged till he has established justice in the earth; and the coastlands wait for his law.

7. His rule will be a light to the Gentiles that the salvation of the Lord will be in effect to the very ends of the earth.
Isa. 49.6 – I will make you as a light for the nations, that my salvation may reach to the end of the earth.

8. He will execute justice and righteousness in the land of God's people.
Jer. 23.5-6 – Behold, the days are coming, declares the Lord, when I will raise up for David a righteous Branch, and he shall reign as king and deal wisely, and shall execute justice and righteousness in the land. [6] In his days Judah will be saved, and Israel will dwell securely. And this is the name by which he will be called: 'The Lord is our righteousness.'

9. David will never lack a successor to sit on his throne.
Jer. 33.17 – For thus says the Lord: David shall never lack a man to sit on the throne of the house of Israel.

10. His majesty, power, and greatness shall extend to the ends of the earth.

a. Great peace shall belong to this earth through him.
Micah 5.4-5 – And he shall stand and shepherd his flock in the strength of the Lord, in the majesty of the name of the Lord his God. And they shall dwell secure, for now he shall be great to the ends of the earth. [5] And he shall be their peace.

b. A Priest will be on his throne.
Zechariah 6:12-13 – And say to him, 'Thus says the Lord of hosts, "Behold, the man whose name is the Branch: for he shall branch out from his place, and he shall build the temple of the Lord. [13] It is he who shall build the temple of the Lord and shall bear royal honor and shall sit and rule on his throne. And there shall be a priest on his throne, and the counsel of peace shall be between them both."

c. He will rule to the ends of the earth.
Zechariah 9:9-10 – Rejoice greatly, O daughter of Zion! Shout aloud, O daughter of Jerusalem! behold, your king is coming to you; righteous and having salvation is he, humble and mounted on a donkey, on a colt, the foal of a donkey. [10] I will cut off the chariot from Ephraim and the war horse from Jerusalem; and the battle bow shall be cut off, and he shall speak peace to the nations; his rule shall be from sea to sea, and from the River to the ends of the earth.

F. Summary

1. Jesus of Nazareth is the fulfillment of the Old Testament promise for an heir on David's throne who would defeat Satan, reverse the effects of the Curse, destroy death, and establish an eternal kingdom of righteousness and peace.

2. The blessed hope, therefore, of the Hebrew and Christian scriptures are one and the same: the hope of the consummation of the Kingdom of God.

3. All things in this age are speedily moving towards the consummation of these promises at a time predetermined and pre-set by the sovereignty of Almighty God.

II. After The Millennium: The Inauguration of the Age to Come

"Today, Sir, I Expect him Today!"

At the *Villa Asconati,* along the shore of Lake Como, Italy, a tourist was introduced to a friendly older man who cared for the castle's garden. The grounds were immaculate, and the gardener was doing everything he could to further improve their beauty. To his surprise, the tourist discovered that the owner of this castle had not been on the property in twelve years. He seemed confused by the man's compulsion for perfection when the owner had not appeared in over a decade.

So he said, "You keep this garden in such fine condition, just as though you expected your master to come tomorrow."

The gardener promptly replied, "Today, sir, today!"

Brian Harbour, *Living Expectantly,* 1990, p.13)

Revelation 21:1-5 – Then I saw a new heaven and a new earth, for the first heaven and the first earth had passed away, and the sea was no more. [2] And I saw the holy city, new Jerusalem, coming down out of heaven from God, prepared as a bride adorned for her husband. [3] And I heard a loud voice from the throne saying, "Behold, the dwelling place of God is with man. He will dwell with them, and they will be his people, and God himself will be with them as their God. [4] He will wipe away every tear from their eyes, and death shall be no more, neither shall there be mourning nor crying nor pain anymore, for the former things have passed away." [5] And he who was seated on

the throne said, "Behold, I am making all things new." Also he said, "Write this down, for these words are trustworthy and true."

A. The apocalyptic focus of the Age to Come: The Holy City, the New Jerusalem.

1. A new heaven and new earth come into being.

    a. Isaiah 65:17-19 – For behold, **I create new heavens and a new earth,** and **the former things shall not be remembered or come into mind.** [18] But be glad and rejoice forever in that which I create; for behold, I create Jerusalem to be a joy, and her people to be a gladness. [19] I will rejoice in Jerusalem and be glad in my people; no more shall be heard in it the sound of weeping and the cry of distress.

    b. Isaiah 66:22 – For as **the new heavens and the new earth that I make shall remain before me,** says the Lord, **so shall your offspring and your name remain.**

    c. 2 Peter 3:13 – But according to his promise **we are waiting for new heavens and a new earth** in which righteousness dwells.

    d. Rev. 21:5 – And he who was seated on the throne said, **"Behold, I am making all things new."** Also he said, "Write this down, for these words are trustworthy and true."

2. The New Jerusalem will descend to the earth. Revelation 21.2-3 – And I saw the holy city, new Jerusalem, coming down out of heaven from God, prepared as a bride adorned for her husband. [3] "Behold, the dwelling place of God is with man. He will dwell with them, and they will be his people, and God himself will be with them as their God.

3. *"Here is an important fact: The ultimate scene of the Kingdom of God is earthly. It is a transformed earth to be sure, but it is still an earthly destiny. Scripture everywhere teaches this. Paul says that "the creation itself will be set free from bondage to decay and obtain the glorious liberty of the children of God." (Rom. 8.21)*

   Ladd, *The Last Things*, p. 112.

4. Excursus:
   Human life begins in a Garden, but it ends and is consummated in a City.

   a. The uncircumcised and unclean will no longer enter it.
      Isaiah 52:1 – Awake, awake, put on your strength, O Zion; put on your beautiful garments, O Jerusalem, the holy city; for **there shall no more come into you the uncircumcised and the unclean.**

   b. It will be a habitation of righteousness, a holy hill.
      Jeremiah 31:23 – Thus says the Lord of hosts, the God of Israel: "Once more they shall use these words in the land of Judah and in its cities, when I restore their fortunes: " '**The Lord bless you, O habitation of righteousness, O holy hill!'**

   c. God is its builder and designer.
      Hebrews 11:10 – For he was looking forward to **the city that has foundations, whose designer and builder is God.** (Cf. John 14.2-3)

   d. We are spiritually of the divine mount of God, Mount Zion.
      Hebrews 12:22 – But **you have come to Mount Zion and to the city of the living God, the heavenly Jerusalem,** and to innumerable angels in festal gathering.

  e. It is our lasting city; we have no city here.
   Hebrews 13:14 – For here we have no lasting city, but **we seek the city that is to come.**

  f. Christ will write upon us: the name of God, the name of the city, and our own new name.
   Rev. 3:12 – The one who conquers, I will make him a pillar in the temple of my God. Never shall he go out of it, and **I will write on him the name of my God, and the name of the city of my God, the new Jerusalem, which comes down from my God out of heaven,** and my own new name.

5. What of its dimensions? (1,500 miles square)
"The description of the new redeemed earth is highly symbolic. The heavenly city, the new Jerusalem, is pictured as a gigantic cube in shape; it is fifteen hundred miles long, fifteen hundred miles wide, and fifteen hundred miles high (Rev. 21.16). This is obviously a symbolic measurement; it staggers the imagination. The city is surrounded by a wall which is only some two hundred feet high. Why does the heavenly Jerusalem need a wall at all? A wall of two hundred feet is utterly out of proportion to a city fifteen hundred miles high. The answer is not difficult: *all ancient cities had walls and John portrayed heavenly realities in earthly language and idiom.* The city has twelve gates, each gate a single pearl, representing the twelve tribes of Israel (Rev. 21.12, 21) The streets of the city are like nothing ever seen on earth: transparent gold (Rev. 21.21)."

Ladd, *The Last Things*, pp. 112-113.

B. The heart of the matter: *The dwelling of God is with humankind.* This will represent the consummation of the entire redemption story, the culmination of the hope of all the sages and saints of the ages, and the appropriate end of salvation itself.

1. Several realities that are currently impossible to be true in this age shall become literally true in the Age to Come.

    a. The very dwelling place of God will forever be with humankind (i.e., no barrier of sin or stain will ever separate us from the presence of God again!).
    Rev. 21:3-4 – And I heard a loud voice from the throne saying, "Behold, **the dwelling place of God is with man**. He will dwell with them, and they will be his people, and **God himself will be with them as their God.**

    b. All forms of human remorse, shame, fear, or dread will be eliminated, with no presence of death ever again to be felt or thought of.
    Rev. 21.4 – **He will wipe away every tear from their eyes, and death shall be no more, neither shall there be mourning nor crying nor pain anymore, for the former things have passed away.**

    c. The redeemed of the Lord will *see his face!*
    Rev. 22:3-5 – No longer will there be anything accursed, but the throne of God and of the Lamb will be in it, and his servants will worship him. [4] They will see his face, and his name will be on their foreheads. [5] And night will be no more. **They will need no light of lamp or sun, for the Lord God will be their light, and they will reign forever and ever.**

2. The impossible reality in this world (e.g., beholding God's "face" directly) will become the life of the Age to Come.

    a. The hope of the Christmas anthem *Messiah* will be seen.
    Isaiah 40:5 – And **the glory of the Lord shall be revealed,** and **all flesh shall see it together,** for the mouth of the Lord has spoken."

b. The blessed joy of the pure in heart will be seen.
Matthew 5:8 – Blessed are **the pure in heart,** for **they shall see God.**

c. We will be with the Lord Jesus *where he is.*
John 12:26 – If anyone serves me, he must follow me; and **where I am, there will my servant be also.** If anyone serves me, the Father will honor him.

d. The heart prayer of the risen Savior is for us to see his glory.
John 17:24 – Father, I desire that they also, whom you have given me, may be with me where I am, **to see my glory that you have given me** because you loved me before the foundation of the world.

e. The apostolic imagination of the Age to Come: "Then I shall know fully."
1 Cor. 13:12 – For now we see in a mirror dimly, but then face to face. Now I know in part; **then I shall know fully, even as I have been fully known.**

f. Holiness is its requirement.
Hebrews 12:14 – Strive for peace with everyone, and **for the holiness without which no one will see the Lord.**

g. The look of glory will transform us.
1 John 3:2 – Beloved, we are God's children now, and what we will be has not yet appeared; but we know that when he appears **we shall be like him, because we shall see him as he is.**

3. The redemptive purpose of God for the universe will be utterly fulfilled.

a. No promises will be left undone or unclaimed.

b. No prophecies will be left unfulfilled.

c. No Scripture will be left without true and eternal fulfillment.

4. All enemies will have been placed under the feet of Christ (the *pluperfect* [future perfect] *tense in the Greek language*).

   a. The devil and his spirit minions will have been forever cast into the lake of fire.

   b. The Antichrist and the beast will meet the same fate as the devil.

   c. All manner of sin and iniquity, along with the curse and its effects on creation will be no more – forever.

   d. Death and its entire entourage of fear, heartache, brokenness, and helplessness will forever be cast away, never to be seen again.

5. All the saints (i.e., those who held on by faith to the promise of eternal life through the Messiah of God, Jesus of Nazareth) will be together united on a redeemed earth in perfected harmony and *koinonia* in worship and service to God.
   Rev. 21:9-12 – Then came one of the seven angels who had the seven bowls full of the seven last plagues and spoke to me, saying, "Come, I will show you the Bride, the wife of the Lamb." [10] And he carried me away in the Spirit to a great, high mountain, and showed me **the holy city Jerusalem coming down out of heaven from God, [11] having the glory of God, its radiance like a most rare jewel, like a jasper, clear as crystal. [12]** It had a great, high wall, with twelve gates, and at the gates twelve angels, and on the gates the names of the twelve

tribes of the sons of Israel were inscribed [13] on the east three gates, on the north three gates, on the south three gates, and on the west three gates. [14] And the wall of the city had twelve foundations, and on them were the twelve names of the twelve apostles of the Lamb.

C. Doxological elements of the Age to Come:

1. Blessedness of communion with God in a new heavens and new earth.
   2 Pet. 3.13 – But according to his promise we are waiting for new heavens and a new earth in which righteousness dwells.

2. Eternal life–never ending days–of meaningful service and worship of God in the midst of his people. This life will be anchored and fed by the inexhaustible life which is in God, the I AM THAT I AM.
   Exo. 3.14 – God said to Moses, "I am who I am." And he said, "Say this to the people of Israel: 'I am has sent me to you.'"

3. The "Vision Beatific and Beautiful:"
   The redeemed will actually dwell in the presence of God, beholding his glory directly. They will see his face.
   Rev. 22:4 – **They will see his face, and his name will be on their foreheads.**

   a. This involves beholding God face to face, described as "knowing even as we are known." (i.e., 1 Cor. 13.12)

   b. This intimate vision will eliminate the need for liturgy as a *means*. All liturgy and worship will be an *end*, for we will be in the very presence of God himself continually and forever. (Could this be the meaning of no need for light, sun, or Temple in the New Jerusalem–*why would there be?*)

(1) Rev. 22:5 – And night will be no more. They will need **no light of lamp or sun, for the Lord God will be their light**, and they will reign forever and ever.

(2) Rev. 21:22-23 – And I saw no temple in the city, for its temple is the Lord God the Almighty and the Lamb. [23] And the city has **no need of sun or moon to shine on it, for the glory of God gives it light, and its lamp is the Lamb.**

c. Its light and glory will illumine the entire world.
Rev. 21.24-26 – **By its light will the nations walk, and the kings of the earth will bring their glory into it,** [25] and its gates will never be shut by day—and there will be no night there. [26] They will bring into it the glory and the honor of the nations.

d. Only those whose names are written in the Lamb's book of life will ever enter this glorious city, or see its beauty.
Rev. 21.27 – But nothing unclean will ever enter it, nor anyone who does what is detestable or false, but **only those who are written in the Lamb's book of life.**

4. The curse and all death will be at an end. All vestiges of the Fall will be abolished and eliminated.
Rev. 21:4 – He will wipe away every tear from their eyes, and death shall be no more, neither shall there be mourning nor crying nor pain anymore, for **the former things have passed away.**

a. The current heaven and earth will be transformed. It will "pass away."
Matthew 24:35 – **Heaven and earth will pass away,** but my words will not pass away.

b. The world in its current form is passing away (i.e., the creation which is subject to bondage, and the

wicked world system under the control of Satan).
1 Cor. 7:31 – and those who deal with the world as though they had no dealings with it. For **the present form of this world is passing away.**

c. A cleansing and refreshing by fire is coming upon the heavens and earth.
2 Peter 3:10 – But the day of the Lord will come like a thief, and then the heavens will pass away with a roar, and **the heavenly bodies will be burned up and dissolved,** and the earth and the works that are done on it will be exposed.

d. The system of the world's greed, lust, and pride are on the way out.
1 John 2:17 – And **the world is passing away along with its desires,** but whoever does the will of God abides forever.

e. The end of the "sea;" chaos is all its forms will be eliminated from existence, and all effects of the Curse will be gone.
Rev. 21:1 – Then I saw a new heaven and a new earth, for the first heaven and the first earth had passed away, and **the sea was no more.**

5. All enemies of God and Christ will have been put down forever.
1 Corinthians 15:25-28 – For he must reign until he has put all his enemies under his feet. [26] The last enemy to be destroyed is death. [27] For " God has put all things in subjection under his feet." But when it says, "all things are put in subjection," it is plain that he is excepted who put all things in subjection under him. [28] **When all things are subjected to him, then the Son himself will also be subjected to him who put all things in subjection under him, that God may be all in all.**

a. All enemies will be thoroughly routed, and the destroyers of humankind will be destroyed.
Psalm 2:6-10 – As for me, I have set my King on Zion, my holy hill. [7] I will tell of the decree: The Lord said to me, "You are my Son; today I have begotten you. [8] Ask of me, and I will make the nations your heritage, and the ends of the earth your possession. [9] **You shall break them with a rod of iron and dash them in pieces like a potter's vessel.**"

b. In this age through the presentation of the Gospel, the Lord Jesus is riding out victoriously through his servants who are announcing his final victory to come.
Psalm 45:3-4 **Gird your sword on your thigh, O mighty one, in your splendor and majesty!** [4] In your majesty ride out victoriously for the cause of truth and meekness and righteousness; let your right hand teach you awesome deeds!

c. The most quoted Messianic text is:
Psalm 110:1 – The Lord says to my Lord: "**Sit at my right hand, until I make your enemies your footstool.**"

d. The effect of Calvary and the Ascension is:
Eph. 1:22 – And he put all things under his feet and gave him as head over all things to the church.

e. It is just a matter of time!
Hebrews 10:12-13 – But when Christ had offered for all time a single sacrifice for sins, he sat down at the right hand of God, [13] **waiting from that time until his enemies should be made a footstool for his feet.**

D. The End of All Things: God will be all-in-all.

1. All things were made by God for himself.
   Proverbs 16:4 – **The Lord has made everything for its purpose**, even the wicked for the day of trouble.

2. Those whom the Lord has made were originally designed to bring him glory and praise, but through sin and disobedience that purpose was marred.

   a. Isaiah 43:7 – everyone who is called by my name, **whom I created for my glory**, whom I formed and made."

   b. Isaiah 43:21 – the people whom **I formed for myself that they might declare my praise.**

3. God is the Source, the Sustainer, and the End of all things, and the coming consummation will make this a continuous, ever-present reality.
   Romans 11:36 – For **from him** and **through him** and **to him** are **all things**. To him be glory forever. Amen.

4. While all things exist and were created for his glory, the consummation will make God in a new way the true center of all things.
   Rev. 4:11 – Worthy are you, our Lord and God, to receive glory and honor and power, for **you created all things, and by your will they existed and were created.**"

   a. All things will be summed up into him in Christ.
   Eph. 1:9-10 – making known to us the mystery of his will, according to his purpose, which he set forth in Christ [10] as a plan for the fullness of time, **to unite all things in him, things in heaven and things on earth.**

b. All things will be One in God; true perfection.
Zech. 14:9 And **the Lord will be king over all the earth.** *On that day* **the Lord will be one and his name one.**

5. The entirety of the whole family in heaven and earth will finally be brought into harmony, a unity and purpose that will never again be challenged, broken, or affected.
Hebrews 12:22-24 – But you have come to Mount Zion and to the city of the living God, the heavenly Jerusalem, and to innumerable angels in festal gathering, [23] and to the assembly of the firstborn who are enrolled in heaven, and to God, the judge of all, and to the spirits of the righteous made perfect, [24] and to Jesus, the mediator of a new covenant, and to the sprinkled blood that speaks a better word than the blood of Abel.

6. God himself (as he is in himself) will become all in all (i.e., a new state of existence for creation which has not seen the likes of which since the Creation).
1 Cor. 15:28 – When all things are subjected to him, then the Son himself will also be subjected to him who put all things in subjection under him, **that God may be all in all.**

a. The triune God and his kingdom will come, and through Christ come to fill all in all in a new way.
Eph. 1:23 – which is his body, **the fullness of him who fills all in all.**

b. Highest level of unity between God, creation, humankind, and all things: God will become all in all.
Col. 3:11 – Here there is not Greek and Jew, circumcised and uncircumcised, barbarian, Scythian, slave, free; but **Christ is all, and in all.**

III. End of the Course: Looking for the End of Time. Let Us Prepare for the Return of Christ!

....

You Tell Me I Am Getting Old

You tell me that I'm gettin' old. I tell you– that's not so!
The "house" I live in all worn out, and that, of course, I know.
It's been in use a long, long while: it's weathered many a gale;
I'm really not surprised you think *I'm* getting old and frail.

The color's changing on the roof, the windows are gettin' dim,
The walls are a little sagging, too, and looking rather thin.
The foundation's not as steady now as once it used to be
My *house* is getting shaky, but know– my *house*– *that* isn't me.

These few short years can't make me old. Inside, I'm in my youth.
Eternity lies right straight ahead, a life of joy and truth.
I'm going to live forever there, in the city of the Great Lamb!
You tell me that *I'm* getting old? You just don't understand.

The one who lives in my little "house" is young and glad and bright;
I just begun that life that'll last, eternal days without night!
You only see the *outside*, which is all that most folks see.
You tell me I am getting old? You mixed up *my house* with *me!*

– Author Unknown

....

2 Cor. 5:1-5 – For we know that if the tent, which is our earthly home, is destroyed, we have a building from God, a house not made with hands, eternal in the heavens. [2] For in this tent we groan, longing to put on our heavenly dwelling, [3] if indeed by putting it on we may not be found naked. [4] For while we are still in this tent, we groan, being burdened– not that we would be unclothed, but that we would be further clothed, so that what is mortal may be swallowed up by life. [5] He who has prepared us for this very thing is God, who has given us the Spirit as a guarantee.

A. Prepare yourself and others for the time to come.

1. Be watchful and prepare yourself.

a. Be watchful.
Romans 13:11-12 – Besides this you know the time, that the hour has come for you to wake from sleep. For salvation is nearer to us now than when we first believed. [12] The night is far gone; the day is at hand. So then let us cast off the works of darkness and put on the armor of light.

b. Be awake and sober.
Matthew 24:42-44 – Therefore, stay awake, for you do not know on what day your Lord is coming. [43] But know this, that if the master of the house had known in what part of the night the thief was coming, he would have stayed awake and would not have let his house be broken into. [44] Therefore you also must be ready, for the Son of Man is coming at an hour you do not expect.

c. Stay dressed for action.
Luke 12:35-38 – Stay dressed for action and keep your lamps burning, [36] and be like men who are waiting for their master to come home from the wedding feast, so that they may open the door to him at once when he comes and knocks. [37] Blessed are those servants whom the master finds awake when he comes. Truly, I say to you, he will dress himself for service and have them recline at table, and he will come and serve them. [38] If he comes in the second watch, or in the third, and finds them awake, blessed are those servants!

d. Be sober.
1 Thess. 5:4-6 – But you are not in darkness, brothers, for that day to surprise you like a thief. [5] For you are all children of light, children of the day. We are not of the night or of the darkness. [6] So then let us not sleep, as others do, but let us keep awake and be sober.

2. Walk in a manner worthy of this calling.

a. 2 Peter 3:11-14 – Since all these things are thus to be dissolved, what sort of people ought you to be in lives of holiness and godliness, [12] waiting for and hastening the coming of the day of God, because of which the heavens will be set on fire and dissolved, and the heavenly bodies will melt as they burn! [13] But according to his promise we are waiting for new heavens and a new earth in which righteousness dwells. [14] Therefore, beloved, since you are waiting for these, be diligent to be found by him without spot or blemish, and at peace. (Cf. Phil. 1.6-11; 1 Thess. 2.12; 3.12-13; 5.23-24

b. Let the grace of God train you for the blessed hope. Titus 2.11-13 – For the grace of God has appeared, bringing salvation for all people, [12] training us to renounce ungodliness and worldly passions, and to live self-controlled, upright, and godly lives in the present age, [13] waiting for our blessed hope, the appearing of the glory of our great God and Savior Jesus Christ,

3. Be zealous and faithful till the end. Turn the heat up! Matthew 24:45-47 – "Who then is the faithful and wise servant, whom his master has set over his household, to give them their food at the proper time? [46] Blessed is that servant whom his master will find so doing when he comes. [47] Truly, I say to you, he will set him over all his possessions. (Cf. Matt. 25.19-21; 2 Cor. 5.9-10; 1 John 2.28)

4. Be prudent and discerning, not wasting even a moment on foolishness and futility.
2 Thessalonians 2:1-3 – Now concerning the coming of our Lord Jesus Christ and our being gathered together to him, we ask you, brothers, [2] not to be quickly shaken in mind or alarmed, either by a spirit or a spoken word, or a letter seeming to be from us, to the effect that the day of the Lord has come. [3] Let no one deceive you in any way. For that day will not come, unless the rebellion

comes first, and the man of lawlessness is revealed, the son of destruction. (Cf. Matt. 24.4-24)

5. Be full of courage and believe with your whole heart in the glory and blessing to come:

   a. Don't be alarmed as things get worse.
      Matthew 24:6 – And you will hear of wars and rumors of wars. See that you are not alarmed, for this must take place, but the end is not yet.

   b. Set your mind to endure to the end.
      Matthew 24:13 – But the one who endures to the end will be saved.

   c. In our endurance we gain our lives, even in the midst of trouble and hardship.
      Luke 21:14-19 – Settle it therefore in your minds not to meditate beforehand how to answer, [15] for I will give you a mouth and wisdom, which none of your adversaries will be able to withstand or contradict. [16] You will be delivered up even by parents and brothers and relatives and friends, and some of you they will put to death. [17] You will be hated by all for my name's sake. [18] But not a hair of your head will perish. [19] By your endurance you will gain your lives.

6. Let this hope permeate every facet of your life. Let it console you and give you joy and comfort in the face of loss and difficulty.

   a. "The countdown's getting closer ev'ry day," even if they get harder to live.
      Luke 21:28 – Now when these things begin to take place, straighten up and raise your heads, because your redemption is drawing near.

b. We have hope! It should make a difference in our disposition towards everything, even the loss of our loved ones.
1 Thessalonians 4:13-14 – But we do not want you to be uninformed, brothers, about those who are asleep, that you may not grieve as others do who have no hope. For since we believe that Jesus died and rose again, even so, through Jesus, God will bring with him those who have fallen asleep. [18] Therefore encourage one another with these words.

c. The testing we experience will be found to our joy at the revelation of Jesus soon.
1 Peter 1:7-9 – so that the tested genuineness of your faith—more precious than gold that perishes though it is tested by fire—may be found to result in praise and glory and honor at the revelation of Jesus Christ. [8] Though you have not seen him, you love him. Though you do not now see him, you believe in him and rejoice with joy that is inexpressible and filled with glory, [9] obtaining the outcome of your faith, the salvation of your souls.

d. As we share in Jesus' sufferings, so we'll share in his joy.
1 Peter 4:13 – But rejoice insofar as you share Christ's sufferings, that you may also rejoice and be glad when his glory is revealed.

7. Stay focused on the prize; consecrate yourself in every way to win the crown.

a. Worldliness is a loss of focus. By its nature, worldly affairs distract you from what counts most of all.
Luke 21:34-35 – But watch yourselves lest your hearts be weighed down with dissipation and drunkenness and cares of this life, and that day come upon you suddenly like a trap. [35] For it will come upon all who dwell on the face of the whole earth.

b. Act like he's coming soon, and you'll change the culture of your life.
1 Corinthians 7:29-31 – This is what I mean, brothers: the appointed time has grown very short. From now on, let those who have wives live as though they had none, [30] and those who mourn as though they were not mourning, and those who rejoice as though they were not rejoicing, and those who buy as though they had no goods, [31] and those who deal with the world as though they had no dealings with it. For the present form of this world is passing away.

c. You're no fool to lose what you can't keep in order to gain what you can't lose.
Phil. 3:12-14 – Not that I have already obtained this or am already perfect, but I press on to make it my own, because Christ Jesus has made me his own. [13] Brothers, I do not consider that I have made it my own. But one thing I do: forgetting what lies behind and straining forward to what lies ahead, [14] I press on toward the goal for the prize of the upward call of God in Christ Jesus.

8. Cultivate an attitude of patience mixed with high expectancy. (You cannot possibly imagine what is to come – don't even try to go there!)

a. Our job in this realm is waiting (which isn't easy!).
1 Thessalonians 1:9-10 – For they themselves report concerning us the kind of reception we had among you, and how you turned to God from idols to serve the living and true God, [10] and to wait for his Son from heaven, whom he raised from the dead, Jesus who delivers us from the wrath to come.

b. Be patient and establish your heart (i.e., don't be snookered by the lure of empty pleasures and petty dreams in this ever-passing-away world).
James 5:7-8 – Be patient, therefore, brothers, until

the coming of the Lord. See how the farmer waits for the precious fruit of the earth, being patient about it, until it receives the early and the late rains. [8] You also, be patient. Establish your hearts, for the coming of the Lord is at hand.

c. Every Christian has to learn how to endure. There's no shortcut to holiness—everybody has to take the "long way 'round."
Hebrews 10:36-38 – For you have need of endurance, so that when you have done the will of God you may receive what is promised. [37]For, "Yet a little while, and the coming one will come and will not delay; [38] but my righteous one shall live by faith, and if he shrinks back, my soul has no pleasure in him."

9. Store up treasures in heaven where nothing can corrode it, or thieves can't take it.

a. Determine to be "the rich and famous" in the place where it matters most.
Matthew 6:19-21 – Do not lay up for yourselves treasures on earth, where moth and rust destroy and where thieves break in and steal, [20] but lay up for yourselves treasures in heaven, where neither moth nor rust destroys and where thieves do not break in and steal. [21] For where your treasure is, there your heart will be also.

b. Look at the kinds of things the King is interested in and invest it all right there.
Matthew 25:34-36, 40 – Then the King will say to those on his right, 'Come, you who are blessed by my Father, inherit the kingdom prepared for you from the foundation of the world. [35] For I was hungry and you gave me food, I was thirsty and you gave me drink, I was a stranger and you welcomed me, [36] I was naked and you clothed me, I was sick and you visited me, I was in prison and you came to me.'

[40] And the King will answer them, 'Truly, I say to you, as you did it to one of the least of these my brothers, you did it to me.'

B. Meditate and pray on these things as often as possible. Integrate this doctrine into every fiber of your worship, service, and discipleship.

1. Pay attention to the prophetic word.
   2 Peter 1:19 – And we have something more sure, the prophetic word, to which you will do well to pay attention as to a lamp shining in a dark place, until the day dawns and the morning star rises in your hearts.

2. A blessing is associated with those who read John's words of prophetic revelation.
   Revelation 1:3 – Blessed is the one who reads aloud the words of this prophecy, and blessed are those who hear, and who keep what is written in it, for the time is near.

3. Realize these times call for self-control, sobriety, and prayer.
   1 Peter 4:7 – The end of all things is at hand; therefore be self-controlled and sober-minded for the sake of your prayers.

4. Stay awake at all times. That's the way to escape the things to come.
   Luke 21:36 – But stay awake at all times, praying that you may have strength to escape all these things that are going to take place, and to stand before the Son of Man."

5. May "Maranatha!" be the cry of your heart.
   Revelation 22:20 – He who testifies to these things says, "Surely I am coming soon." Amen. Come, Lord Jesus!

✢✢✢✢✢

IV. Conclusion

Thy Kingdom Come! Go and Stand at the Window of Expectation

It is no exaggeration to say that this prayer releases powers and that we are often unconscious of what we are doing when we pray for the coming of the Kingdom. The temptation to say with the scoffers of 2 Peter 3 that nothing has changed since the beginning of creation is probably greater than we superficially realize it to be. But just as the prayer of the saints in Revelation 8 immediately released visible and audible power on earth — "peals of thunder, loud noises, flashes of lightning, and an earthquake" (vs. 5) — so the prayer "Thy Kingdom come" is no stammering monologue, but a prayer that expects an answer. And every time we pray the Lord's Prayer there is reason for us to go and stand at the window of expectation.

How often in the congregation of the Lord the glow of this expectation is extinguished. On the basis of the apocalyptic structure of the eschatological promise, the church has—even within the bounds of traditional eschatology — distanced itself inwardly from the future, and set its eye on what might happen on the way to the future. In this obscuring of the expectation, a crisis arises for life itself, and "de-eschatologizing" sets in, more and more overshadowing the meaning of the present. The church must dare to assume responsibility for the prayer "Thy Kingdom come," without reservations. This courage before the face of Him who hears prayer is essential to the doxology that begins already in this life, and will someday change into the new song. It is a hymn to the acts of God, made manifest in history, celebrated and proclaimed. which call time and again —in hiddenness — to a new confidence that does not disappoint. Thy Kingdom come! . . .

G. C. Berkouwer, *The Return of Christ*.
Grand Rapids: Eerdmans Publishing Company, 1972, pp. 452-53.

Jude 1:24-25 – Now to him who is able to keep you from stumbling and to present you blameless before the presence of his glory with great joy, [25] to the only God, our Savior, through Jesus Christ our Lord, be glory, majesty, dominion, and authority, before all time and now and forever. Amen.

- Does your personal devotion, meditation, and spiritual formation consider the weight of the NT vision of the future, the consummation of the Kingdom of God?

- Are you preparing yourself as best you can each day for the return of Jesus Christ?

- Does your preaching, teaching, and ministry reflect the dominance of this doctrine in the Bible?

- Are you fighting the good fight of faith, striving to finish your course, and hopeful to receive the crown of righteousness that all true warriors of Christ will receive in the reckoning to come?

Therefore, brothers, be all the more diligent to make your calling and election sure, for if you practice these qualities you will never fall. For in this way there will be richly provided for you an entrance into the eternal kingdom of our Lord and Savior Jesus Christ.

– The Apostle Peter (2 Peter 1:10-11)

The Bottom Line _____

Appendix

267 *Appendix 1*
The Nicene Creed

268 *Appendix 2*
The Nicene Creed with Biblical Support

270 *Appendix 3*
We Believe: Confession of the Nicene Creed (8.7.8.7)

271 *Appendix 4*
We Believe: Confession of the Nicene Creed (Common Meter)

272 *Appendix 5*
The Story of God: Our Sacred Roots

273 *Appendix 6*
Once Upon a Time:
The Cosmic Drama through a Biblical Narrative of the World

275 *Appendix 7*
The Theology of Christus Victor

276 *Appendix 8*
Christus Victor: An Integrated Vision for the Christian Life and Witness

277 *Appendix 9*
Old Testament Witness to Christ and His Kingdom

278 *Appendix 10*
Summary Outline of the Scriptures

282 *Appendix 11*
From Before to Beyond Time: The Plan of God and Human History

283 *Appendix 12*
There Is a River:
Identifying the Streams of a Revitalized Authentic Christian Community in the City

284 *Appendix 13*
A Schematic for a Theology of the Kingdom and the Church

285	*Appendix 14* Living in the Already and the Not Yet Kingdom
286	*Appendix 15* Jesus of Nazareth: Presence of the Future
287	*Appendix 16* Traditions (Paradosis)
295	*Appendix 17* Documenting Your Work: A Guide to Help You Give Credit Where Credit Is Due
299	*Appendix 18* Comparative Chart of the Millennial Views
303	*Appendix 19* Compass of Narrative Elements
302	*Appendix 20* Ethics of the NT: Living in the Upside-Down Kingdom of God
302	*Appendix 21* Kingdom of God Timeline
303	*Appendix 22* Spectra of Orientation
304	*Appendix 23* The Historic Hope of the Church
305	*Appendix 24* Translating the Story of God

Appendix 1
The Nicene Creed
The Urban Ministry Institute

We believe in one God, the Father Almighty, Maker of heaven and earth and of all things visible and invisible.

We believe in one Lord Jesus Christ, the only Begotten Son of God, begotten of the Father before all ages, God from God, Light from Light, True God from True God, begotten not created, of the same essence as the Father, through whom all things were made.

Who for us men and for our salvation came down from heaven and was incarnate by the Holy Spirit and the Virgin Mary and became human. Who for us too, was crucified under Pontius Pilate, suffered and was buried. The third day he rose again according to the Scriptures, ascended into heaven, and is seated at the right hand of the Father. He will come again in glory to judge the living and the dead, and his Kingdom will have no end.

We believe in the Holy Spirit, the Lord and life-giver, who proceeds from the Father and the Son, who together with the Father and Son is worshiped and glorified, who spoke by the prophets.

We believe in one holy, catholic, and apostolic Church.

We acknowledge one baptism for the forgiveness of sin, and we look for the resurrection of the dead and the life of the age to come. Amen.

Appendix 2
The Nicene Creed
With Biblical Support
The Urban Ministry Institute

We believe in one God, *(Deut. 6.4-5; Mark 12.29; 1 Cor. 8.6)*
    the Father Almighty, *(Gen. 17.1; Dan. 4.35; Matt. 6.9; Eph. 4.6; Rev. 1.8)*
    Maker of heaven and earth *(Gen. 1.1; Isa. 40.28; Rev. 10.6)*
    and of all things visible and invisible. *(Ps. 148; Rom. 11.36; Rev. 4.11)*

We believe in one Lord Jesus Christ, the only Begotten Son of God, begotten of the Father before all ages, God from God, Light from Light, True God from True God, begotten not created, of the same essence as the Father,
    (John 1.1-2; 3.18; 8.58; 14.9-10; 20.28; Col. 1.15, 17; Heb. 1.3-6)
through whom all things were made. *(John 1.3; Col. 1.16)*

Who for us men and for our salvation came down from heaven and was incarnate by the Holy Spirit and the Virgin Mary and became human.
    (Matt. 1.20-23; John 1.14; 6.38; Luke 19.10)
Who for us too, was crucified under Pontius Pilate, suffered and was buried.
    (Matt. 27.1-2; Mark 15.24-39, 43-47; Acts 13.29; Rom. 5.8; Heb. 2.10; 13.12)
The third day he rose again according to the Scriptures,
    (Mark 16.5-7; Luke 24.6-8; Acts 1.3; Rom. 6.9; 10.9; 2 Tim. 2.8)
ascended into heaven, and is seated at the right hand of the Father.
    (Mark 16.19; Eph. 1.19-20)
He will come again in glory to judge the living and the dead, and his Kingdom will have no end. *(Isa. 9.7; Matt. 24.30; John 5.22; Acts 1.11; 17.31; Rom. 14.9; 2 Cor. 5.10; 2 Tim. 4.1)*

We believe in the Holy Spirit, the Lord and life-giver, *(Gen. 1.1-2; Job 33.4; Ps. 104.30; 139.7-8; Luke 4.18-19; John 3.5-6; Acts 1.1-2; 1 Cor. 2.11; Rev. 3.22)*
who proceeds from the Father and the Son, *(John 14.16-18, 26; 15.26; 20.22)*
who together with the Father and Son is worshiped and glorified,
    (Isa. 6.3; Matt. 28.19; 2 Cor. 13.14; Rev. 4.8)
who spoke by the prophets. *(Num. 11.29; Mic. 3.8; Acts 2.17-18; 2 Pet. 1.21)*

We believe in one holy, catholic, and apostolic Church.
    (Matt. 16.18; Eph. 5.25-28; 1 Cor. 1.2; 10.17; 1 Tim. 3.15; Rev. 7.9)

We acknowledge one baptism for the forgiveness of sin, *(Acts 22.16; 1 Pet. 3.21; Eph. 4.4-5)*
And we look for the resurrection of the dead and the life of the age to come.
    (Isa. 11.6-10; Mic. 4.1-7; Luke 18.29-30; Rev. 21.1-5; 21.22-22.5)
Amen.

The Nicene Creed with Biblical Support – Memory Verses

Below are suggested memory verses, one for each section of the Creed.

The Father
Revelation 4.11

The Son
John 1.1

The Son's Mission
1 Corinthians 15.3-5

The Holy Spirit
Romans 8.11

The Church
1 Peter 2.9

Our Hope
1 Thessalonians 4.16-17

Appendix 3

We Believe: Confession of the Nicene Creed (8.7.8.7 meter*)

Rev. Dr. Don L. Davis, 2007. All Rights Reserved.

* This song is adapted from the Nicene Creed, and set to 8.7.8.7. meter, meaning it can be sung to tunes of the same meter, such as: Joyful, Joyful, We Adore Thee; I Will Sing of My Redeemer; What a Friend We Have in Jesus; Come, Thou Long Expected Jesus

Father God Almighty rules, the Maker of both earth and heav'n.
All things seen and those unseen, by him were made, by him were giv'n!
We believe in Jesus Christ, the Lord, God's one and only Son,
Begotten, not created, too, he and our Father God are one!

Begotten from the Father, same, in essence, as both God and Light;
Through him by God all things were made, in him all things were giv'n life.
Who for us all, for our salvation, did come down from heav'n to earth,
Incarnate by the Spirit's pow'r, and through the Virgin Mary's birth.

Who for us too, was crucified, by Pontius Pilate's rule and hand,
Suffered, and was buried, yet on the third day, he rose again.
According to the Sacred Scriptures all that happ'ned was meant to be.
Ascended high to God's right hand, in heav'n he sits in glory.

Christ will come again in glory to judge all those alive and dead.
His Kingdom rule shall never end, for he will rule and reign as Head.
We worship God, the Holy Spirit, Lord and the Life-giver known;
With Fath'r and Son is glorified, Who by the prophets ever spoke.

And we believe in one true Church, God's holy people for all time,
Cath'lic in its scope and broadness, built on the Apostles' line!
Acknowledging that one baptism, for forgiv'ness of our sin,
And we look for Resurrection, for the dead shall live again.

Looking for unending days, the life of the bright Age to come,
When Christ's Reign shall come to earth, the will of God shall then be done!
Praise to God, and to Christ Jesus, to the Spirit–triune Lord!
We confess the ancient teachings, clinging to God's holy Word!

Appendix 4
We Believe: Confession of the Nicene Creed (Common Meter*)
Rev. Dr. Don L. Davis, 2007

* This song is adapted from the Nicene Creed, and set to common meter (8.6.8.6.), meaning it can be sung to tunes of the same meter, such as: O, for a Thousand Tongues to Sing; Alas, and Did My Savior Bleed; Amazing Grace; All Hail the Power of Jesus' Name; There Is a Fountain; Joy to the World

The Father God Almighty rules, Maker of earth and heav'n.
Yes, all things seen and those unseen, by him were made, and given!

We hold to one Lord Jesus Christ, God's one and only Son,
Begotten, not created, too, he and our Lord are one!

Begotten from the Father, same, in essence, God and Light;
Through him all things were made by God, in him were given life.

Who for us all, for salvation, came down from heav'n to earth,
Was incarnate by the Spirit's pow'r, and the Virgin Mary's birth.

Who for us too, was crucified, by Pontius Pilate's hand,
Suffered, was buried in the tomb, on third day rose again.

According to the Sacred text all this was meant to be.
Ascended to heav'n, to God's right hand, now seated high in glory.

He'll come again in glory to judge all those alive and dead.
His Kingdom rule shall never end, for he will reign as Head.

We worship God, the Holy Spirit, our Lord, Life-giver known,
With Fath'r and Son is glorified, Who by the prophets spoke.

And we believe in one true Church, God's people for all time,
Cath'lic in scope, and built upon the apostolic line.

Acknowledging one baptism, for forgiv'ness of our sin,
We look for Resurrection day–the dead shall live again.

We look for those unending days, life of the Age to come,
When Christ's great Reign shall come to earth, and God's will shall be done!

APPENDIX 5
The Story of God: Our Sacred Roots
Rev. Dr. Don L. Davis

The LORD God is the source, sustainer, and end of all things in the heavens and earth. All things were formed and exist by his will and for his eternal glory, the triune God, Father, Son, and Holy Spirit, Rom. 11.36.

	The Alpha and the Omega	Christus Victor	Come, Holy Spirit	Your Word Is Truth	The Great Confession	His Life in Us	Living in the Way	Reborn to Serve
	THE TRIUNE GOD'S UNFOLDING DRAMA — God's Self-Revelation in Creation, Israel, and Christ				**THE CHURCH'S PARTICIPATION IN GOD'S UNFOLDING DRAMA** — Fidelity to the Apostolic Witness to Christ and His Kingdom			
	The Objective Foundation: The Sovereign Love of God — God's Narration of His Saving Work in Christ				*The Subjective Practice: Salvation by Grace through Faith — The Redeemed's Joyous Response to God's Saving Work in Christ*			
The Author of the Story	The Champion of the Story	The Interpreter of the Story	The Testimony of the Story	The People of the Story	Re-enactment of the Story	Embodiment of the Story	Continuation of the Story
The Father as Director	Jesus as Lead Actor	The Spirit as Narrator	Scripture as Script	As Saints, Confessors	As Worshipers, Ministers	As Followers, Sojourners	As Servants, Ambassadors
Christian Worldview	Communal Identity	Spiritual Experience	Biblical Authority	Orthodox Theology	Priestly Worship	Congregational Discipleship	Kingdom Witness
Theistic and Trinitarian Vision	Christ-centered Foundation	Spirit-Indwelt and -Filled Community	Canonical and Apostolic Witness	Ancient Creedal Affirmation of Faith	Weekly Gathering in Christian Assembly	Corporate, Ongoing Spiritual Formation	Active Agents of the Reign of God
Sovereign Willing	Messianic Representing	Divine Comforting	Inspired Testifying	Truthful Retelling	Joyful Excelling	Faithful Indwelling	Hopeful Compelling
Creator — True Maker of the Cosmos	**Recapitulation** — Typos and Fulfillment of the Covenant	**Life-Giver** — Regeneration and Adoption	**Divine Inspiration** — God-breathed Word	**The Confession of Faith** — Union with Christ	**Song and Celebration** — Historical Recitation	**Pastoral Oversight** — Shepherding the Flock	**Explicit Unity** — Love for the Saints
Owner — Sovereign Disposer of Creation	**Revealer** — Incarnation of the Word	**Teacher** — Illuminator of the Truth	**Sacred History** — Historical Record	**Baptism into Christ** — Communion of Saints	**Homilies and Teachings** — Prophetic Proclamation	**Shared Spirituality** — Common Journey through the Spiritual Disciplines	**Radical Hospitality** — Evidence of God's Kingdom Reign
Ruler — Blessed Controller of All Things	**Redeemer** — Reconciler of All Things	**Helper** — Endowment and the Power	**Biblical Theology** — Divine Commentary	**The Rule of Faith** — Apostles' Creed and Nicene Creed	**The Lord's Supper** — Dramatic Re-enactment	**Embodiment** — Anamnesis and Prolepsis through the Church Year	**Extravagant Generosity** — Good Works
Covenant Keeper — Faithful Promisor	**Restorer** — Christ, the Victor over the powers of evil	**Guide** — Divine Presence and Shekinah	**Spiritual Food** — Sustenance for the Journey	**The Vincentian Canon** — Ubiquity, antiquity, universality	**Eschatological Foreshadowing** — The Already/Not Yet	**Effective Discipling** — Spiritual Formation in the Believing Assembly	**Evangelical Witness** — Making Disciples of All People Groups

Appendix 6

Once upon a Time

The Cosmic Drama through a Biblical Narration of the World

Rev. Dr. Don L. Davis

From Everlasting to Everlasting, Our Lord Is God

From everlasting, in that matchless mystery of existence before time began, our Triune God dwelt in perfect splendor in eternal community as Father, Son, and Holy Spirit, the I AM, displaying his perfect attributes in eternal relationship, needing nothing, in boundless holiness, joy, and beauty. According to his sovereign will, our God purposed out of love to create a universe where his splendor would be revealed, and a world where his glory would be displayed and where a people made in his own image would dwell, sharing in fellowship with him and enjoying union with himself in relationship, all for his glory.

Who, as the Sovereign God, Created a World That Would Ultimately Rebel against His Rule

Inflamed by lust, greed, and pride, the first human pair rebelled against his will, deceived by the great prince, Satan, whose diabolical plot to supplant God as ruler of all resulted in countless angelic beings resisting God's divine will in the heavenlies. Through Adam and Eve's disobedience, they exposed themselves and their heirs to misery and death, and through their rebellion ushered creation into chaos, suffering, and evil. Through sin and rebellion, the union between God and creation was lost, and now all things are subject to the effects of this great fall – alienation, separation, and condemna-tion become the underlying reality for all things. No angel, human being, or creature can solve this dilemma, and without God's direct intervention, all the universe, the world, and all its creatures would be lost.

Yet, in Mercy and Loving-kindness, the Lord God Promised to Send a Savior to Redeem His Creation

In sovereign covenantal love, God determined to remedy the effects of the universe's rebellion by sending a Champion, his only Son, who would take on the form of the fallen pair, embrace and over-throw their separation from God, and suffer in the place of all humankind for its sin and disobedience. So, through his covenant faithfulness, God became directly involved in human history for the sake of their salvation. The Lord God stoops to engage his creation for the sake of restoring it, to put down evil once and for all, and to establish a people out of which his Champion would come to establish his reign in this world once more.

So, He Raised Up a People from Which the Governor Would Come

And so, through Noah, he saves the world from its own evil, through Abraham, he selects the clan through which the seed would come. Through Isaac, he continues the promise to Abraham, and through Jacob (Israel) he establishes his nation, identifying the tribe out of which he will come (Judah). Through Moses, he delivers his own from oppression and gives them his covenantal law, and through Joshua, he brings his people into the land of promise. Through judges and leaders he superintends his people, and through David, he covenants to bring a King from his clan who will reign forever. Despite his promise, though, his people fall short of his covenant time after time. Their stubborn and persistent rejection of the Lord finally leads to the nation's judgment, invasion, overthrow, and captivity. Mercifully, he remembers his covenant and allows a remnant to return – for the promise and the story were not done.

Who, as Champion, Came Down from Heaven, in the Fullness of Time, and Won through the Cross

Some four hundred years of silence occurred. Yet, in the fullness of time, God fulfilled his covenant promise by entering into this realm of evil, suffering, and alienation through the incarnation. In the person of Jesus of Nazareth, God came down from heaven and lived among us, displaying the Father's glory, fulfilling the requirements of God's moral law, and demonstrating the power of the Kingdom of God in his words, works, and exorcisms. On the Cross he took on our rebellion, destroyed death, overcame the devil, and rose on the third day to restore creation from the Fall, to make an end of sin, disease, and war, and to grant never-ending life to all people who embrace his salvation.

And, Soon and Very Soon, He Will Return to This World and Make All Things New

Ascended to the Father's right hand, the Lord Jesus Christ has sent the Holy Spirit into the world, forming a new people made up of both Jew and Gentile, the Church. Commissioned under his headship, they testify in word and deed the gospel of reconciliation to the whole creation, and when they have completed their task, he will return in glory and complete his work for creation and all creatures. Soon, he will put down sin, evil, death, and the effects of the Curse forever, and restore all creation under its true rule, refreshing all things in a new heavens and new earth, where all beings and all creation will enjoy the shalom of the Triune God forever, to his glory and honor alone.

And the Redeemed Shall Live Happily Ever After . . .

The End

Appendix 7

The Theology of Christus Victor
Rev. Dr. Don L. Davis

	The Promised Messiah	The Word Made Flesh	The Son of Man	The Suffering Servant	The Lamb of God	The Victorious Conqueror	The Reigning Lord in Heaven	The Bridegroom and Coming King
Biblical Framework	Israel's hope of Yahweh's anointed who would redeem his people	In the person of Jesus of Nazareth, the Lord has come to the world	As the promised king and divine Son of Man, Jesus reveals the Father's glory and salvation to the world	As Inaugurator of the Kingdom of God, Jesus demonstrates God's reign present through his words, wonders, and works	As both High Priest and Paschal Lamb, Jesus offers himself to God on our behalf as a sacrifice for sin	In his resurrection from the dead and ascension to God's right hand, Jesus is proclaimed as Victor over the power of sin and death	Now reigning at God's right hand till his enemies are made his footstool, Jesus pours out his benefits on his body	Soon the risen and ascended Lord will return to gather his Bride, the Church, and consummate his work
Scripture References	Isa. 9.6-7 Jer. 23.5-6 Isa. 11.1-10	John 1.14-18 Matt. 1.20-23 Phil. 2.6-8	Matt. 2.1-11 Num. 24.17 Luke 1.78-79	Mark 1.14-15 Matt. 12.25-30 Luke 17.20-21	2 Cor. 5.18-21 Isa. 52-53 John 1.29	Eph. 1.16-23 Phil. 2.5-11 Col. 1.15-20	1 Cor. 15.25 Eph. 4.15-16 Acts. 2.32-36	Rom. 14.7-9 Rev. 5.9-13 1 Thess. 4.13-18
Jesus' History	The pre-incarnate, only begotten Son of God in glory	His conception by the Spirit, and birth to Mary	His manifestation to the Magi and to the world	His teaching, exorcisms, miracles, and mighty works among the people	His suffering, crucifixion, death, and burial	His resurrection, with appearances to his witnesses, and his ascension to the Father	The sending of the Holy Spirit and his gifts, and Christ's session in heaven at the Father's right hand	His soon return from heaven to earth as Lord and Christ: the Second Coming
Description	The biblical promise for the seed of Abraham, the prophet like Moses, the son of David	In the Incarnation, God has come to us; Jesus reveals to humankind the Father's glory in fullness	In Jesus, God has shown his salvation to the entire world, including the Gentiles	In Jesus, the promised Kingdom of God has come visibly to earth, demonstrating his binding of Satan and rescinding the Curse	As God's perfect Lamb, Jesus offers himself up to God as a sin offering on behalf of the entire world	In his resurrection and ascension, Jesus destroyed death, disarmed Satan, and rescinded the Curse	Jesus is installed at the Father's right hand as Head of the Church, Firstborn from the dead, and supreme Lord in heaven	As we labor in his harvest field in the world, so we await Christ's return, the fulfillment of his promise
Church Year	Advent	Christmas	Season after Epiphany Baptism and Transfiguration	Lent	Holy Week Passion	Eastertide Easter, Ascension Day, Pentecost	Season after Pentecost Trinity Sunday	Season after Pentecost All Saints Day, Reign of Christ the King
	The Coming of Christ	The Birth of Christ	The Manifestation of Christ	The Ministry of Christ	The Suffering and Death of Christ	The Resurrection and Ascension of Christ	The Heavenly Session of Christ	Reign of Christ
Spiritual Formation	As we await his Coming, let us proclaim and affirm the hope of Christ	O Word made flesh, let us every heart prepare him room to dwell	Divine Son of Man, show the nations your salvation and glory	In the person of Christ, the power of the reign of God has come to earth and to the Church	May those who share the Lord's death be resurrection with him	Let us participate by faith in the victory of Christ over the power of sin, Satan, and death	Come, indwell us, Holy Spirit, and empower us to advance Christ's Kingdom in the world	We live and work in expectation of his soon return, seeking to please him in all things

Appendix 8

Christus Victor: An Integrated Vision for the Christian Life and Witness

Rev. Dr. Don L. Davis

For the Church

- The Church is the primary extension of Jesus in the world
- Ransomed treasure of the victorious, risen Christ
- *Laos:* The people of God
- God's new creation: presence of the future
- Locus and agent of the Already/Not Yet Kingdom

For Gifts

- God's gracious endowments and benefits from *Christus Victor*
- Pastoral offices to the Church
- The Holy Spirit's sovereign dispensing of the gifts
- Stewardship: divine, diverse gifts for the common good

For Theology and Doctrine

- The authoritative Word of Christ's victory: the Apostolic Tradition: the Holy Scriptures
- Theology as commentary on the grand narrative of God
- *Christus Victor* as the core theological framework for meaning in the world
- The Nicene Creed: the Story of God's triumphant grace

Christus Victor
*Destroyer of Evil and Death
Restorer of Creation
Victor o'er Hades and Sin
Crusher of Satan*

For Evangelism and Mission

- Evangelism as unashamed declaration and demonstration of *Christus Victor* to the world
- The Gospel as Good News of kingdom pledge
- We proclaim God's Kingdom come in the person of Jesus of Nazareth
- The Great Commission: go to all people groups making disciples of Christ and his Kingdom
- Proclaiming Christ as Lord and Messiah

For Spirituality

- The Holy Spirit's presence and power in the midst of God's people
- Sharing in the disciplines of the Spirit
- Gatherings, lectionary, liturgy, and our observances in the Church Year
- Living the life of the risen Christ in the rhythm of our ordinary lives

For Worship

- People of the Resurrection: unending celebration of the people of God
- Remembering, participating in the Christ event in our worship
- Listen and respond to the Word
- Transformed at the Table, the Lord's Supper
- The presence of the Father through the Son in the Spirit

For Justice and Compassion

- The gracious and generous expressions of Jesus through the Church
- The Church displays the very life of the Kingdom
- The Church demonstrates the very life of the Kingdom of heaven right here and now
- Having freely received, we freely give (no sense of merit or pride)
- Justice as tangible evidence of the Kingdom come

Appendix 9

Old Testament Witness to Christ and His Kingdom

Rev. Dr. Don L. Davis

Christ Is Seen in the OT's:	Covenant Promise and Fulfillment	Moral Law	Christophanies	Typology	Tabernacle, Festival, and Levitical Priesthood	Messianic Prophecy	Salvation Promises
Passage	Gen. 12.1-3	Matt. 5.17-18	John 1.18	1 Cor. 15.45	Heb. 8.1-6	Mic. 5.2	Isa. 9.6-7
Example	The Promised Seed of the Abrahamic covenant	The Law given on Mount Sinai	Commander of the Lord's army	Jonah and the great fish	Melchizedek, as both High Priest and King	The Lord's Suffering Servant	Righteous Branch of David
Christ As	Seed of the woman	The Prophet of God	God's present Revelation	Antitype of God's drama	Our eternal High Priest	The coming Son of Man	Israel's Redeemer and King
Where Illustrated	Galatians	Matthew	John	Matthew	Hebrews	Luke and Acts	John and Revelation
Exegetical Goal	To see Christ as heart of God's sacred drama	To see Christ as fulfillment of the Law	To see Christ as God's revealer	To see Christ as antitype of divine typos	To see Christ in the Temple *cultus*	To see Christ as true Messiah	To see Christ as coming King
How Seen in the NT	As fulfillment of God's sacred oath	As telos of the Law	As full, final, and superior revelation	As substance behind the historical shadows	As reality behind the rules and roles	As the Kingdom made present	As the One who will rule on David's throne
Our Response in Worship	God's veracity and faithfulness	God's perfect righteousness	God's presence among us	God's inspired Scripture	God's ontology: his realm as primary and determinative	God's anointed servant and mediator	God's resolve to restore his kingdom authority
How God Is Vindicated	God does not lie: he's true to his word	Jesus fulfills all righteousness	God's fullness is revealed to us in Jesus of Nazareth	The Spirit spoke by the prophets	The Lord has provided a mediator for humankind	Every jot and tittle written of him will occur	Evil will be put down, creation restored, under his reign

Appendix 10
Summary Outline of the Scriptures
Rev. Dr. Don L. Davis

The Old Testament

1. **Genesis** – *Beginnings*
   a. Adam
   b. Noah
   c. Abraham
   d. Isaac
   e. Jacob
   f. Joseph

2. **Exodus** – *Redemption (out of)*
   a. Slavery
   b. Deliverance
   c. Law
   d. Tabernacle

3. **Leviticus** – *Worship and Fellowship*
   a. Offerings and sacrifices
   b. Priests
   c. Feasts and festivals

4. **Numbers** – *Service and Walk*
   a. Organized
   b. Wanderings

5. **Deuteronomy** – *Obedience*
   a. Moses reviews history and law
   b. Civil and social laws
   c. Palestinian Covenant
   d. Moses' blessing and death

6. **Joshua** – *Redemption (into)*
   a. Conquer the land
   b. Divide up the land
   c. Joshua's farewell

7. **Judges** – *God's Deliverance*
   a. Disobedience and judgment
   b. Israel's twelve judges
   c. Lawless conditions

8. **Ruth** – *Love*
   a. Ruth chooses
   b. Ruth works
   c. Ruth waits
   d. Ruth rewarded

9. **1 Samuel** – *Kings, Priestly Perspective*
   a. Eli
   b. Samuel
   c. Saul
   d. David

10. **2 Samuel** – *David*
    a. King of Judah (9 years - Hebron)
    b. King of all Israel (33 years - Jerusalem)

11. **1 Kings** – *Solomon's Glory, Kingdom's Decline*
    a. Solomon's glory
    b. Kingdom's decline
    c. Elijah the prophet

12. **2 Kings** – *Divided Kingdom*
    a. Elisha
    b. Israel (Northern Kingdom falls)
    c. Judah (Southern Kingdom falls)

13. **1 Chronicles** – *David's Temple Arrangements*
    a. Genealogies
    b. End of Saul's reign
    c. Reign of David
    d. Temple preparations

14. **2 Chronicles** – *Temple and Worship Abandoned*
    a. Solomon
    b. Kings of Judah

15. **Ezra** – *The Minority (Remnant)*
    a. First return from exile - Zerubbabel
    b. Second return from exile - Ezra (priest)

16. **Nehemiah** – *Rebuilding by Faith*
    a. Rebuild walls
    b. Revival
    c. Religious reform

17. **Esther** – *Female Savior*
    a. Esther
    b. Haman
    c. Mordecai
    d. Deliverance: Feast of Purim

18. **Job** – *Why the Righteous Suffer*
    a. Godly Job
    b. Satan's attack
    c. Four philosophical friends
    d. God lives

19. **Psalms** – *Prayer and Praise*
    a. Prayers of David
    b. Godly suffer; deliverance
    c. God deals with Israel
    d. Suffering of God's people - end with the Lord's reign
    e. The Word of God (Messiah's suffering and glorious return)

20. **Proverbs** – *Wisdom*
    a. Wisdom vs. folly
    b. Solomon
    c. Solomon - Hezekiah
    d. Agur
    e. Lemuel

21. **Ecclesiastes** – *Vanity*
   a. Experimentation
   b. Observation
   c. Consideration
	31. **Obadiah** – *Edom's Destruction*
	   a. Destruction prophesied
	   b. Reasons for destruction
	   c. Israel's future blessing

22. **Song of Solomon** – *Love Story*	32. **Jonah** – *Gentile Salvation*
	   a. Jonah disobeys
	   b. Others suffer
	   c. Jonah punished
	   d. Jonah obeys; thousands saved
	   e. Jonah displeased, no love for souls

23. **Isaiah** – *The Justice (Judgment) and Grace (Comfort) of God*
   a. Prophecies of punishment
   b. History
   c. Prophecies of blessing	

24. **Jeremiah** – *Judah's Sin Leads to Babylonian Captivity*
   a. Jeremiah's call; empowered
   b. Judah condemned; predicted Babylonian captivity
   c. Restoration promised
   d. Prophesied judgment inflicted
   e. Prophecies against Gentiles
   f. Summary of Judah's captivity
	33. **Micah** – *Israel's Sins, Judgment, and Restoration*
	   a. Sin and judgment
	   b. Grace and future restoration
	   c. Appeal and petition

	34. **Nahum** – *Nineveh Condemned*
	   a. God hates sin
	   b. Nineveh's doom prophesied
	   c. Reasons for doom

25. **Lamentations** – *Lament over Jerusalem*
   a. Affliction of Jerusalem
   b. Destroyed because of sin
   c. The prophet's suffering
   d. Present desolation vs. past splendor
   e. Appeal to God for mercy
	35. **Habakkuk** – *The Just Shall Live by Faith*
	   a. Complaint of Judah's unjudged sin
	   b. Chaldeans will punish
	   c. Complaint of Chaldeans' wickedness
	   d. Punishment promised
	   e. Prayer for revival; faith in God

26. **Ezekiel** – *Israel's Captivity and Restoration*
   a. Judgment on Judah and Jerusalem
   b. Judgment on Gentile nations
   c. Israel restored; Jerusalem's future glory
	36. **Zephaniah** – *Babylonian Invasion Prefigures the Day of the Lord*
	   a. Judgment on Judah foreshadows the Great Day of the Lord
	   b. Judgment on Jerusalem and neighbors foreshadows final judgment of all nations
	   c. Israel restored after judgments

27. **Daniel** – *The Time of the Gentiles*
   a. History; Nebuchadnezzar, Belshazzar, Daniel
   b. Prophecy	

28. **Hosea** – *Unfaithfulness*
   a. Unfaithfulness
   b. Punishment
   c. Restoration
	37. **Haggai** – *Rebuild the Temple*
	   a. Negligence
	   b. Courage
	   c. Separation
	   d. Judgment

29. **Joel** – *The Day of the Lord*
   a. Locust plague
   b. Events of the future Day of the Lord
   c. Order of the future Day of the Lord
	38. **Zechariah** – *Two Comings of Christ*
	   a. Zechariah's vision
	   b. Bethel's question; Jehovah's answer
	   c. Nation's downfall and salvation

30. **Amos** – *God Judges Sin*
   a. Neighbors judged
   b. Israel judged
   c. Visions of future judgment
   d. Israel's past judgment blessings
	39. **Malachi** – *Neglect*
	   a. The priest's sins
	   b. The people's sins
	   c. The faithful few

The New Testament

1. **Matthew** – *Jesus the King*
   a. The Person of the King
   b. The Preparation of the King
   c. The Propaganda of the King
   d. The Program of the King
   e. The Passion of the King
   f. The Power of the King

2. **Mark** – *Jesus the Servant*
   a. John introduces the Servant
   b. God the Father identifies the Servant
   c. The temptation initiates the Servant
   d. Work and word of the Servant
   e. Death burial, resurrection

3. **Luke** – *Jesus Christ the Perfect Man*
   a. Birth and family of the Perfect Man
   b. Testing of the Perfect Man; hometown
   c. Ministry of the Perfect Man
   d. Betrayal, trial, and death of the Perfect Man
   e. Resurrection of the Perfect Man

4. **John** – *Jesus Christ is God*
   a. Prologue - the Incarnation
   b. Introduction
   c. Witness of works and words
   d. Witness of Jesus to his apostles
   e. Passion - witness to the world
   f. Epilogue

5. **Acts** – *The Holy Spirit Working in the Church*
   a. The Lord Jesus at work by the Holy Spirit through the apostles at Jerusalem
   b. In Judea and Samaria
   c. To the uttermost parts of the Earth

6. **Romans** – *The Righteousness of God*
   a. Salutation
   b. Sin and salvation
   c. Sanctification
   d. Struggle
   e. Spirit-filled living
   f. Security of salvation
   g. Segregation
   h. Sacrifice and service
   i. Separation and salutation

7. **1 Corinthians** – *The Lordship of Christ*
   a. Salutation and thanksgiving
   b. Conditions in the Corinthian body
   c. Concerning the Gospel
   d. Concerning collections

8. **2 Corinthians** – *The Ministry of the Church*
   a. The comfort of God
   b. Collection for the poor
   c. Calling of the Apostle Paul

9. **Galatians** – *Justification by Faith*
   a. Introduction
   b. Personal - Authority of the apostle and glory of the Gospel
   c. Doctrinal - Justification by faith
   d. Practical - Sanctification by the Holy Spirit
   e. Autographed conclusion and exhortation

10. **Ephesians** – *The Church of Jesus Christ*
    a. Doctrinal - the heavenly calling of the Church
       - A Body
       - A Temple
       - A Mystery
    b. Practical - the earthly conduct of the Church
       - A New Man
       - A Bride
       - An Army

11. **Philippians** – *Joy in the Christian Life*
    a. Philosophy for Christian living
    b. Pattern for Christian living
    c. Prize for Christian living
    d. Power for Christian living

12. **Colossians** – *Christ the Fullness of God*
    a. Doctrinal - Christ, the fullness of God; in Christ believers are made full
    b. Practical - Christ, the fullness of God; Christ's life poured out in believers, and through them

13. **1 Thessalonians** – *The Second Coming of Christ:*
    a. Is an inspiring hope
    b. Is a working hope
    c. Is a purifying hope
    d. Is a comforting hope
    e. Is a rousing, stimulating hope

14. **2 Thessalonians** – *The Second Coming of Christ*
    a. Persecution of believers now; judgment of unbelievers hereafter (at coming of Christ)
    b. Program of the world in connection with the coming of Christ
    c. Practical issues associated with the coming of Christ

15. **1 Timothy** – *Government and Order in the Local Church*
    a. The faith of the Church
    b. Public prayer and women's place in the Church
    c. Officers in the Church
    d. Apostasy in the Church
    e. Duties of the officer of the Church

16. **2 Timothy** – *Loyalty in the Days of Apostasy*
    a. Afflictions of the Gospel
    b. Active in service
    c. Apostasy coming; authority of the Scriptures
    d. Allegiance to the Lord

17. **Titus** – *The Ideal New Testament Church*
    a. The Church is an organization
    b. The Church is to teach and preach the Word of God
    c. The Church is to perform good works

18. **Philemon** – *Reveal Christ's Love and Teach Brotherly Love*
    a. Genial greeting to Philemon and family
    b. Good reputation of Philemon
    c. Gracious plea for Onesimus
    d. Guiltless substitutes for guilty
    e. Glorious illustration of imputation
    f. General and personal requests

19. **Hebrews** – *The Superiority of Christ*
    a. Doctrinal - Christ is better than the Old Testament economy
    b. Practical - Christ brings better benefits and duties

20. **James** – *Ethics of Christianity*
    a. Faith tested
    b. Difficulty of controlling the tongue
    c. Warning against worldliness
    d. Admonitions in view of the Lord's coming

21. **1 Peter** – *Christian Hope in the Time of Persecution and Trial*
    a. Suffering and security of believers
    b. Suffering and the Scriptures
    c. Suffering and the sufferings of Christ
    d. Suffering and the Second Coming of Christ

22. **2 Peter** – *Warning against False Teachers*
    a. Addition of Christian graces gives assurance
    b. Authority of the Scriptures
    c. Apostasy brought in by false testimony
    d. Attitude toward return of Christ: test for apostasy
    e. Agenda of God in the world
    f. Admonition to believers

23. **1 John** – *The Family of God*
    a. God is light
    b. God is love
    c. God is life

24. **2 John** – *Warning against Receiving Deceivers*
    a. Walk in truth
    b. Love one another
    c. Receive not deceivers
    d. Find joy in fellowship

25. **3 John** – *Admonition to Receive True Believers*
    a. Gaius, brother in the Church
    b. Diotrephes
    c. Demetrius

26. **Jude** – *Contending for the Faith*
    a. Occasion of the epistle
    b. Occurrences of apostasy
    c. Occupation of believers in the days of apostasy

27. **Revelation** – *The Unveiling of Christ Glorified*
    a. The person of Christ in glory
    b. The possession of Jesus Christ - the Church in the World
    c. The program of Jesus Christ - the scene in Heaven
    d. The seven seals
    e. The seven trumpets
    f. Important persons in the last days
    g. The seven vials
    h. The fall of Babylon
    i. The eternal state

Appendix 11

From Before to Beyond Time
The Plan of God and Human History

Adapted from Suzanne de Dietrich. *God's Unfolding Purpose*. Philadelphia: Westminster Press, 1976.

I. **Before Time (Eternity Past) 1 Cor. 2.7**
   A. The Eternal Triune God
   B. God's Eternal Purpose
   C. The Mystery of Iniquity
   D. The Principalities and Powers

II. **Beginning of Time (Creation and Fall) Gen. 1.1**
   A. Creative Word
   B. Humanity
   C. Fall
   D. Reign of Death and First Signs of Grace

III. **Unfolding of Time (God's Plan Revealed Through Israel) Gal. 3.8**
   A. Promise (Patriarchs)
   B. Exodus and Covenant at Sinai
   C. Promised Land
   D. The City, the Temple, and the Throne (Prophet, Priest, and King)
   E. Exile
   F. Remnant

IV. **Fullness of Time (Incarnation of the Messiah) Gal. 4.4-5**
   A. The King Comes to His Kingdom
   B. The Present Reality of His Reign
   C. The Secret of the Kingdom: the Already and the Not Yet
   D. The Crucified King
   E. The Risen Lord

V. **The Last Times (The Descent of the Holy Spirit) Acts 2.16-18**
   A. Between the Times: the Church as Foretaste of the Kingdom
   B. The Church as Agent of the Kingdom
   C. The Conflict Between the Kingdoms of Darkness and Light

VI. **The Fulfillment of Time (The Second Coming) Matt. 13.40-43**
   A. The Return of Christ
   B. Judgment
   C. The Consummation of His Kingdom

VII. **Beyond Time (Eternity Future) 1 Cor. 15.24-28**
   A. Kingdom Handed Over to God the Father
   B. God as All in All

Appendix 12

"There Is a River"

Identifying the Streams of a Revitalized Authentic Christian Community in the City[1]

Rev. Dr. Don L. Davis • Psalm 46.4 (ESV) - There is a river whose streams make glad the city of God, the holy habitation of the Most High.

Tributaries of Authentic Historic Biblical Faith			
Recognized Biblical Identity	*Revived Urban Spirituality*	*Reaffirmed Historical Connectivity*	*Refocused Kingdom Authority*
The Church Is **One**	The Church Is **Holy**	The Church Is **Catholic**	The Church Is **Apostolic**
A Call to Biblical Fidelity *Recognizing the Scriptures as the anchor and foundation of the Christian faith and practice*	A Call to the Freedom, Power, and Fullness of the Holy Spirit *Walking in the holiness, power, gifting, and liberty of the Holy Spirit in the body of Christ*	A Call to Historic Roots and Continuity *Confessing the common historical identity and continuity of authentic Christian faith*	A Call to the Apostolic Faith *Affirming the apostolic tradition as the authoritative ground of the Christian hope*
A Call to Messianic Kingdom Identity *Rediscovering the story of the promised Messiah and his Kingdom in Jesus of Nazareth*	A Call to Live as Sojourners and Aliens as the People of God *Defining authentic Christian discipleship as faithful membership among God's people*	A Call to Affirm and Express the Global Communion of Saints *Expressing cooperation and collaboration with all other believers, both local and global*	A Call to Representative Authority *Submitting joyfully to God's gifted servants in the Church as undershepherds of true faith*
A Call to Creedal Affinity *Embracing the Nicene Creed as the shared rule of faith of historic orthodoxy*	A Call to Liturgical, Sacramental, and Catechetical Vitality *Experiencing God's presence in the context of the Word, sacrament, and instruction*	A Call to Radical Hospitality and Good Works *Expressing kingdom love to all, and especially to those of the household of faith*	A Call to Prophetic and Holistic Witness *Proclaiming Christ and his Kingdom in word and deed to our neighbors and all peoples*

---

[1] *This schema is an adaptation and is based on the insights of the **Chicago Call** statement of May 1977, where various leading evangelical scholars and practitioners met to discuss the relationship of modern evangelicalism to the historic Christian faith.*

Appendix 13

A Schematic for a Theology of the Kingdom and the Church

The Urban Ministry Institute

The Reign of the One, True, Sovereign, and Triune God, the LORD God, Yahweh, God the Father, Son, and Holy Spirit

The Father	**The Son**	**The Spirit**
Love - 1 John 4.8	Faith - Heb. 12.2	Hope - Rom. 15.13
Maker of heaven and earth and of all things visible and invisible	Prophet, Priest, and King	Lord of the Church

Creation	**Kingdom**	**Church**
All that exists through the creative action of God.	The Reign of God expressed in the rule of his Son Jesus the Messiah.	The one, holy, apostolic community which functions as a witness to (Acts 28.31) and a foretaste of (Col. 1.12; James 1.18; 1 Pet. 2.9; Rev. 1.6) the Kingdom of God.

		The Church is an Apostolic Community Where the Word is Rightly Preached, Therefore it is a Community of:
The eternal God, sovereign in power, infinite in wisdom, perfect in holiness, and steadfast in love, is the source and goal of all things.	**Freedom** (Slavery) Jesus replied, "I tell you the truth, everyone who sins is a slave to sin. Now a slave has no permanent place in the family but a son belongs to it forever. So if the Son sets you free, you will be free indeed." - John 8.34-36 (NIV)	**Calling** - It is for freedom that Christ has set us free. Stand firm, then, and do not let yourselves be burdened again by a yoke of slavery. - Gal. 5.1 (NIV) (cf. Rom. 8.28-30; 1 Cor. 1.26-31; Eph. 1.18; 2 Thess. 2.13-14; Jude 1.1) **Faith** - "If you do not believe that I am the one I claim to be, you will indeed die in your sins". . . . To the Jews who had believed him Jesus said, "If you hold to my teaching you are really my disciples. Then you will know the truth and the truth will set you free." - John 8.24b, 31-32 (NIV) (cf. Ps. 119.45; Rom. 1.17; 5.1-2; Eph. 2.8-9; 2 Tim. 1.13-14; Heb. 2.14-15; James 1.25) **Witness** - The Spirit of the Lord is upon me because he has anointed me to preach good news to the poor. He has sent me to proclaim freedom for the prisoners and recovery of sight for the blind, to release the oppressed, to proclaim the year of the Lord's favor. - Luke 4.18-19 (NIV) (cf. Lev. 25.10; Prov. 31.8; Matt. 4.17; 28.18-20; Mark 13.10; Acts 1.8; 8.4, 12; 13.1-3; 25.20; 28.30-31)

Rev. 8.18-31 →

		The Church is One Community Where the Sacraments are Rightly Administered, Therefore it is a Community of:
O, the depth of the riches of the wisdom and knowledge of God! How unsearchable his judgments, and his paths beyond tracing out! Who has known the mind of the Lord? Or who has been his counselor? Who has ever given to God, that God should repay him? For from him and through him and to him are all things. To him be glory forever! Amen. - Rom. 11.33-36 (NIV) (cf. 1 Cor. 15.23-28; Rev.)	**Wholeness** (Sickness) But he was pierced for our transgressions, he was crushed for our iniquities; the punishment that brought us peace was upon him and by his wounds we are healed. - Isa. 53.5 (NIV)	**Worship** - Worship the Lord your God, and his blessing will be on your food and water. I will take away sickness from among you. - Exod. 23.25 (NIV) (cf. Ps. 147.1-3; Heb. 12.28; Col. 3.16; Rev. 15.3-4; 19.5) **Covenant** - The Holy Spirit also testifies to us about this. First he says: "This is the covenant I will make with them after that time, says the Lord. I will put My laws in their hearts, and I will write them on their minds." Then he adds: "Their sins and lawless acts I will remember no more." - Heb. 10.15-17 (NIV) (cf. Isa. 54.10-17; Ezek. 34.25-31; 37.26-27; Mal. 2.4-5; Luke 22.20; 2 Cor. 3.6; Col. 3.15; Heb. 8.7-13; 12.22-24; 13.20-21) **Presence** - And in him you too are being built together to become a dwelling in which God lives by his Spirit. - Eph. 2.22 (NIV) (cf. Exod. 40.34-38; Ezek. 48.35; Matt. 18.18-20)

Rev. 21.1-5 →

		The Church is a Holy Community Where Discipline is Rightly Ordered, Therefore it is a Community of:
	Justice (Selfishness) Here is my servant whom I have chosen, the one I love, in whom I delight; I will put my spirit on him and he will proclaim justice to the nations. He will not quarrel or cry out; no one will hear his voice in the streets. A bruised reed he will not break and a smoldering wick he will not put out till he leads justice to victory. - Matt. 12.18-20 (NIV)	**Reconciliation** - For he himself is our peace, who has made the two one and has destroyed the barrier, the dividing wall of hostility by abolishing in his flesh the law with its commandments and regulations. His purpose was to create one new man out of two, thus making peace and in this one body to reconcile both of them to God through the cross, by which he put to death their hostility. He came and preached peace to those who were far off and peace to those who were near. For through him we have access to the Father by one Spirit. - Eph. 2.14-18 (NIV) (cf. Exod. 23.4-9; Lev. 19.34; Deut. 10.18-19; Ezek. 22.29; Mic. 6.8; 2 Cor. 5.16-21) **Suffering** - Therefore, since Christ suffered in his body, arm yourselves also with the same attitude, because he who has suffered in his body is done with sin. As a result, he does not live the rest of his earthly life for evil human desires, but rather for the will of God. - 1 Pet. 4.1-2 (NIV) (cf. Luke 6.22; 10.3; Rom. 8.17; 2 Tim. 2.3; 3.12; 1 Pet. 2.20-24; Heb. 5.8; 13.11-14) **Service** - Jesus called them together and said, "You know that the rulers of the Gentiles lord it over them, and their high officials exercise authority over them. Not so with you. Instead, whoever wants to become great among you must be your servant, and whoever wants to be first must be your slave - just as the Son of Man did not come to be served, but to serve and to give his life as a ransom for many." - Matt. 20.25-27 (NIV) (cf. 1 John 4.16-18; Gal. 2.10)

Isa. 11.6-9 →

Appendix 14
Living in the Already and the Not Yet Kingdom
Rev. Dr. Don L. Davis

The Spirit: The pledge of the inheritance *(arrabon)*
The Church: The foretaste *(aparche)* of the Kingdom
"In Christ": The rich life *(en Christos)* we share as citizens of the Kingdom

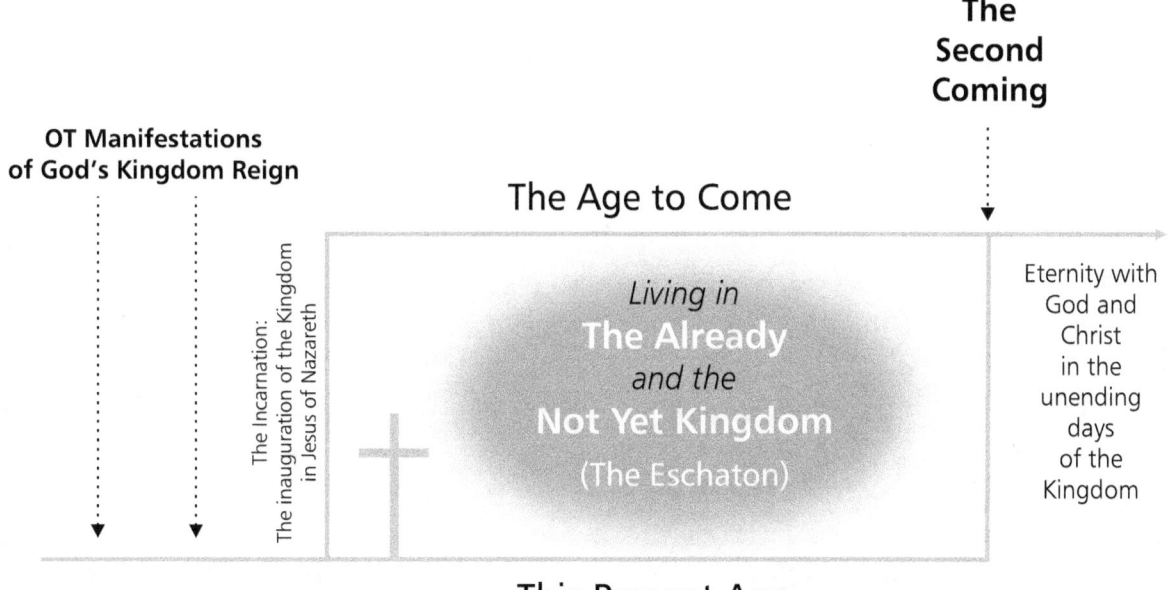

Internal enemy: The flesh (*sarx*) and the sin nature
External enemy: The world (*kosmos*) the systems of greed, lust, and pride
Infernal enemy: The devil (*kakos*) the animating spirit of falsehood and fear

Jewish View of Time

This Present Age | The Age to Come

The Coming of Messiah
The restoration of Israel
The end of Gentile oppression
The return of the earth to Edenic glory
Universal knowledge of the Lord

Appendix 15
Jesus of Nazareth: The Presence of the Future
Rev. Dr. Don L. Davis

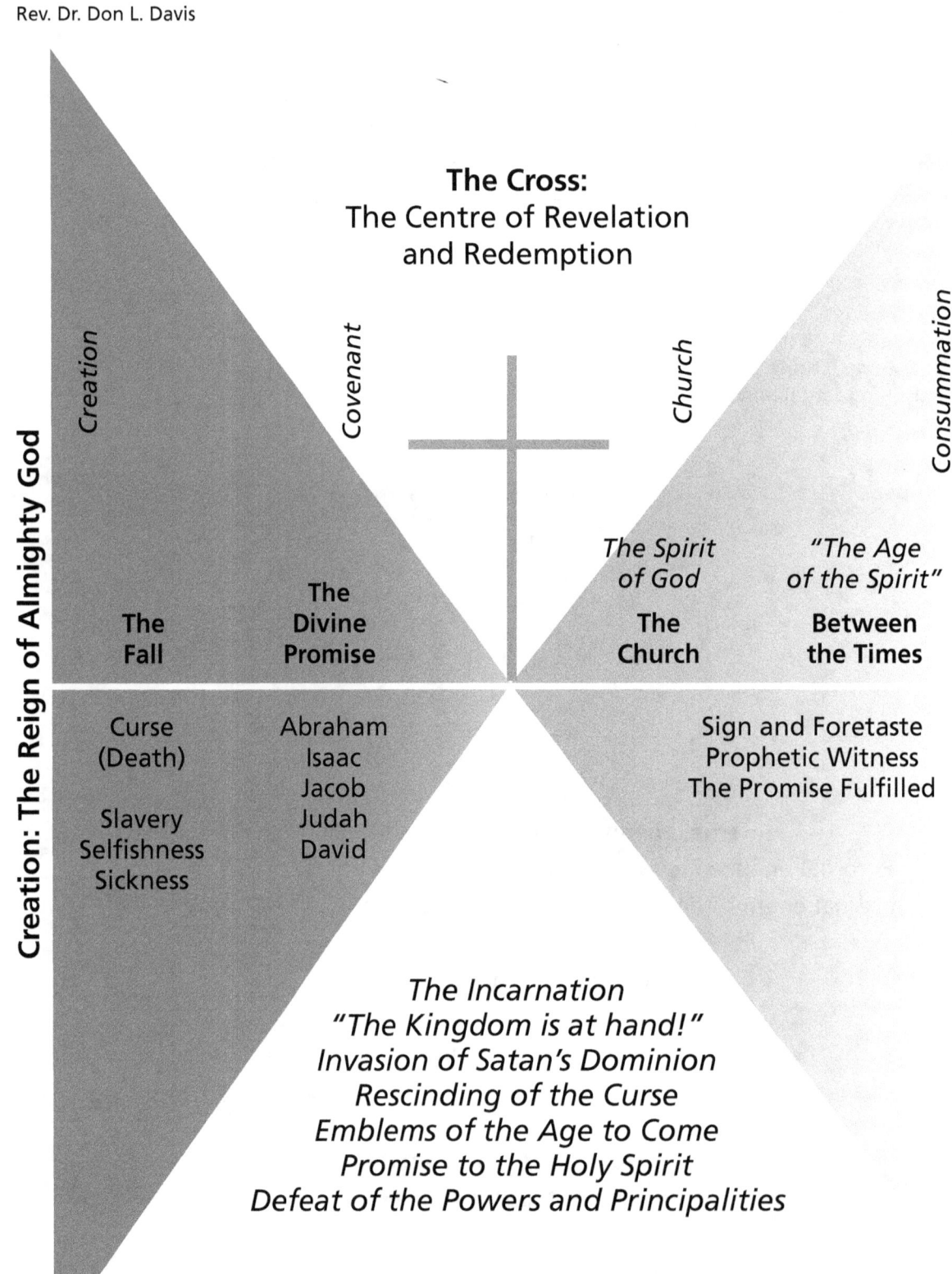

Appendix 16
Traditions
(Paradosis)
Dr. Don L. Davis and Rev. Terry G. Cornett

Strong's Definition

Paradosis. Transmission, i.e. (concretely) a precept; specifically, the Jewish traditionary law

Vine's Explanation

denotes "a tradition," and hence, by metonymy, (a) "the teachings of the rabbis," . . . (b) "apostolic teaching," . . . of instructions concerning the gatherings of believers, of Christian doctrine in general . . . of instructions concerning everyday conduct.

1. **The concept of tradition in Scripture is essentially positive.**

   Jer. 6.16 (ESV) – Thus says the Lord: "Stand by the roads, and look, and ask for the ancient paths, where the good way is; and walk in it, and find rest for your souls. But they said, 'We will not walk in it'" (cf. Exod. 3.15; Judg. 2.17; 1 Kings 8.57-58; Ps. 78.1-6).

   2 Chron. 35.25 (ESV) – Jeremiah also uttered a lament for Josiah; and all the singing men and singing women have spoken of Josiah in their laments to this day. They made these a rule in Israel; behold, they are written in the Laments (cf. Gen. 32.32; Judg. 11.38-40).

   Jer. 35.14-19 (ESV) – "The command that Jonadab the son of Rechab gave to his sons, to drink no wine, has been kept, and they drink none to this day, for they have obeyed their father's command. I have spoken to you persistently, but you have not listened to me. I have sent to you all my servants the prophets, sending them persistently, saying, 'Turn now every one of you from his evil way, and amend your deeds, and do not go after other gods to serve them, and then you shall dwell in the land that I gave to you and your fathers.' But you did not incline your ear or listen to me. The sons of Jonadab the son of Rechab have kept the command that their father gave them, but this people has

Traditions, continued

not obeyed me. Therefore, thus says the Lord, the God of hosts, the God of Israel: Behold, I am bringing upon Judah and all the inhabitants of Jerusalem all the disaster that I have pronounced against them, because I have spoken to them and they have not listened, I have called to them and they have not answered." But to the house of the Rechabites Jeremiah said, "Thus says the Lord of hosts, the God of Israel: Because you have obeyed the command of Jonadab your father and kept all his precepts and done all that he commanded you, therefore thus says the Lord of hosts, the God of Israel: Jonadab the son of Rechab shall never lack a man to stand before me."

2. **Godly tradition is a wonderful thing, but not all tradition is godly.**

   Any individual tradition must be judged by its faithfulness to the Word of God and its usefulness in helping people maintain obedience to Christ's example and teaching.[1] In the Gospels, Jesus frequently rebukes the Pharisees for establishing traditions that nullify rather than uphold God's commands.

   Mark 7.8 (ESV) – You leave the commandment of God and hold to the tradition of men (cf. Matt. 15.2-6; Mark 7.13).

   Col. 2.8 (ESV) – See to it that no one takes you captive by philosophy and empty deceit, according to human tradition, according to the elemental spirits of the world, and not according to Christ.

3. **Without the fullness of the Holy Spirit, and the constant edification provided to us by the Word of God, tradition will inevitably lead to dead formalism.**

   Those who are spiritual are filled with the Holy Spirit, whose power and leading alone provides individuals and congregations a sense of freedom and vitality in all they practice and believe. However, when the practices and teachings of any given tradition are no longer infused by the power of the Holy Spirit and the Word of God, tradition loses its effectiveness, and may actually become counterproductive to our discipleship in Jesus Christ.

---

[1] "All Protestants insist that these traditions must ever be tested against Scripture and can never possess an independent apostolic authority over or alongside of Scripture." (J. Van Engen, "Tradition," ***Evangelical Dictionary of Theology***, Walter Elwell, Gen. ed.) We would add that Scripture is itself the "authoritative tradition" by which all other traditions are judged. See "Appendix A, The Founders of Tradition: Three Levels of Christian Authority," at the end of this document.

Traditions, continued

Eph. 5.18 (ESV) – And do not get drunk with wine, for that is debauchery, but be filled with the Spirit.

Gal. 5.22-25 (ESV) – But the fruit of the Spirit is love, joy, peace, patience, kindness, goodness, faithfulness, gentleness, self-control; against such things there is no law. And those who belong to Christ Jesus have crucified the flesh with its passions and desires. If we live by the Spirit, let us also walk by the Spirit.

2 Cor. 3.5-6 (ESV) – Not that we are sufficient in ourselves to claim anything as coming from us, but our sufficiency is from God, who has made us competent to be ministers of a new covenant, not of the letter but of the Spirit. For the letter kills, but the Spirit gives life.

4. **Fidelity to the Apostolic Tradition (teaching and modeling) is the essence of Christian maturity.**

   2 Tim. 2.2 (ESV) – and what you have heard from me in the presence of many witnesses entrust to faithful men who will be able to teach others also.

   1 Cor. 11.1-2 (ESV) – Be imitators of me, as I am of Christ. Now I commend you because you remember me in everything and maintain the traditions even as I delivered them to you (cf. 1 Cor. 4.16-17, 2 Tim. 1.13-14, 2 Thess. 3.7-9, Phil. 4.9).

   1 Cor. 15.3-8 (ESV) – For I delivered to you as of first importance what I also received: that Christ died for our sins in accordance with the Scriptures, that he was buried, that he was raised on the third day in accordance with the Scriptures, and that he appeared to Cephas, then to the twelve. Then he appeared to more than five hundred brothers at one time, most of whom are still alive, though some have fallen asleep. Then he appeared to James, then to all the apostles. Last of all, as to one untimely born, he appeared also to me.

5. **The Apostle Paul often includes an appeal to the tradition for support in doctrinal practices.**

Traditions, continued

> 1 Cor. 11.16 (ESV) – If anyone is inclined to be contentious, we have no such practice, nor do the churches of God (cf. 1 Cor. 1.2, 7.17, 15.3).
>
> 1 Cor. 14.33-34 (ESV) – For God is not a God of confusion but of peace. As in all the churches of the saints, the women should keep silent in the churches. For they are not permitted to speak, but should be in submission, as the Law also says.

6. **When a congregation uses received tradition to remain faithful to the "Word of God," they are commended by the apostles.**

   > 1 Cor. 11.2 (ESV) – Now I commend you because you remember me in everything and maintain the traditions even as I delivered them to you.
   >
   > 2 Thess. 2.15 (ESV) – So then, brothers, stand firm and hold to the traditions that you were taught by us, either by our spoken word or by our letter.
   >
   > 2 Thess. 3.6 (ESV) – Now we command you, brothers, in the name of our Lord Jesus Christ, that you keep away from any brother who is walking in idleness and not in accord with the tradition that you received from us.

Appendix A

The Founders of Tradition Three Levels of Christian Authority

Exod. 3.15 (ESV) – God also said to Moses, "Say this to the people of Israel, 'The Lord, the God of your fathers, the God of Abraham, the God of Isaac, and the God of Jacob, has sent me to you.' This is my name forever, and thus I am to be remembered throughout all generations."

1. **The Authoritative Tradition: The Apostles and the Prophets (The Holy Scriptures)**

   > Eph. 2.19-21 (ESV) – So then you are no longer strangers and aliens, but you are fellow citizens with the saints and members of the house-

Traditions, continued

hold of God, built on the foundation of the apostles and prophets, Christ Jesus himself being the cornerstone, in whom the whole structure, being joined together, grows into a holy temple in the Lord.

~ The Apostle Paul

God revealed his saving work to those who would give eyewitness testimony to his glory, first in Israel, and ultimately in Jesus Christ the Messiah. This testimony is binding for all people, at all times, and in all places. It is the authoritative tradition by which all subsequent tradition is judged.

[2] See Appendix B, "Defining the Great Tradition," at the end of this document.

2. The Great Tradition: the Ecumenical Councils and their Creeds[2]

What has been believed everywhere, always, and by all.

~ Vincent of Lerins

The Great Tradition is the core dogma (doctrine) of the Church. It represents the teaching of the Church as it has understood the Authoritative Tradition (the Holy Scriptures), and summarizes those essential truths that Christians of all ages have confessed and believed. To these doctrinal statements the whole Church (Catholic, Orthodox, and Protestant)[3] gives its assent. The worship and theology of the Church reflects this core dogma, which finds its summation and fulfillment in the person and work of Jesus Christ. From earliest times, Christians have ex-pressed their devotion to God in its Church calendar, a yearly pattern of worship which summarizes and reenacts the events of Christ's life.

[3] Even the more radical wing of the Protestant reformation (Anabaptists) who were the most reluctant to embrace the creeds as dogmatic instruments of faith, did not disagree with the essential content found in them. "They assumed the Apostolic Creed– they called it 'The Faith,' *Der Glaube*, as did most people." See John Howard Yoder, **Preface to Theology: Christology and Theological Method**. Grand Rapids: Brazos Press, 2002. pp. 222-223.

3. Specific Church Traditions: the Founders of Denominations and Orders

The Presbyterian Church (U.S.A.) has approximately 2.5 million members, 11,200 congregations and 21,000 ordained ministers. Presbyterians trace their history to the 16th century and the Protestant Reformation. Our heritage, and much of what we believe, began with the French lawyer John Calvin (1509-1564), whose writings crystallized much of the Reformed thinking that came before him.

~ The Presbyterian Church, U.S.A.

Christians have expressed their faith in Jesus Christ in various ways through specific movements and traditions which embrace

Traditions, continued

and express the Authoritative Tradition and the Great Tradition in unique ways. For instance, Catholic movements have arisen around people like Benedict, Francis, or Dominic, and among Protestants people like Martin Luther, John Calvin, Ulrich Zwingli, and John Wesley. Women have founded vital movements of Christian faith (e.g., Aimee Semple McPherson of the Foursquare Church), as well as minorities (e.g., Richard Allen of the African Methodist Episcopal Church or Charles H. Mason of the Church of God in Christ, who also helped to spawn the Assemblies of God), all which attempted to express the Authoritative Tradition and the Great Tradition in a specific way consistent with their time and expression.

The emergence of vital, dynamic movements of the faith at different times and among different peoples reveal the fresh working of the Holy Spirit throughout history. Thus, inside Catholicism, new communities have arisen such as the Bene-dictines, Franciscans, and Dominicans; and outside Catholicism, new denominations have emerged (Lutherans, Presbyterians, Methodists, Church of God in Christ, etc.). Each of these specific traditions have "founders," key leaders whose energy and vision helped to establish a unique expression of Christian faith and practice. Of course, to be legitimate, these movements must adhere to and faithfully express both the Authoritative Tradition and the Great Tradition. Members of these specific traditions embrace their own practices and patterns of spirituality, but these particular features are not necessarily binding on the Church at large. They represent the unique expressions of that community's understanding of and faithfulness to the Authoritative and Great Traditions.

Specific traditions seek to express and live out this faithfulness to the Authoritative and Great Traditions through their worship, teaching, and service. They seek to make the Gospel clear within new cultures or sub-cultures, speaking and modeling the hope of Christ into new situations shaped by their own set of questions posed in light of their own unique circumstances. These move-ments, therefore, seek to contextualize the Authoritative tradition in a way that faithfully and effectively leads new groups of people to faith in Jesus Christ, and incorporates those who believe into the community of faith that obeys his teachings and gives witness of him to others.

Traditions, continued

Appendix B

Defining the "Great Tradition"

The Great Tradition (sometimes called the "classical Christian tradition") is defined by Robert E. Webber as follows:

> [It is] the broad outline of Christian belief and practice developed from the Scriptures between the time of Christ and the middle of the fifth century.
> ~ Webber. *The Majestic Tapestry*.
> Nashville: Thomas Nelson Publishers, 1986. p. 10.

This tradition is widely affirmed by Protestant theologians both ancient and modern.

> Thus those ancient Councils of Nicea, Constantinople, the first of Ephesus, Chalcedon, and the like, which were held for refuting errors, we willingly embrace, and reverence as sacred, in so far as relates to doctrines of faith, for they contain nothing but the pure and genuine interpretation of Scripture, which the holy Fathers with spiritual prudence adopted to crush the enemies of religion who had then arisen.
> ~ John Calvin. *Institutes*. IV, ix. 8.

> . . most of what is enduringly valuable in contemporary biblical exegesis was discovered by the fifth century.
> ~ Thomas C. Oden. *The Word of Life*.
> San Francisco: HarperSanFrancisco, 1989. p. xi

> The first four Councils are by far the most important, as they settled the orthodox faith on the Trinity and the Incarnation.
> ~ Philip Schaff. *The Creeds of Christendom*. Vol. 1.
> Grand Rapids: Baker Book House, 1996. p. 44.

Our reference to the Ecumenical Councils and Creeds is, therefore, focused on those Councils which retain a widespread agreement in the Church among Catholics, Orthodox, and Protestants. While Catholic and Orthodox share common agreement on the first seven councils, Protestants tend to affirm and use primarily the first four. Therefore, those councils which continue to be shared by the whole Church are completed with the Council of Chalcedon in 451.

Traditions, continued

It is worth noting that each of these four Ecumenical Councils took place in a pre-European cultural context and that none of them were held in Europe. They were councils of the whole Church and they reflected a time in which Christianity was primarily an eastern religion in it's geographic core. By modern reckoning, their par- ticipants were African, Asian, and European. The councils reflected a church that ". . . has roots in cultures far distant from Europe and preceded the development of modern European identity, and [of which] some of its greatest minds have been African" (Oden, The *Living God*, San Francisco: HarperSanFrancisco, 1987, p. 9).

Perhaps the most important achievement of the Councils was the creation of what is now commonly called the Nicene Creed. It serves as a summary statement of the Christian faith that can be agreed on by Catholic, Orthodox, and Protestant Christians.

The first four Ecumenical Councils are summarized in the following chart:

Name/Date/Location	Purpose	
First Ecumenical Council 325 A.D. Nicea, Asia Minor	Defending against: Question answered: Action:	*Arianism* *Was Jesus God?* *Developed the initial form of the Nicene Creed to serve as a summary of the Christian faith*
Second Ecumenical Council 381 A.D. Constantinople, Asia Minor	Defending against: Question answered: Action:	*Macedonianism* *Is the Holy Spirit a personal and equal part of the Godhead?* *Completed the Nicene Creed by expanding the article dealing with the Holy Spirit*
Third Ecumenical Council 431 A.D. Ephesus, Asia Minor	Defending against: Question answered: Action:	*Nestorianism* *Is Jesus Christ both God and man in one person?* *Defined Christ as the Incarnate Word of God and affirmed his mother Mary as theotokos (God-bearer)*
Fourth Ecumenical Council 451 A.D. Chalcedon, Asia Minor	Defending against: Question answered: Action:	*Monophysitism* *How can Jesus be both God and man?* *Explained the relationship between Jesus' two natures (human and Divine)*

Appendix 17
Documenting Your Work
A Guide to Help You Give Credit Where Credit Is Due
The Urban Ministry Institute

Avoiding Plagiarism

Plagiarism is using another person's ideas as if they belonged to you without giving them proper credit. In academic work it is just as wrong to steal a person's ideas as it is to steal a person's property. These ideas may come from the author of a book, an article you have read, or from a fellow student. The way to avoid plagiarism is to carefully use "notes" (textnotes, footnotes, endnotes, etc.) and a "Works Cited" section to help people who read your work know when an idea is one you thought of, and when you are borrowing an idea from another person.

Using Citation References

A citation reference is required in a paper whenever you use ideas or information that came from another person's work.

All citation references involve two parts:

- Notes in the body of your paper placed next to each quotation which came from an outside source.

- A "Works Cited" page at the end of your paper or project which gives information about the sources you have used

Using Notes in Your Paper

There are three basic kinds of notes: parenthetical notes, footnotes, and endnotes. At The Urban Ministry Institute, we recommend that students use parenthetical notes. These notes give the author's last name(s), the date the book was published, and the page number(s) on which you found the information. Example:

> In trying to understand the meaning of Genesis 14.1-24, it is important to recognize that in biblical stories "the place where dialogue is first introduced will be an important moment in revealing the character of the speaker . . ." (Kaiser and Silva 1994, 73). This is certainly true of the character of Melchizedek who speaks words of blessing. This identification of Melchizedek as a positive spiritual influence is reinforced by the fact that he is the King of Salem, since Salem means "safe, at peace" (Wiseman 1996, 1045).

Documenting Your Work, *continued*

Creating a Works Cited Page

A "Works Cited" page should be placed at the end of your paper. This page:

- lists every source you quoted in your paper
- is in alphabetical order by author's last name
- includes the date of publication and information about the publisher

The following formatting rules should be followed:

1. **Title**

   The title "Works Cited" should be used and centered on the first line of the page following the top margin.

2. **Content**

   Each reference should list:

   - the author's full name (last name first)
   - the date of publication
   - the title and any special information (Revised edition, 2nd edition, reprint) taken from the cover or title page should be noted
   - the city where the publisher is headquartered followed by a colon and the name of the publisher

3. **Basic form**

   - Each piece of information should be separated by a period.
   - The second line of a reference (and all following lines) should be indented.
   - Book titles should be underlined (or italicized).
   - Article titles should be placed in quotes.

   Example:

   Fee, Gordon D. 1991. *Gospel and Spirit: Issues in New Testament Hermeneutics*. Peabody, MA: Hendrickson Publishers.

Documenting Your Work, continued

4. **Special Forms**

   A book with multiple authors:

   Kaiser, Walter C., and Moisés Silva. 1994. *An Introduction to Biblical Hermeneutics: The Search for Meaning.* Grand Rapids: Zondervan Publishing House.

   An edited book:

   Greenway, Roger S., ed. 1992. *Discipling the City: A Comprehensive Approach to Urban Mission.* 2nd ed. Grand Rapids: Baker Book House.

   A book that is part of a series:

   Morris, Leon. 1971. *The Gospel According to John.* Grand Rapids: Wm. B. Eerdmans Publishing Co. The New International Commentary on the New Testament. Gen. ed. F. F. Bruce.

   An article in a reference book:

   Wiseman, D. J. "Salem." 1982. In *New Bible Dictionary.* Leicester, England - Downers Grove, IL: InterVarsity Press. Eds. I. H. Marshall and others.

   (*An example of a "Works Cited" page is located at the end of this appendix.*)

For Further Research

Standard guides to documenting academic work in the areas of philosophy, religion, theology, and ethics include:

Atchert, Walter S., and Joseph Gibaldi. 1985. *The MLA Style Manual.* New York: Modern Language Association.

The Chicago Manual of Style. 1993. 14th ed. Chicago: The University of Chicago Press.

Turabian, Kate L. 1987. *A Manual for Writers of Term Papers, Theses, and Dissertations.* 5th edition. Bonnie Bertwistle Honigsblum, ed. Chicago: The University of Chicago Press.

Documenting Your Work, continued

Works Cited

Fee, Gordon D. 1991. *Gospel and Spirit: Issues in New Testament Hermeneutics*. Peabody, MA: Hendrickson Publishers.

Greenway, Roger S., ed. 1992. *Discipling the City: A Comprehensive Approach to Urban Mission*. 2nd ed. Grand Rapids: Baker Book House.

Kaiser, Walter C., and Moisés Silva. 1994. *An Introduction to Biblical Hermeneutics: The Search for Meaning*. Grand Rapids: Zondervan Publishing House.

Morris, Leon. 1971. *The Gospel According to John*. Grand Rapids: Wm. B. Eerdmans Publishing Co. *The New International Commentary on the New Testament*. Gen. ed. F. F. Bruce.

Wiseman, D. J. "Salem." 1982. In *New Bible Dictionary*. Leicester, England-Downers Grove, IL: InterVarsity Press. Eds. I. H. Marshall and others.

Appendix 18

Comparative Chart of the Millennial Views
Rev. Dr. Don L. Davis

A Chart Concerning the Millennium: Comparative outline of evangelical opinion on the Millennial Reign of Christ Adapted from *The Moody Handbook of Theology*.

Categories	VIEWS CONCERNING LAST THINGS			
	Amillennialism	Postmillennialism	Historic Premillennialism	Dispensational Premillennialism
Second Coming of Christ	Single event; no distinction between rapture and second coming; Introduces eternal state.	Single event; no distinction between rapture and second coming; Christ returns after Millennium.	Rapture and second coming simultaneous; Christ returns to reign on earth.	Second coming in two phases: rapture for church; second coming to earth 7 years later.
Resurrection	General resurrection of believers and unbelievers at second coming of Christ.	General resurrection of believers and unbelievers at second coming of Christ.	Resurrection of believers at beginning of Millennium. Resurrection of unbelievers at end of Millennium.	Distinction in resurrections: 1. Church at rapture. 2. Old Testament/Tribulation saints at second coming. 3. Unbelievers at end of Millennium.
Judgments	General judgment of all people.	General judgment of all people.	Judgment at second coming. Judgment at end of Tribulation.	Distinction in judgment: 1. Believers works at rapture; 2. Jews/Gentiles at end of Tribulation. 3. Unbelievers at end of Millennium.
Tribulation	Tribulation is experienced in the present age.	Tribulation is experienced in this present age.	Posttrib view: church goes through the future Tribulation.	Pretrib view: church is raptured prior to Tribulation.
Millennium	No literal Millennium on earth after second coming. Kingdom present in church age.	Present age blends into Millennium because of progress of gospel.	Millennium is both present and future. Christ is reigning in heaven. Millennium is not necessarily 1,000 years.	At second coming Christ inaugurates literal 1,000-year Millennium on earth.
Israel and the Church	Church is the new Israel. No distinction between Israel and church	Church is the new Israel. No distinction between Israel and church	Some distinction between Israel and church. Future for Israel but church is spiritual Israel.	Complete distinction between Israel and church. Distinct program for each.
Adherents	L. Berkhof O.T. Allis G.C. Berkhouwer	Charles Hodge B.B. Warfield W.G.T. Shedd A.H. Strong	G.E. Ladd A. Reese M.J. Erickson	L.S. Chafer J.D. Pentecost C.C. Ryrie J.F. Walvoord

Appendix 19
Compass of Narrative Elements
Rev. Dr. Don L. Davis

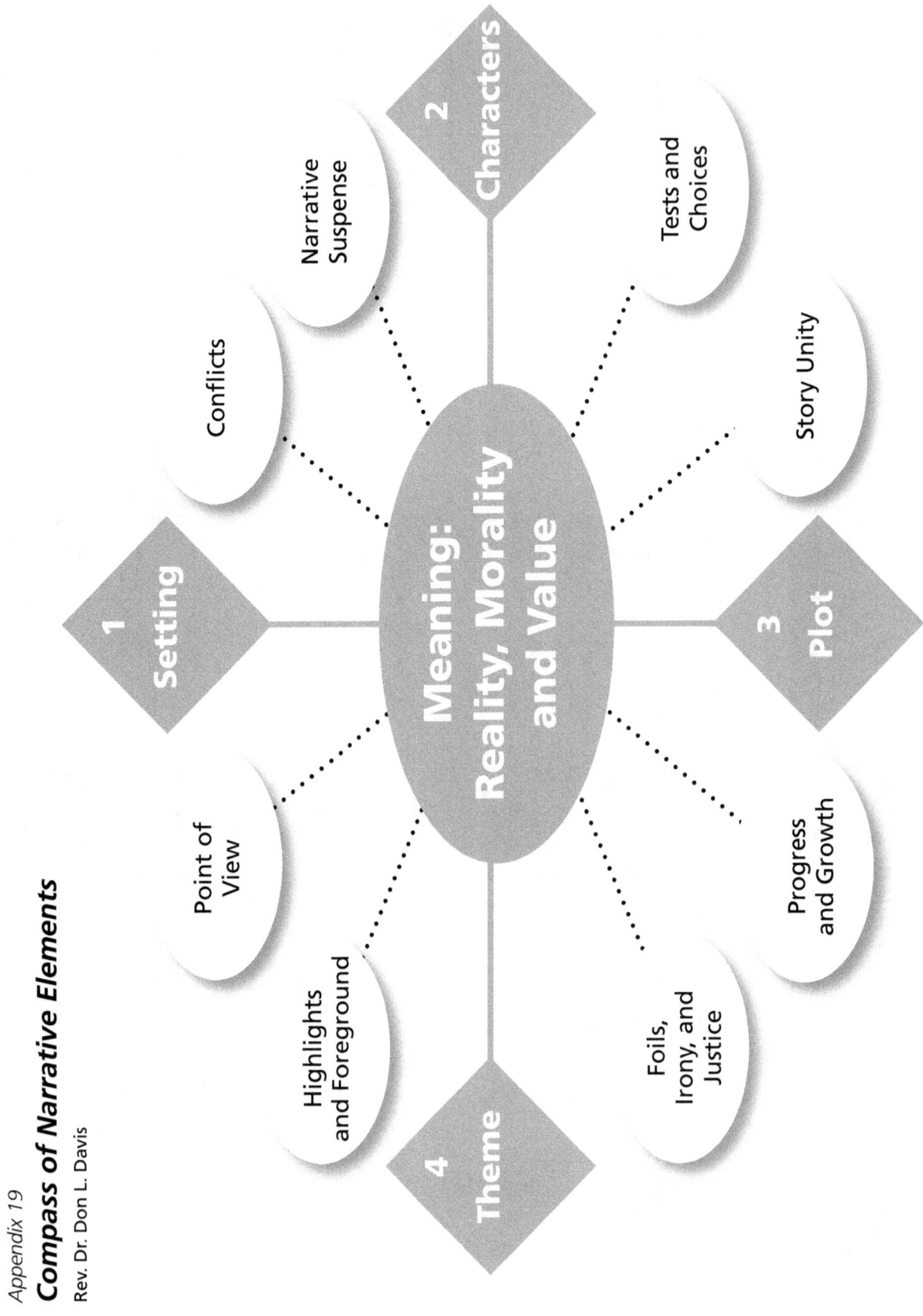

Appendix 20
Ethics Of The New Testament
Living in the Upside-Down Kingdom of God
Rev. Dr. Don L. Davis

The Principle of Reversal

The Principle Expressed	Scripture
The poor shall become rich, and the rich shall become poor	Luke 6.20-26
The law breaker and the undeserving are saved	Matt. 21.31-32
Those who humble themselves shall be exalted	1 Pet. 5.5-6
Those who exalt themselves shall be brought low	Luke 18.14
The blind shall be given sight	John 9.39
Those claiming to see shall be made blind	John 9.40-41
We become free by being Christ's slave	Rom. 12.1-2
God has chosen what is foolish in the world to shame the wise	1 Cor. 1.27
God has chosen what is weak in the world to shame the strong	1 Cor. 1.27
God has chosen the low and despised to bring to nothing things that are	1 Cor. 1.28
We gain the next world by losing this one	1 Tim. 6.7
Love this life and you'll lose it; hate this life, and you'll keep the next	John 12.25
You become the greatest by being the servant of all	Matt. 10.42-45
Store up treasures here, you forfeit heaven's reward	Matt. 6.19
Store up treasures above, you gain heaven's wealth	Matt. 6.20
Accept your own death to yourself in order to live fully	John 12.24
Release all earthly reputation to gain heaven's favor	Phil. 3.3-7
The first shall be last, and the last shall become first	Mark 9.35
The grace of Jesus is perfected in your weakness, not your strength	2 Cor. 12.9
God's highest sacrifice is contrition and brokenness	Ps. 51.17
It is better to give to others than to receive from them	Acts 20.35
Give away all you have in order to receive God's best	Luke 6.38

Appendix 21
Kingdom of God Timeline
Rev. Dr. Don L Davis

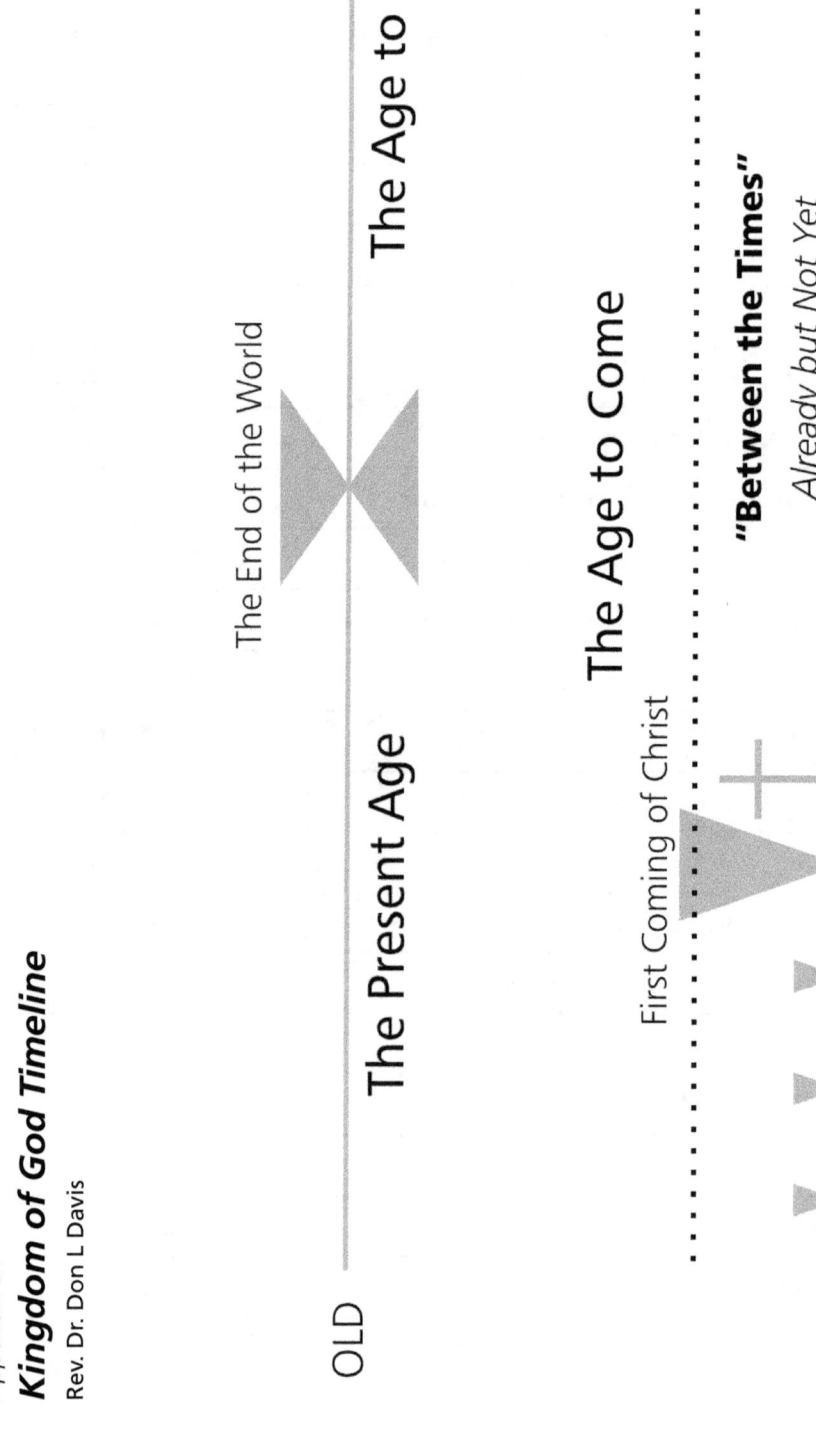

Appendix 22

Spectra of Orientation

Rev. Dr. Don L Davis

Galatians 5:16-18 But I say, walk by the Spirit, and you will not gratify the desires of the flesh. [17] For the desires of the flesh are against the Spirit, and the desires of the Spirit are against the flesh, for these are opposed to each other, to keep you from doing the things you want to do. [18] But if you are led by the Spirit, you are not under the law.

Romans 8:5-6 For those who live according to the flesh set their minds on the things of the flesh, but those who live according to the Spirit set their minds on the things of the Spirit. [6] To set the mind on the flesh is death, but to set the mind on the Spirit is life and peace.

Romans 8:13 For if you live according to the flesh you will die, but if by the Spirit you put to death the deeds of the body, you will live.

Orienting Our Stories to God's Biblical Story:
Beginning, Middle, and End

1. No BME -- Worldly, fleshly orientation
2. BME-- Nostalgic, overly sentimental orientation
3. BMe-- Preoccupation with "now" orientation
4. BME-- "Prophecy bug" event-finding orientation
5. "My Personal" BME-- Narcissistic self-centered orientation
6. B-M-E-- "Already/Not Yet" NT orientation

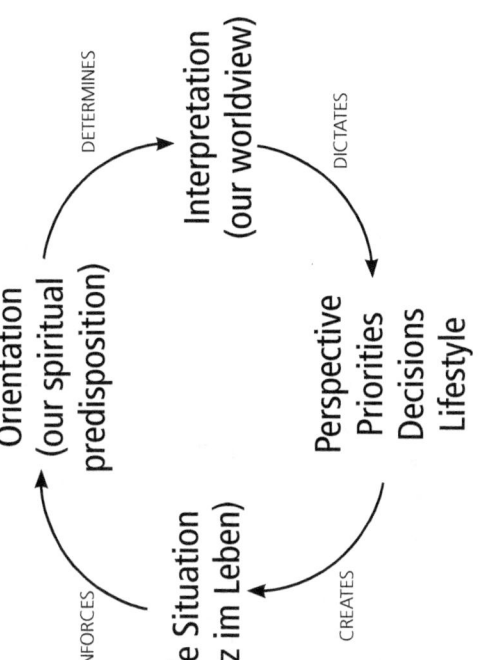

The Role of Prophecy in Worldview Orientation

Orientation (our spiritual predisposition) — DETERMINES → Interpretation (our worldview) — DICTATES → Perspective / Priorities / Decisions / Lifestyle — CREATES → Life Situation (sitz im Leben) — REINFORCES →

Dr. Don L. Davis.
February 2006.

Appendix 23
The Historic Hope of the Church
Adapted from George E. Ladd, *The Blessed Hope*.

	Date	Author	Gist of it	How the Hope is viewed	The Rapture?	Implications
The Didache	First quarter of the second century	Uncertain	One of the earliest pieces of Christian literature: Christian instruction	Invokes a spirit of watchfulness, warnings against falling away, the appearance of Antichrist, prepare Church for Great Tribulation	Author expects the Church to suffer in the Tribulation at Antichrist's hands	The coming of Christ to occur at the end of a time of woe and suffering
Barnabas	Same period as Didache	Anonymous	An epistle warning believers to prepare for the suffering ahead	Looking for the coming of Christ and for the last time of trouble, shun works of lawlessness and wicked folk, Antichrist is at hand	Expected the Church to go through the Tribulation; end will come after Empire falls	A clear belief that Antichrist would arise after Roman empire would fall
The Shepherd of Hermas	cir. 150 A.D.	Hermas	Letter to warn believers to be prepared	Believers will be preserved in and through Tribulation; deliverance is not from the presence but in the presence of it	Hermas is admonished to prepare the Church for the Tribulation	If the Church is prepared, it need not fear the sufferings to come
Justin Martyr	cir. 150 A.D.	Early Church father	Premillennial Instructions for Christians to ready themselves for persecution	Expectation of the Church to go through the Tribulation and be persecuted by the Antichrist; no fear of persecution: "the more things happen, the more do others and in larger numbers become faithful	Justin became a martyr, felt that the sufferings inflicted by the Antichrist would not be similar to sufferings then	Christians suffer thru beheadings, crucifixions, thrown to wild beasts, chains, and fire–they have and always endure
Irenaeus	Late second century	Bishop of Lyons	Premillennial system of interpretation of Church	Looked forward to a series of historical events within the Roman empire before Antichrist could arise and Christ return to earth; did not believe it was immediately at hand, Antichrist will persecute Christians, Christ will come at end of the Great Tribulation	Looked for the overthrow of Rome and the division of the Empire among ten kings, Tribulation will purify the Church	Time line highlighted Christ's return in glory to punish Antichrist and deliver saints who suffered under his terror
Tertullian	Late 2nd and 3rd centuries	North African church father	Premillennial apologist confessing the coming of Christ in glory	Applied the restoration of the Jews as the figurative interpretation of Christ and his church, the end would come heralded by signs of warning, exhortations to watch and prayer to be accounted worthy to escape the things to come	Object of his hope was to stand before the Son of Man after a series of cosmic signs appeared	The Day of the Lord and the resurrection of the dead will occur after of a series of preceding signs and events
Lactantius	Late 3rd and early 4th century	Latin father of the church	"Divine Institutes" devoted considerable attention to the end time	Expected a series of signs which would precede the end, history would run a 6,000 year course, followed by millennium; all this demanded profound changes in Roman empire, deterioration in society, with the Church undergoing persecution and woe	Much of human race would be destroyed, and the Church is destined to suffer the evils of the end times	No sense of an immediate, any-moment coming of Christ or saving Church from end time horrors
Hippolytus	First decades of the 3rd century	Bishop of Rome	Applies prophecy to the end of the Roman empire	Antichrist to arise out of the Roman empire, tribulation and persecution to fall upon the saints, the resurrection and kingdom of saints occurs after the return of Christ; read Revelation in terms of futurist view: things to come	God will purify the church through suffering at the hands of the Antichrist	Christians will endure the Tribulation, after which Christ will come and establish his kingdom
Middle Ages	5th through 15th centuries	Numerous interpreters	Revelation gives a symbolic form of the outline of Church history	Antichrist was argued to be the Saracens, false prophet Mohammed; popes used Revelation to gain support for Crusades	Text seen in largely historical and symbolic ways	Focus is on the present power and reign of the Church in the world
Protestantism	15th century to the present	Reformers and their progeny	Historical interpretations that associated the Antichrist with papal Rome	History of the Church is embodied in the book of Revelation, Church of Rome is connected with the Antichrist: Calvin, Luther, Zwingli, Tyndale, Melanchton, etc.	The Roman church and the Papacy identified in varying degrees with the Antichrist	Early Reformers shared the historical view with little hint of a futurist view

Appendix 24
Translating the Story of God
Rev. Dr. Don L Davis

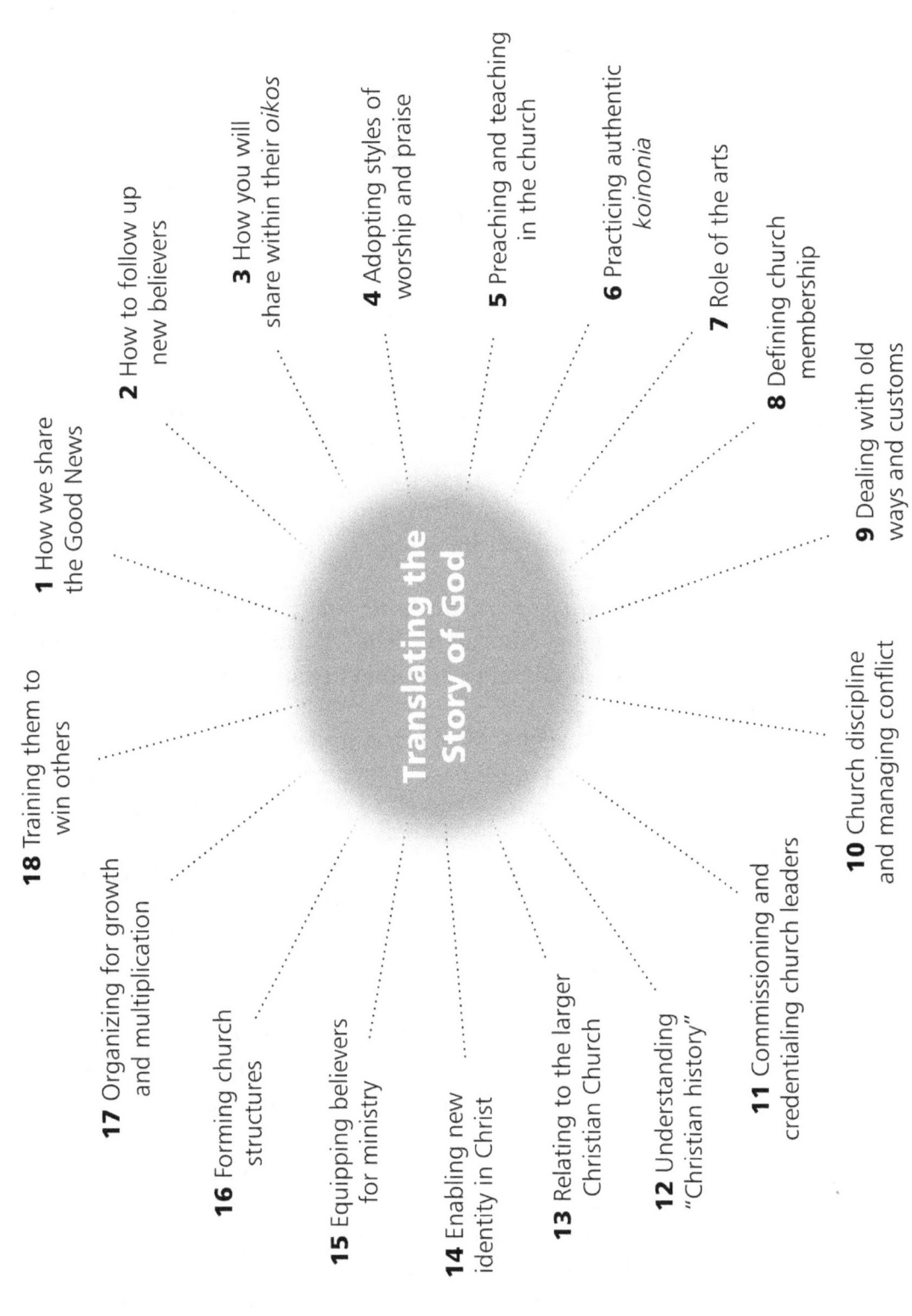

Translating the Story of God

1. How we share the Good News
2. How to follow up new believers
3. How you will share within their *oikos*
4. Adopting styles of worship and praise
5. Preaching and teaching in the church
6. Practicing authentic *koinonia*
7. Role of the arts
8. Defining church membership
9. Dealing with old ways and customs
10. Church discipline and managing conflict
11. Commissioning and credentialing church leaders
12. Understanding "Christian history"
13. Relating to the larger Christian Church
14. Enabling new identity in Christ
15. Equipping believers for ministry
16. Forming church structures
17. Organizing for growth and multiplication
18. Training them to win others

About Us

Many urban churches and ministries suffer with discouragement because there is little lasting fruit. Often there is no plan for leadership development. The biggest obstacle to successfully planting churches is training indigenous leaders to be pastors, to be able to rightly divide the Word of Truth without losing their cultural distinctive. For decades the Church in America has told the urban poor, "If you want a theological education, you have to change cultures and know someone who is rich." We have basically said, "Do not bother to apply to get Bible training." Consequently, biblically sound, evangelical urban leadership is uncommon.

The Urban Ministry Institute (TUMI) overcomes four barriers that urban leaders face in their efforts to receive theological education:

1. *Cost:* Many urban pastors could never afford to attend a traditional seminary.

2. *Academic requirements:* Many of God's chosen leaders in the inner city have little more than a high school education and would not be admitted to most seminaries.

3. *Proximity:* Most urban leaders have a full-time ministry, a family, and a full-time job, so uprooting their family and abandoning their ministry to go away to Bible college is out of the question.

4. *Cultural relevance:* Most of what is taught in traditional seminaries does not equip an urban pastor to lead a flock in the inner city, so even if he/she could afford to go to Bible school, what is taught there is not relevant to daily life.

In 1995 we launched TUMI in Wichita, Kansas, and have equipped hundreds of pastors since then. In 2000 we began establishing satellite training centers in other inner cities across the country and around the world. We have satellites in partnership with denominations, ministries, and schools, hosted in such places as churches, missions, prisons, and seminaries, and located all over the United States with international partners in places such as Canada, Puerto Rico, Ghana, Guatemala, Mexico, Pakistan, and Liberia. Check our website *www.tumi.org* for all of our satellite locations.

We offer a variety of training materials and resources (visit *www.tumi.org*). Take advantage of our rich experience in church planting, urban ministry, and evangelism by ordering resources for your church or personal ministry. These can be used in your church, Sunday school class, small group or personal study.

- Sermons
- Prayer devotionals (series) and resources to lead groups in prayer concerts
- The Capstone Curriculum: courses on DVD with Student Workbooks and Mentor Guides
- Artwork for the urban church
- Books and workbooks with built-in study questions

Helping Churches to Rediscover Vital Spirituality!
We believe that in order to renew our personal and corporate walks in the contemporary church we must simply return and rediscover our Sacred Roots, i.e., the core beliefs, practices, and commitments of the Christian faith. These roots are neither sectarian nor provincial, but are rather cherished and recognized by all believers everywhere, at all times, and by everyone. Paul exhorted the Thessalonians, "So then, brothers, stand firm and hold to the traditions that you were taught by us, either by our spoken word or by our letter" (2 Thess. 2.15). Our Sacred Roots necessarily suggest that all who believe (wherever and whenever they have lived) affirm their common rootedness in the saving work of God, the same Lord who created, covenanted with Israel, was incarnate in Christ, and is being witnessed to by his people, the Church.

Jesus Cropped from the Picture
Why Christians Get Bored and How to Restore Them to Vibrant Faith
by Rev. Don Allsman
Why are many churches shrinking? Why are so many Christians bored? Could it be that the well-meaning attempt to simplify the gospel message for contemporary culture has produced churches full of discouraged people secretly longing for something more? *Jesus Cropped from the Picture* describes this phenomenon and proposes a return to our sacred roots as a guard against spiritual lethargy and a way to enhance spiritual vibrancy.

Sacred Roots
A Primer on Retrieving the Great Tradition
by Dr. Don L. Davis

The Christian Faith is anchored on the person and work of Jesus of Nazareth, the Christ, whose incarnation, crucifixion, and resurrection forever changed the world. Between the years 100 and 500 C.E. those who believed in him grew from a small persecuted minority to a strong aggressive movement reaching far beyond the bounds of the Roman empire. The roots this era produced gave us our canon (the Scriptures), our worship, and our conviction (the major creeds of the Church, and the central tenets of the Faith, especially regarding the doctrine of the Trinity and Christ). This book suggests how we can renew our contemporary faith again, by rediscovering these roots, our Sacred Roots, by retrieving the Great Tradition of the Church that launched the Christian revolution.

Participating in Urban Church Planting Movements

If you are interested in more of Dr. Davis's ideas on how to facilitate or participate in urban church planting movements and how you can help sustain them through retrieving the Great Tradition, be sure to get your own copies of the following three *Foundations for Ministry Series* courses. These three courses are central to discussing what we understand the focus of urban mission to be, both in terms of the aim of it (i.e., to multiply churches rapidly among the urban poor), and the substance of it (i.e., retrieving and expressing The Great Tradition with churches that contextualize it).

Winning the World: Facilitating Urban Church Planting Movements

At a time when our definitions of the Church have become more and more individualized, this study analyzes church plant and growth theories as they relate to the more communal Nicene-based marks of church life. Using these marks as the basis for a more biblical view of the Church, this study discusses and investigates the con-nection between church planting, world evangelization, church growth, leadership development, and urban mission. It clearly identifies the underlying principles which have contributed to the explosive multiplication of churches in places like India, Latin America, and China, and proposes the possibility of similar move-ments of revival, renewal, and reproduction among the poor in American cities. This course lays the foundation for the necessary principles underlying key elements of a Church Planting Movement and what it would take to facilitate and participate in one [workbook and MP3 audio – visit *www.tumi.org/foundations*].

Church Matters: Retrieving the Great Tradition

At a time of turbulence and dramatic change in society and uneasiness and compromise in the Church, it is critical for believers to retain a sense of the history of the body of Christ. What is needed today is a sense of perspective, i.e., coming to view and understand current events through the lens of God's working through the Church through the ages. Armed with a sense of history, we will be both encouraged and challenged that our current situation is neither unique nor unresolvable. Through the great movements of the Church, the Holy Spirit has shown that even in the face of schism, compromise, difficulty, and persecution, the people of God can learn, grow, and fulfill God's plan for them. This course shows that you can rediscover the power of the living biblical tradition of the Church, anchored in the person and work of Jesus Christ, and how essential it is to ground our Church Planting on something larger than us. Throughout its history, the Church has proven that God's unique plan can unfold even in the face of schism and persecution. Such wisdom is critical to renew and revive the urban church today [workbook and MP3 audio – visit *www.tumi.org/foundations*].

Marking Time: Forming Spirituality through the Christian Year

In this course, we explore the origins and meaning of the Christian Year and how it represents the profound yet simple remembrance and re-enactment of the life of Christ in real time during the calendar year. Beginning with an overview of the Bible's teaching in connection to time and history, this course explores the dominant view of the atonement, Christus Victor, which reigned in the ancient Church for a thousand years. We look at how this dynamic vision of Jesus' victory over sin and death was captured in the worship of the Church in the Church Year. This course, then, lays out the argument and rationale for embracing the Church Year as a structure that enables us to enhance spiritual formation in the urban church setting [workbook and MP3 audio – visit *www.tumi.org/foundations*].